D0034833

DRIVING WHILE BLACK

LORIDA 40
7126

DRIVING WHILE BLACK

African American Travel and the Road to Civil Rights

Gretchen Sorin

LIVERIGHT PUBLISHING CORPORATION
A Division of W. W. Norton & Company
Independent Publishers Since 1923
New York London

Frontispiece: *Library of Congress Collection, Farm Security Administration*

Printed in the United States of America
First Edition

For information about special discounts for bulk purchases, please contact W. W. Norton Special Sales at specialsales@wwnorton.com or 800-233-4830

Manufacturing by Lake Book
Book design by Lovedog Studio
Production manager: Anna Oler

ISBN 978-1-63149-569-4

Liveright Publishing Corporation, 500 Fifth Avenue, New York, N.Y. 10110
www.wwnorton.com

W. W. Norton & Company Ltd., 15 Carlisle Street, London W1D 3BS

1 2 3 4 5 6 7 8 9 0

For

Alvenia Wooten Sullivan

(1919–2009)

and

Clyde Eugene Sullivan

(1909–1983)

Strivers, Nurturers, Storytellers

And for Gary (1954–1992), with whom

I shared a childhood

CONTENTS

INTRODUCTION

Good roads beckon to you and me, daily we grow more motor-wise. The nomad in the poorest and the mightiest of us, sends us behind the wheel, north, south, east, and west, in answer to the call of the road. . . . [T]here is still a small cloud that stands between us and complete motor-travel freedom. On the trail, this cloud rarely troubles us in the mornings, but as the afternoon wears on it casts a shadow of apprehension on our hearts and sours us a little. "Where," it asks us, "will you stay tonight?"

—Alfred Edgar Smith,
"Through the Windshield," *Opportunity*, 1933

We obtained the most important book needed for Negroes who traveled anywhere in the United States. It was called the Green Book. The "Green Book" was the bible of every Negro highway traveler in the 1950s and early 1960s. You literally didn't dare leave home without it.

—Earl Hutchinson Sr.,
A Colored Man's Journey Through 20th Century Segregated America

SINCE THE BEGINNING OF THE TWENTIETH CENTURY, no feature of modern life has been more emblematic of, or deeply connected to, American identity and the American dream than the automobile. The automobile dramatically changed life in the United States, a subject documented extensively in both popular culture and scholarly works of social, economic, and cultural history. Cars altered the physical landscape of the nation and transformed its culture. As large numbers of Americans moved from the cities to the suburbs, they used their cars to commute to work. Highways traversed and connected cities but bypassed many rural communities, often leaving them in difficult economic circumstances. The national economy flourished with the factory production of automobiles, car parts, and tires. Automobile workers were among those who joined the ranks of the middle class and purchased cars of their own. Anyone who could buy a car could usually also afford leisure travel, and cars took families on vacations, expanding tourism to become one of the nation's largest industries. As women became car buyers and drivers, their lives changed as well, giving them more independence. Cars even changed courtship patterns, as the backseat provided opportunities for teenage sexual encounters. Automobiles enabled people and goods to move through the country rapidly and increased interconnectedness across a vast nation, while at the same time creating a new pastime—driving.

Not everyone, however, celebrated the automobile. Over the decades, and even into the present, many commentators argued that it was an atomizing force—not to mention one causing widespread environmental harm and loss of life through traffic accidents. Still, the dominant view of the car was as a symbol of freedom, independence, and possibility. Yet those who celebrated the automobile and the ideal of the open road, in most cases, wittingly or not, limited their perspective to white Americans.

For African Americans, the automobile held distinct importance and promise. It made self-directed travel a possibility when travel by bus and train, controlled by others, could lead to humiliating or even life-threatening encounters. Owning a car demonstrated black American success in a nation where that success was often thwarted. With a growing black middle class, more and more black Americans could purchase automobiles, and they used their cars and their consumer dollars not merely to vacation—though they did do that—but also as weapons against segregation. Even many who were not in the middle class found ways to buy cars, seeking any alternative to public transportation, since they were often barred, by law and custom, from securing mortgages and buying houses. Still, each car trip could be fraught with anxiety, and it required special preparations and careful planning to ensure success.

This is one of the first books to tell the story of the African American experience with the automobile, and my hope is that it shows how access to cars completely transformed black life in ways that were both far-reaching and totally unexpected. The automobile expanded the freedom of movement and the opportunity to travel throughout the country for all Americans, but this freedom meant something different—and often, simply more—to blacks than to whites. Automobiles provided a means of escape from the Jim Crow South. They were a tremendous source of pride for African Americans and they changed the etiquette of travel on the road. Most important, the automobile became a tool in the battle to end discrimination in public accommodations.

From the founding of the republic, the right to move about without restrictions and at will was considered fundamental to basic civil rights and American democracy. In the twentieth century, in the 1920 case of *United States v. Wheeler*, the Supreme Court affirmed the entitlement of every person to move freely from place to place and state to state, a right denied to African Americans: . . . *and the people of each State shall have free ingress and egress to and from any other State, and shall enjoy therein all the privileges of trade and commerce, subject to the same.*

For black people, mobility was always most highly prized because it was often and had historically been an impossibility. Masters confined their enslaved persons to their property, and free black people found themselves regularly stopped, questioned to determine their status, and sometimes even kidnapped and sold into slavery. These restrictions on movement before emancipation carried on, in different forms, into the post–Civil War Reconstruction era and beyond, despite passage of the Thirteenth, Fourteenth, and Fifteenth Amendments to the Constitution, designed to end slavery and protect the due-process and citizenship rights of African Americans.

For much of the twentieth century, many white Americans felt comfortable denying their black countrymen not only the right to travel freely but also the ability to use public accommodations—everything from swimming pools to restaurants, movie theaters, and hotels. Black Americans attempting to exercise their rights as citizens faced Jim Crow railroad cars and buses, segregated taxicabs and water fountains, even separate sections in public libraries. A tradition of deeply entrenched racism—including baseless fears about black men being dangerous, and the idea that all black people were naturally inferior—fed beliefs that African Americans should be literally kept in their places and restricted to segregated neighborhoods. The physical separation of black people from the white population excluded African Americans from quality education, housing, and employment, and also reinforced notions of white superiority. But the automobile made it more difficult, although not impossible, to enforce racial apartheid while cruising along the highways at forty-five miles per hour.

The growth of an automobile culture changed the physical environment as well and made reliable roads essential. Narrow carriage paths of mud or hard-packed dirt and meandering cowpaths needed to be replaced with macadamized highways and concrete streets. These old thoroughfares suited a culture that had moved slowly behind horse-drawn vehicles, but automobiles became stuck in these rutted roads, and the dust stirred up on unpaved surfaces clogged internal-combustion engines. Cars required smooth surfaces and at least two lanes wide, enough to accommodate vehicles traveling in opposite directions. And, to keep drivers from getting lost, planners needed to establish national and statewide systems of route numbers.

The intricate pattern of interstate highways was designed to make car travel safer and more efficient, to support national defense, to boost the economy, and later to provide a method for citizens to evacuate the cities in the event of a nuclear war. As early as 1916, the federal government passed legislation to finance the building of roads. Throughout the twentieth century, the US Army argued for the building of a system of highways in the event that troops and supplies needed to be deployed quickly. President Dwight D. Eisenhower made passage of the 1956 Federal Aid Highway Act (also known as the National Interstate and Defense Highways Act) a signature piece of his administration. It soon led to a vast network of highways coursing through every state and connecting major cities and rural areas. Existing roads, the president argued, represented an "appalling problem of waste, danger, and death." In his annual State of the Union address in January 1955, Eisenhower told the nation: "A modern highway system is essential to meet the needs of a growing population, our expanding economy and our national security."

This national network of roads was used primarily by ordinary drivers, bringing Americans from different places and different backgrounds into contact with one another. Even when they stayed on the highways and away from town centers, drivers needed to stop for gasoline and sometimes for repairs. Each year, as African Americans who had migrated to the North, Midwest, and West during the Great Migration returned to the South to visit relatives, they dramatically increased the number of black people traveling on the nation's highways. Turnpikes, highways, and parkways wound through areas of the country that had previously been entirely white and isolated from outsiders. Black people were traveling in these spaces for the first time, inadvertently challenging traditional customs. These drivers were not supposed to be in all-white neighborhoods without good reason, yet they pushed back against the laws and routines of segregated communities, crossing back and forth between "white spaces" and "black spaces."

African Americans faced a wide variety of difficulties and potential dangers on and off the interstate highways and whenever they traveled—whether for vacation, to visit family, or for business. They encountered racist law-enforcement officers and gas-station attendants, bigoted auto repairmen, threatening road signs, restaurants and hotels that denied them service. They faced the possibility of mob violence. Even though the fear of such unpleasant or even violent encounters left many black drivers continuously on edge, they embraced the automobile as their preferred method of travel. To navigate safely, they devised many strategies, both individually and through group action. They carried detailed maps and itineraries and carefully watched the faces of the people they encountered, looking for any indication of hostility. They bypassed specific communities reputed to be "sundown towns" and places that had reputations for being particularly hostile to black people. The automobile supported travel for blacks in private, comfortable circumstances, but it also required new thinking and habits.

A network of black businesses that catered to and supported black travelers grew organically across the country. Women operated many overnight lodging spaces—home businesses that gave them extra income and helped them support their families. From coast to coast, mom-and-pop guesthouses and tourist homes, beauty parlors, and even large hotels (including New York's Hotel Theresa, the Hampton House Motel in Miami, and the Dunbar Hotel in Los Angeles), as well as nightclubs and restaurants (such as New Orleans' Dooky Chase's or Atlanta's Paschal's), and a growing number of black-owned service stations kept automobiles on the road, people fed, and provided places to stay the night. Many of these businesses, most of which have not survived, were known only to the black citizens who frequented them—they existed in a parallel, segregated world. Nonetheless, these establishments also reflected a vibrant entrepreneurial spirit within the black community that helped them "make a way out of no way."

This parallel world of black travelers generated a number of guidebooks, none more famous than *The Negro Motorist Green Book* (later *The Negro Travelers' Green Book*), founded by Victor and Alma Green in 1936. This and other travel guides listed black businesses, promoted them, and made them accessible to the traveling public, thus helping travelers navigate the ever-changing landscape. Not only did the guides aid travelers, but they opened small black family businesses to a national market—exposure that most could never have afforded otherwise.

THIS BOOK opens in the antebellum period, as any history of black freedom and mobility must. In the twentieth century, it charts the growth of the automobile as the preferred method of travel for African Americans and recounts the experiences of black travelers in cars as well as on public conveyances that made their race an issue of central concern whenever they left their neighborhoods. The poignant stories of these travelers explain the necessity for the wide variety of specialized black travel guides that grew with the popularity of the automobile. World War II led African American soldiers and industrial workers to demand an end to segregation—a moral stain on a nation that fought Nazism and an obstacle on the path to middle-class life. After the war, family, business, and pleasure travelers purchased automobiles in even larger numbers. The opportunity to own a car brought new freedom to black people, and many embraced it with delight. But as they looked out through their windshields, with their children safely ensconced in the backseats, African Americans saw a landscape of demeaning and frightening imagery—signs, billboards, souvenirs, even menus at roadside restaurants. Most drivers' mishaps on the road resulted in travel delays, but encounters with the police, traffic accidents, angry mobs, or simple car trouble could turn deadly for African Americans.

As this history reveals, black drivers took many precautions to protect themselves and their families from these dangers. They had specific criteria for the selection of the makes and models of their cars and they carried a variety of supplies to ensure the success of every trip. Beginning in the 1930s, the guidebooks began appearing. *The Green Book* was distinctive not only because of its success but because of its ambitious and high-minded goal. Its writers saw travel as transformative—something that would elevate not only the traveler but also those whom the traveler encountered along the way. The guide hoped to encourage black Americans to use their vacations and business trips as a means of defeating racism. "Travel is fatal to prejudice, bigotry, and narrow-mindedness, and many of our people need it sorely on these accounts," wrote Mark Twain in his 1869 travel book *The Innocents Abroad*.[1] Victor Green adopted these words and made them his mantra. Many white people only knew African Americans through stereotyped images in everything from magazines and postcards to cookie jars and films. If white Americans could only meet and talk with African Americans, Green reasoned, they would change their attitudes. *The Green Book* promoted travel by rail, bus, and eventually plane, but the focus was on the automobile, coveted by almost every American family.

Victor and Alma Green did not produce the first African American travel guide, and *The Negro Motorist Green Book* would not be the last. But theirs had the largest readership and the greatest impact, and it provides a crucial perspective on gender, discrimination, automobile culture, black entrepreneurship, and national identity in Jim Crow America. As we will see, Victor Green's mantra would be, to some extent, borne out by history: This book advances the claim that travel contributed to changes in American behavior.

The latter chapters tell that story, moving from Kittery Point, Maine, to Birmingham, Alabama, and New Orleans, Louisiana, looking at the role of black-owned businesses that assisted travelers. When seen from this angle, the civil rights movement becomes a broad struggle—not only of marches and demonstrations but also of many thousands working quietly behind the scenes. The epilogue briefly explores the legacy of this history in the present day, when driving a car remains for African Americans a potentially dangerous activity, especially when it comes to police traffic stops. We should see these dismal events not simply as a legacy of slavery and racism but also as the continuation of restrictions on mobility that have been placed on African Americans from the start.

Current restrictions on African American mobility contribute to ongoing deep divisions between black people and white people about their views of law enforcement. Seventy-three percent of African Americans today believe that black people are treated unfairly by the justice system, while 53 percent of white Americans view the justice system as fair and equal. Similarly, a 2016 Pew Research Center study revealed a huge disparity between black and white Americans in their beliefs about the treatment of black citizens by law-enforcement officers, with black Americans far more mistrustful of police officers, and far more convinced that police officers are inclined to use excessive force, and rarely are held accountable, when dealing with people of color.[2] The shooting of Philando Castile in his car in Falcon Heights, Minnesota, on July 6, 2016, and fifteen-year-old Jordan Edwards, a passenger in a car leaving a party in Dallas on April 29, 2017, are frightening reminders that black lives remain captives to history.

As Americans, we share certain values: the freedom to travel, the joy of driving, the sense of wonder and adventure in a national park, the fear of seeing police lights in the rearview mirror. But there are also experiences that divide us and point to a deeply troubling, but at the same time often inspiring, history of struggle, perseverance, and transformation.

THE RESEARCH and writing of *Driving While Black* was for me intensely personal and a journey in itself. Unexpectedly, I came to a much greater understanding of my parents, and the courage and determination of everyone who, like them, grew up amid the humiliation, violence, and discrimination of the Jim Crow era. The experiences they never divulged to my brother and me—the segregated schools and Jim Crow signs, a stay in a segregated hospital, living in the volatile community of Fayetteville, North Carolina, during World War II—must have been debilitating, even as they silently endured them. They were strivers who always kept moving forward. The intransigent nature of racial discrimination in the United States, sanctioned by law, and the determination of many Americans to keep African Americans from being successful, makes their accomplishments all the more remarkable. Going out on the road was for them, as it was for so many black Americans, an act of quiet rebellion. "Driving while black" is a phrase first used sarcastically in the 1990s, but it refers to a problem that predates its coinage—encountering danger, harassment, and even violence while operating a car on the road in the United States. My parents knew the feeling, even if they would not have used these words. I realized it would have been impossible for me to write this book without reflecting on their journeys, literal and metaphorical. This is a reality that they lived with all of their lives and that every African American family still lives with each and every day. But this is a story that is not simply about African Americans, although it is told through that lens. I hope it is a story that broadens and deepens our understanding of the automobile's role in American life and history and encourages us to consider the context within which today's race relations developed. Looking back often provides a way to move forward.

DRIVING WHILE BLACK

Chapter 1

THE JOURNEY

Undoubtedly the right of locomotion, the right to move from one place to another according to inclination, is an attribute of personal liberty, and the right, ordinarily, of free transit from or through the territory of any State is a right secured by the 14th amendment and by other provisions of the Constitution.

—*Shachtman v. Dulles*, 1955

During the antebellum era and in the decades after emancipation, most African Americans, at least those living in the South, traveled very little. My father's family, the Sullivans, had lived in Chesterfield County, South Carolina, at least since the early nineteenth century. Even after the Civil War, when General William Sherman, bent on harshly punishing South Carolina, burned his way through the state, the Sullivans stayed in the only place they knew. My grandmother, Josephine, still a child herself, gave birth to my father at the age of fifteen; my father's father was a white man. This was the family secret. No one in the family knew his name—or, if they knew, they wouldn't tell me. From the time I first heard this story as a twenty-five-year-old, I wondered about the nature of Josephine's "relationship" with my biological grandfather. One year after the child's birth, according to the census records, Josephine and baby Clyde Eugene were living in the South Carolina home of her mother, a widow named Chaney Sullivan.

The family matriarch, Great-Grandmother Chaney, was by all accounts a formidable woman. Born a slave in 1853, she bore thirteen children and outlived her husband, Handy, by many years, dying in 1936 after a very hard life. She played a large role in my father's earliest memories. One memory was so profoundly painful that it was seared into his mind, even at the tender age of five.

He told me about it when I was in my twenties, staring past me as the mental image gradually came into focus. He had been sitting, he told me, on the porch of Grandmother Chaney's house.

"Do you remember the house?" I asked.

"Yes," he said. "It was a small, two-room house with a shallow porch. Grandma Chaney told me to sit on the porch and to stay there."

"Don't move," she said, for inside the house his grandmother attended, as midwife, to his twenty-year-old mother, who was in labor. The tiny house had no room for a five-year-old underfoot. He sat alone, playing quietly for a long time, until his grandmother came out to fetch him.

"She's gone," she said. "She's gone."

Josephine had not survived, and the baby girl, known only as "Toots," died as well. In 1914, in a poor black community in the South, the death of a young mother and her baby in childbirth must certainly have been commonplace, but it was nevertheless tragic.

When I heard this story, I ached for this five-year-old who had just lost his mother. But the historian in me was dumbfounded. The house he described, where my father had lived as a child, was either a sharecropper's cabin or, perhaps, even a former slave cabin. I was just one generation removed from slave housing. But, like so many other families who had been enslaved, the Sullivans stayed on or near the plantation.

THE RESTRICTIONS on African American mobility in the United States began four centuries ago, with the involuntary journey from Africa to the New World. Kidnapped from their villages and marched to the sea, the enslaved Africans forcibly embarked on the first leg of their migration, the Middle Passage. Men were shackled together and packed into the ships' holds so tightly that they could not stand or reach the buckets provided as their toilets. The oppressive heat, the stench, and disease overcame many on the crossing. Some committed suicide or sank into deep melancholy. Olaudah Equiano, an enslaved African, later wrote a memoir describing the confusion, hopelessness, and fear that overwhelmed the prisoners during the ocean voyage. He assumed that the red-faced "white men with horrible looks and long hair" collected the Africans for food, and they surely would be eaten.[1]

The beginning of the slaves' journey to the New World, the Atlantic crossing, could take as little as six weeks, but rough weather often extended the voyage to thirteen weeks of seasickness, dysentery, scurvy, and misery. Thousands died of suicide, malnutrition, disease, or brutality. In the New World, the slavers sold the Africans at auction, after which they began a second phase of involuntary travel to the places where they would establish new family relationships and would toil for generations. Slaveowners designed draconian measures to restrict their slaves' movements to their property.

"We would be sorry when dark, as de patrollers would walk through de quarters and home of de slaves wid pine torch lights to whip de niggers found away from deir home," remembered eighty-three-year-old Ida Henry, describing the enforcers who intimidated slaves trying to sneak away from the plantation at night. But, she recalled, after cooking for the master all day, her mother often slipped through the woods to visit relatives on a nearby farm, despite the danger.[2] An enslaved person like Ida might spend her entire lifetime involuntarily confined to one master's plantation—prevented from leaving or moving about freely even to visit relatives nearby, except clandestinely. Another enslaved woman, Patsy Southwell, commented that she spent her entire life restricted to

Rock Hill, a Texas plantation.[3] Rural slaves, who worked the cotton or tobacco fields, were so restricted in their movements that they rarely encountered other enslaved Africans on neighboring plantations. In Georgia's cities, including Savannah, Atlanta, or Augusta, the slave patrollers' duties often merged with what we would think of as the duties of an urban police force, although they actually were organized to prevent blacks from freely moving about without the knowledge of their owners. Southern as well as some northern cities and states passed official prohibitions on the free movement of enslaved persons.[4]

For white Americans, freedom of movement has always been a fundamental right. The Articles of Confederation, the original agreement among the thirteen states establishing the United States, reads in part: "[T]he people of each State shall have free ingress and regress to and from any other State, and shall enjoy therein all the privileges of trade and commerce."[5] The right was considered so fundamental as not to be required for inclusion in the Constitution. Indeed, at the time of the writing of the Constitution, the government had little ability to control the mobility of most of its citizens if they chose to cross colonial borders or to board a ship to another country. It was simply assumed that they could move about as they wished. In multiple cases in the nineteenth and twentieth centuries, the Supreme Court reiterated the right to the freedom of movement based on the privileges and immunities clause of the Constitution. The court held that this authority was situated with the states and not with the federal government. Thus, it guaranteed white men the liberty to move about as they chose, but black codes—laws covering only black people—enacted at the state level, controlled and criminalized mobility for enslaved persons.

These legal constraints on the movement of slaves came early in the development of American democracy. Throughout the colonial period, state governments passed increasingly restrictive limitations on both movement and assembly. Groups of enslaved people gathering for festivals, worship, or burials terrified slaveowners, who, despite claiming slaves were intellectually inferior, also believed that groups of slaves were developing sophisticated plots to overthrow their masters or commit mass murder. They pushed for laws prohibiting black people from any form of public congregation. Paranoia that a staff, a club, a gun, or a sword might be used against the master led to further prohibitions on carrying anything that might be taken up as a weapon. Slaveowners also feared that unfettered mobility gave their enslaved people the opportunity to learn the landscape, to see the locations of its physical features, and to plot methods of escape. Keeping them ignorant of their surroundings made it more difficult for them to successfully run away.

The black codes also barred slaves from purchasing or drinking alcoholic beverages that slaveowners believed might lead to wild behavior and loss of inhibitions—which in turn might lead to rebellion. The most restrictive statutes kept enslaved persons strictly confined to the master's property and as isolated from one another as possible. In Virginia, for example, the extensive slave code required the constable to give any slave who departed from his master's grounds without permission and without a pass "twenty lashes on his bare back well layd on, and soe sent home to his said master, mistress or overseer."[6] Comparable laws existed throughout the colonies, and later the states added restrictions in the United States Constitution. The fugitive slave clause further criminalized mobility, making enslaved individuals lawbreakers if they sought their freedom by running away.[7]

African Americans who were free suffered from the same restrictions placed on their enslaved brethren, and they faced many indignities when moving about in public. The Code of Virginia even kept free black people from entering the state without permission. As the slaveowner class saw it, the presence of free black individuals threatened the institution of slavery and could incite slaves. "If a free negro, not authorized by law to do so, come into or remain in this state," stipulated Virginia's law, "any person may, and every sheriff, sergeant and constable is required to, apprehend and carry him before some justice of the county."[8] On public conveyances such as stagecoaches or carriages, free men and women might be pushed off to make way for white riders. As methods of transportation changed, so too did methods of exclusion for black citizens. Trains had separate Jim Crow cars that typically were filthy and located directly behind the engine, which belched soot and smoke directly onto the riders. In 1842, abolitionist William Lloyd Garrison was so incensed by the separate Jim Crow railcars that he published a directory for travelers in his newspaper, *The Liberator*. The directory ranked the railroad companies based on the level of human dignity afforded black travelers.[9] When taking the train, Garrison often showed solidarity with his black countrymen by riding with them in the Jim Crow car.

White passengers hurled insults and racial epithets at black people who attempted to occupy spaces they viewed as white. Frederick Douglass was repeatedly and rudely ejected from train cars as he traveled the country in support of abolition. Even when leaving the house or walking down a local road, any black person might hear the racial slur "nigger." At any time or place outside of one's own family, the word would be used liberally and often.[10] Children's books used "nigger" to clearly establish, in the minds of young white people, a social order in which whites were superior and blacks inferior.

Slaves doing the master's business away from home required signed passes giving them special permission to travel or even to be out of sight of their owners.[11] Charleston, South Carolina, and other southern cities issued metal badges to be worn around the necks of enslaved men or women permitted to work away from their official places of residence. The tags enabled slaveowners to make additional money by hiring out their skilled slaves when their labor was not needed at home. Sometimes these arrangements also permitted the enslaved person to earn some extra money and

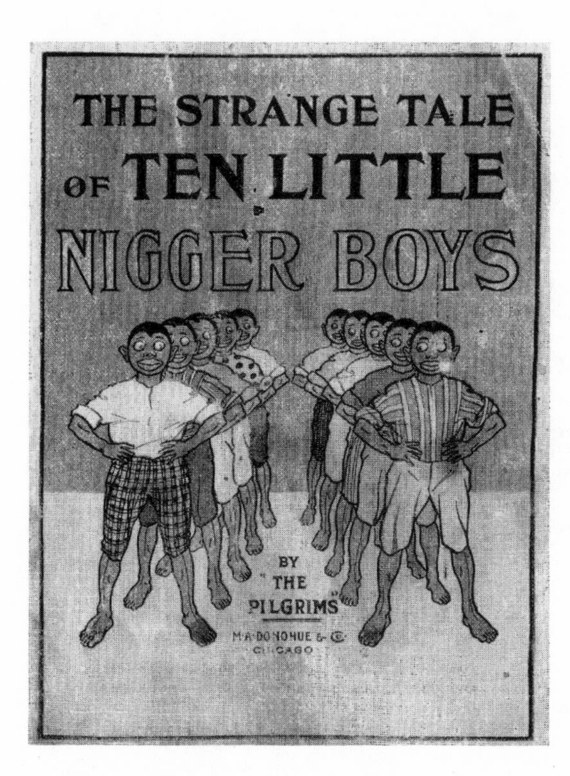

This children's book, published in Chicago, teaches children to count down from ten while learning to demean African Americans. The highly stereotyped and grisly images depict monkeylike boys whose exploits include being swallowed by a giant herring and killed by a bear. (The Strange Tale of Ten Little Nigger Boys, *"The Pilgrims," M. A. Donohue & Co., Chicago, Fenimore Art Museum Research Library, Cooperstown, NY, Special Collections 808.899zzP643.)*

eventually purchase his freedom or even the freedom of his family. Evoking nothing else but a modern-day dog tag, the badges identified the wearer by number and also listed his or her specific expertise—blacksmith, perhaps, or potter or furniture maker. The badges made running away more difficult and ensured that the master could more easily keep track of his property.

Handwritten passes penned on small slips of paper were much more commonly used to control slave mobility. Fearing that a literate black community might more ably fight against slavery, the colonies (and later the states) prohibited enslaved persons from learning to read and criminalized those who taught them. With such strict laws, most slaves were illiterate, making it difficult to forge travel passes or read maps or road signs when running away. But resourceful individuals used careful planning and subterfuge to seek freedom, and forged passes were common. Historian

In Charleston, South Carolina, slave tags like these were worn by enslaved persons as identifiers so their masters could control their movements. (*National Museum of American History, Smithsonian Institution Archives.*)

John Wood Sweet documented one example of a daring escape and attempt to subvert the system of passes. Two enslaved men in Newport, Rhode Island, asked a literate fellow slave (Isaac) to create fictitious identities and counterfeit papers to get them from Rhode Island to New York. Unfortunately, the plan failed. Caught in New London, Connecticut, the runaways were shipped back to Newport, where their friend Isaac was punished.[12] Still, failures did not deter many other would-be fugitives.

Checking passes, slave patrols roamed the countryside to enforce the black codes and catch those illegally away from their quarters. These early groups of law enforcers—often the first policing units in a community—stopped any black person they encountered, enslaved or free, and forced them to produce papers proving their status, an early form of racial profiling. Most of these groups consisted of white men, and very occasionally women. Sometimes they included local slaveowners with a vested interest in ensuring that their slaves were kept in line and constantly under surveillance. The often-compulsory participation in these patrols pitted all

Please to let Benjamin McDaniel pass to Dr. Henkal's in New-Market, Shenandoah County Va. and return on Monday or Tuesday next to Montpelier, for Mrs Madison

June 1st 1843.

Passes like this one enabled slaves to travel, but only within the limits determined by the master. This 1843 pass gave Benjamin McDaniel permission to travel from Montpelier, the plantation where he lived, to New Market, Shenandoah County, Virginia, and back again. (*Schomburg Center for Research in Black Culture, Manuscripts, Archives and Rare Books Division, New York Public Library.*)

white people against all black people, slave or free, and gave them free rein to stop, harass, invade, and search individuals and homes.

An extant logbook from South Carolina carefully documented, in fine script, the five-man squads the town of Aiken sent out regularly on day and night patrols to guard roads and to hunt for enslaved men and women who did not have permission to be away from their plantations. After hours, the squads often socialized together, which helped to solidify participants' beliefs in white superiority as rich and poor collaborated to oppress the local black residents. A "Negro Slave's Pass" issued to a man named Charles revealed how strictly the squads monitored slave movements. Charles' pass enabled him to "pass and repass" between the town of Aiken and Mr. John Glover's plantation on Saturday, September 8, 1860. But the pass expired on Monday at noon, at which time Charles would be at the mercy of the slave patrols.[13]

Not surprisingly, the patrollers frightened and intimidated the local black populations. Some men joined the groups simply because they wanted to establish themselves as dominant over the slave population or because they found a perverse enjoyment in meting out corporal punishment. The work gave them the opportunity to beat other human beings without repercussions. "[The patrol] evinced rather a joyful expectancy," wrote nineteenth-century abolitionist Austin Steward in his memoir about his slave days, "of the many they should find there without a pass, and the flogging they would give them for that, if not guilty of any other offence. . . ."[14]

The black codes severely limited slave mobility. Designed to safeguard the economic interests of white slaveowners, the slave patrols not only protected their human property but also began the process of creating the American caste system that reinforced the notion of black people as second-class citizens (even though they were in fact citizens), and as people who needed to be controlled and contained. Many scholars now argue that slave patrols, as government-sponsored groups, became the modern enforcers of Jim Crow and the precursors of some of today's police departments.[15]

Despite the slave codes and the patrols, enslaved African Americans still found ways to travel clandestinely, or to escape to freedom. The Underground Railroad—the prime symbol of the importance of the freedom of mobility—played a critical role for generations of African Americans. Stories of escape and the allure of the Underground Railroad became a source of pride and hope, not only in the nineteenth century but even into the present.

Indeed, the Underground Railroad resonates well beyond African American communities. It has moved into the realm of American folklore and myth because it speaks broadly to American values and to the nation's founding ideas about freedom and mobility. Today, many people who are not black claim the Underground Railroad as a part of their own heritage. Ordinary homeowners became guardians of democracy, and people of all colors stood up with courage to an unjust law. Communities throughout upstate New York, for example, still speak with pride of regional participation in abolition efforts—from harrowing pursuits to daring escapes, and particularly the clandestine stops on the escape route to Canada. Yet the vast majority of Underground Railroad sites may have been hidden in black communities, where fugitives blended in with the local residents and were more able to hide in plain sight.

AFTER EMANCIPATION, in 1863, 90 percent of the nation's black residents still lived in the southern states. For the first time, their decision of when and where to migrate was based on free choice. Between about 1916 and the 1970s, as many as five million of these descendants of former slaves packed up whatever possessions they could and moved by train, bus, or automobile to the cities of the Northeast, Midwest, or West. The Great Migration remains the greatest mass movement of people in the history of the United States. Aiming to escape intimidation, Jim Crow laws, and the sharecropping that became another method of re-enslaving the black population, many of the migrants had to sneak out of town to escape, as southern whites tried to prevent their labor force from leaving. Letters to *The Chicago Defender* (one of the nation's most influential black newspapers) seeking positions and housing in the North often requested that the paper keep the writers' names confidential to avoid alerting white employers that "their Negroes" were trying to move away. Escaping the South became the critical next step in the freedom of mobility—and, simply, in gaining their freedom—for many African Americans.

Once settled in their new homes, the migrants found the ability to move freely throughout the country essential for annual trips home to visit family. Most took the train or drove their cars between their new urban homes and their southern home communities. My family made an annual sojourn to Fayetteville, North Carolina, from Newark, New Jersey, for a week or two each summer to visit the Wootens—"your mother's people," as my father referred to them. On the way south, we might stop to visit Uncle Richard, my mother's brother, whose Great Migration destination had been Philadelphia. My grandmother—as well as uncles, aunts, and a host of other family members—still lived in the South.

While the growing tide of Jim Crow laws and practices determined almost every aspect of their lives—where black people could live, work, eat, sleep, and go to school—the train and later the automobile became tools of defiance and dignity in the journey to full equality. For a people restricted in movement for so many generations, the pilgrimage back to the South to visit family and friends became a tradition, and traveling as they pleased came to be an essential part of citizenship.

Despite the large number of black migrants moving north, those who traveled regularly and most often were musicians, athletes, and businessmen. Their work required them to be on the road and to find accommodations away from home. For musicians, the importance of mobility and travel could be seen in the frequency of travel-related lyrics in their music. The notion of physical, metaphorical, and metaphysical travel—representing actual geographic places of freedom and safety and the spiritual journey to freedom—appears in the music of both male and female blues singers as well as instrumentalists. The words of their songs spoke of mobility and the necessity of escape from the South. Ma Rainey, "Mother of the Blues," sang about getting her independence in "Walking Blues," "Runaway Blues," and "Traveling Blues":

I'm dangerous and blue, can't stay here no more
I'm dangerous and blue, can't stay here no more
Here comes my train folks, and I've got to go.[16]

The words of slave spirituals provided inspiration for later music and symbolized the importance of the journey from the land of Jim Crow to the new, hoped-for "promised land"—a place of equality. Couched in Christian imagery and rhetoric, and sung by enslaved men and women working in the fields, spirituals evoked travel to heaven and the Promised Land while referring, at the same time, to improving one's lot in this life. Lyrics such as "I'm goin' home," "going home to Canaan," "ain't but one more river to cross," "wade in the water," and "bound to go" described the trip north to freedom as well as a spiritual journey. The "land of Jordan," the "free country," and "steal away" offered metaphors for leaving the oppression of slavery.

In the twentieth century, Martin Luther King Jr. intoned the words of this metaphorical journey—"I will get to the promised land"—to bring to mind his vision for a people finally liberated. In the speech that he gave the day before his death from an assassin's bullet, King prophetically spoke of the continuing struggle for liberation and the hope that black people would someday reach the journey's end: "I may not get there with you."

Other genres of African American music told stories of travel by car. Ike Turner and Jackie Brenston wrote about the popular, stylish, and fast Oldsmobile—the Rocket 88—in the 1951 song by the same name. "Now that you've ridden in my Rocket 88, I'll be around every night about eight." For the Dixie Hummingbirds, a jubilee-quartet–style gospel group most popular from the 1920s to the 1950s but still performing today (with new members), the African American journey was and remains one of religious exploration and the certainty of redemption in the song "Christian Automobile." No longer was the route to heaven found by following the North Star to freedom, as it was during the days of the Underground Railroad. Travel in your car symbolized the twentieth-century approach to redemption. The lyrics speak of the car as a metaphor for the road to salvation: "Prayer is your driver's license: Faith is your steering wheel."

Headed in the opposite direction, Chuck Berry's "Down Bound Train" also revealed his religious upbringing. On the titular train, the devil himself was the engineer and the lyrics warned of the dangers of Satan's wrath on the road to hell, with deliverance coming only through prayer. In his popular rock-and-roll song "You Can't Catch Me," Berry, who adored his automobiles, most of them

Cadillacs, humorously recounted the fantastic story of the car of his imagination—a car so fast that it can evade the police. The powerful engine of Berry's imaginary car flies past the state troopers on the New Jersey Turnpike. The song was inspired by an experience Berry had in the wee hours of the morning when he decided to race a hot rod rumbling beside him and got caught speeding. He wished that his car had wings.[17]

So I let out my wings and then I blew my horn
Bye bye New Jersey, I've become airborne.

Bandleader Duke Ellington often chose his favorite mode of travel, the train, to evoke the freedom to travel. Titles of his songs often include trains—"Daybreak Express," "Build That Railroad," and "Across the Track Blues." He chose "Take the 'A' Train" as

Chuck Berry and his Cadillac. Berry wrote many songs about automobiles, including one of his greatest hits, named for his guitar, Maybelline. (*Danny Clinch, photographed for* Esquire/Contour *by Getty Images.*)

the theme song for his band. This instrumental piece, written by his arranger and lyricist Billy Strayhorn, sets Harlem's energy to music and refers to the subway trip uptown to the center of black America. Some of Ellington's pieces musically imitated the sounds of a train's movement, steam, and whistles. Ellington loved train travel of any kind. When he and the band went on the road, they often traveled luxuriously by private Pullman car (until the 1940s, when the US Army requisitioned all of the Pullman cars for the war effort and they were forced to travel by rented train coach or by bus). Private train cars allowed the band to avoid the discomfort and humiliation of sitting in the Jim Crow train car.[18]

While musicians traveled regularly for work, ordinary African Americans exercised their right to travel freely for vacations whenever they could. They chose to "hit the road as soon as the warm weather" set in, as travel writer Victor Green put it: "They want to get away from their old surroundings to see—to learn how people live—to meet old and new friends."[19] The importance of mobility also fulfilled the long-standing goal of the black middle class to provide opportunities for education and enrichment for their children. Green supported and encouraged African Americans to schedule annual vacations through *The Negro Motorist Green Book*, whose first edition was published in 1936. He and other black travel writers believed that road trips provided a path to Negro self-improvement as well as self-actualization.

Not every African American stood on the front lines of a civil rights march or a sit-in, but many were able to nudge the cause forward by exercising their freedom of mobility. Resistance could take many forms. "Negroes are fed up," wrote lawyer and activist Pauli Murray in a 1943 article in the progressive magazine *Common Sense*. "The Negroes in America are determined to obtain justice and nothing will stop them. The determination is unanimous. It is expressed at every level of Negro life from zoot suiter to college president, from sharecropper to soldier, from preacher to labor leader."[20] Murray's resolve mirrored the views of African Americans throughout the United States, a resolve cemented by World War II and reflected in the Double V Campaign aimed at defeating Nazism abroad and racism at home. Conceived by the *Pittsburgh Courier* staff as a way to galvanize African American support for the war effort and to fight, at the same time, "for the preservation of democracy" at home, the campaign urged Negro Americans not to "soft pedal" demands for "Complete freedom and citizenship." A poll of readers showed that they wholeheartedly agreed.[21]

In the 1950s, James Avery, a black corporate executive for Esso, whose job was to build relationships with black communities, described the experience of being on the front lines of a major American corporation fighting bigotry subtly, yet consistently. Black executives did not have to face guns, "like those [black students] trying to go to school in Alabama," Avery remembered, but they faced constant indignities, verbal assaults, and rejections from hotels where their white colleagues stayed and restaurants where their white colleagues conducted business meetings.[22]

Famed *Life* photographer Gordon Parks referred to the camera as his weapon of choice—a weapon that enabled him to illuminate the plight of his fellow African Americans. Academic and TIAA chief Dr. Clifton Wharton used that phrase to describe his work in the corporate world. "In terms of fighting, you always have a choice of weapons," Wharton told *Fortune* magazine. Avery and Wharton were among the early African American corporate travelers to demand equal lodgings. Wharton viewed the behavior that he and his colleagues demonstrated in their relationships with other employees—during corporate business trips and in the boardroom—as a surreptitious approach to resistance and a discrete way to bring about change. "Some of us chose to do our fighting on the inside," he said.[23]

Similarly, with each mile they traveled, ordinary African Americans challenged prohibitions that prevented them from traveling and from entering segregated spaces. They used travel to claim the rights of citizenship and push the boundaries of racism. For thousands of black Americans, the automobile became their weapon, just as the camera was for Gordon Parks.

Chapter 2

"HUMILIATION STALKS THEM"

They say this is a war
For Freedom Over There
Say, Mr. F.D.R.
How 'bout some Freedom Here?

—From "The Ballad of Ned Turman,"
Arthur L. Drayton, 1942
(*Pittsburgh Courier* Archives)

In 1940, with war looming, the US government instituted the Selective Training and Service Act, the first peacetime draft in the nation's history. My father, a slight man at only 127 pounds, seemed an unlikely military recruit, but in June 1941 the draft swept hundreds of thousands of men between the ages of eighteen and forty-five into the army. He was thirty years old. In July, after a series of aptitude tests and interviews, Private Clyde Sullivan shipped out by segregated troop train with 242 other trainees from Fort Dix, New Jersey, to Fort Bragg in Fayetteville, North Carolina, to join the 16th Battalion Field Replacement Center. The segregated train was just the first of the indignities the new soldiers would endure. Like my father, many of Fort Bragg's black recruits came from northern cities, so Fayetteville's overt Jim Crow practices, including constraints on their movements, did not sit well with them. As they came up against Jim Crow for the first time, they often rebelled, and sometimes violence ensued, as my father was soon to discover.

In 1941, Fayetteville, North Carolina, was a small city of 17,500 residents, 40 percent of them African American. In 1918, the US Army had built Fort Bragg nine miles north of the city. The only method of travel for those men who went into Fayetteville proper seeking a brief respite from the base was a military bus—a segregated bus. Scheduled to run every hour, though rarely ever on time, the "Negro" bus that summer was packed with angry, sweaty men worried that they might not get to their work shifts. In August, the temperature rose to 94 degrees and the humidity was so heavy that spontaneous thundershowers drenched anyone unlucky enough to be caught outside.

On August 6, tempers flared on the last segregated and overcrowded bus of the night. Amid the yelling and jostling for space on the bus, the MPs arrived and used their usual method of defusing conflict—their billy clubs. All of the MPs were white, and they regularly exerted their power on the heads of the black soldiers. Twenty-seven-year-old Private Ned Turman, of Ashton, North Carolina, tired of the treatment black soldiers endured, would have no more of it. He grabbed the .45 holstered on the MP's hip and shot him. Soldiers outside the bus scattered at the sound of gunfire. More MPs arrived. In the melee that followed, seven black soldiers were injured. Sergeant Edwin Hargraves, the military policeman shot by Turman, died. Sergeant Russell Owens, another MP, boarded the bus and killed Ned Turman.

In response, the army rushed to do something—or at least to appear to be doing something—about the dissatisfaction among black soldiers with North Carolina's Jim Crow practices and the lack of sanitary and recreational facilities for them at Fort Bragg. This incident was one of dozens of racial melees on military bases and in communities that housed bases all over the country. Each was an embarrassment—not only to the army but also to the nation. Black soldiers had shone the light on the racism and violence they faced every day in their own country. Officials at Fort Bragg then aggressively publicized the two young black recruits—

the new "public relations bureau"—assigned as liaisons between the press and the army. A photograph placed in a number of black newspapers across the country depicted (to my surprise, when I first saw it) a reporter, Walter McLean of Louisville, Kentucky, and a photographer, Clyde Sullivan of Staten Island, New York, whose task it was to demonstrate to the press and to the nation that things were improving.

The years in the Jim Crow South were traumatic for my father, and he would never talk about his experiences, even though he received promotions to the rank of sergeant and received training in watch and chronometer repair, a skill that he continued to practice as a hobby for the rest of his life. Other than meeting my mother during his time off in Fayetteville, there was nothing in his military years that he cared to remember. Aside from brief visits and funerals, he returned to Fayetteville only on rare occasions after his discharge from the US Army. When we made weeklong visits with my mother to my grandmother's house during the 1960s, my father always chose to drop us off and to pick us up, never staying more than one overnight. He always hurried back north.

World War II highlighted the contradictions between the nation's democratic ideals and its treatment of black Americans. But the war also aided the black freedom struggle. In 1941, President Franklin Roosevelt issued executive order 8802, prohibiting discrimination in defense industries. This ensured that African Americans were hired into many jobs that had been unavailable to them before the war. Despite considerable resistance, many African Americans, particularly in the northern states, received training that not only aided the war effort but also provided unemployed or underemployed workers with new skills useful to them after the war ended. The Pittsburgh Courier *announced courses to train tool-and-die makers, machinists, welders, and engineers. In Baltimore, more than 365 students—forty of them women—registered in short order for classes in auto mechan-*

ics, aircraft riveting, cabinetmaking, blueprint reading, electrical work, and radio work.[1]

For many, service in the military ultimately facilitated movement into the middle class. After the war, black citizens used their increasing disposable income to purchase cars and other consumer goods. They had money to take vacations and to travel across the country—and thus to push against the limits imposed by Jim Crow. As my father learned firsthand during the war, public transportation was the site of great indignities for black people. It was, as a result, where they began to resist in greater numbers.

WHEN CHARLIE MCGARLAND and his wife were barred from boarding a train in Wake Forest, North Carolina, on January 2, 1942, despite having purchased reserved seats, they wrote to NAACP (National Association for the Advancement of Colored People) Attorney Thurgood Marshall. According to McGarland's letter, the conductor informed the couple that "no colored passengers rides [sic] this train," and then he proceeded to seat several white passengers. The black couple watched the train pull away from the platform, wondering, ". . . what part is the Negro going to play in this war? Why should we fight when we are discriminated [sic] on the train and in other places?"[2] During World War II, a barrage of such letters to the NAACP—the nation's oldest and largest civil rights organization—described similar indignities suffered by black people, whether or not they were in uniform.

One railroad official even used the war as justification for the terrible treatment of black passengers. C. H. Gattis, assistant traffic manager of the Seaboard Coast Line, the rail line running along the east coast from New York City to Florida, rationalized the exclusion of black soldiers from the train by explaining that holiday travel, and "added large movements of a military nature," necessitated the "difficulties in boarding. We are sure you can appreciate the trying conditions under which the railroads and all transportation agencies are working during these war times, and it is not our policy to discriminate against anyone."[3] Such euphemisms or outright lies may have been convincing to officials like Gattis, but African Americans, despite their support for the war, refused to allow such pressures to hinder their opposition to racist policies.

While black passengers could easily obtain tickets for the "colored" railroad car, the humiliations of segregated train cars were significant. As a result of conversations at the National Baptist Convention in 1908, Reverend R. H. Boyd wrote a 25-cent guidebook to assist passengers as they attempted to navigate the complicated Jim Crow system, which was implemented differently across each of the southern states. Some states required separate coaches divided by race. Others permitted partitioned cars. Some defined the words *color* or *Negro*. Special provisions could be made for prisoners and nurses, presumably because they might have been riding in the car with a white person. The writer urged readers to "keep the tiny volume as a constant companion in the pocket or hand of every self-respecting, law-abiding Negro who is compelled to travel by rail in any of the fourteen states of the Union that have passed separate or 'jim crow' car laws for the purpose of humiliating and degrading the Negro race in the eye of all the civilized world."[4] The author hoped that the book would provide a way to make train travel less onerous, and he naively believed that conductors and trainmen violating the separate-but-equal requirements might be punished.

Less clean, less comfortable, and more crowded accommodations almost always defined these segregated railroad cars. A 1939 Seaboard Coast Line timetable for the New York-to-Miami route described comfortable, "reclining, de luxe seats" in the main coaches, but it warned African American passengers that the "Colored Coach [is] not Air-Conditioned."[5] Bathrooms were often cleaned less frequently in the "colored" coach, if they were cleaned at all, and train travelers complained of dirty and threadbare seats. Passengers traveling south might secure a regular seat in

Chicago, Detroit, New York, or Newark, only to be asked to move to the "colored" car once the train crossed that symbolic Mason–Dixon Line.

Of all the Jim Crow practices, none denoted second-class citizenship or was more offensive than the requirement that African Americans sit in the back of the bus. Forcing people to sit in the rear, or to stand and give up their seats when white people entered a bus, continuously reinforced white supremacy and stripped passengers of their dignity as well as their civil rights. Movable signs placed in the middle of the bus indicated the point where the Negro section began, but the signs were constantly shifted as more white passengers boarded, reducing the number of seats for black riders. Jim Crow municipal buses, owned and operated by cities, delivered the undeniable message that racism was sanctioned and codified by the state.

The national system of highways, efficiently paved with macadam, brought with it the proliferation of bus lines, both privately owned and municipal. Unlike railroads tied to the locations of the train tracks, buses could take riders anywhere and everywhere. Local municipal bus travel was inexpensive and convenient, with frequent stops and inexpensive tickets. In different states, bus travel was either segregated or not, depending on state laws.

Interstate bus travel posed other problems. As buses crossed a border separating a state that did not require segregation from one that by law enforced the separation of black and white passengers, drivers would often stop the bus and humiliate the black riders by ordering them to move to the seats in the rear or even to exit the bus.

Bus companies like Greyhound and Trailways, two of the largest interstate carriers, refused to take any stand, moral or otherwise, on bus segregation, even though segregation imposed significant costs on them. The expense of building and maintaining separate facilities—separate bus waiting rooms, bathrooms, water fountains, ticket windows, dining facilities, and entrances—

Segregated bus in Chattanooga, Tennessee, where black riders were required by law to sit in the back. (*Jim Mooney photograph,* Chattanooga Times.)

dramatically increased the cost of operating southern bus terminals, adding as much as 50 percent to construction costs and also requiring additional staff.[6] From a public relations perspective, Jim Crow practices also hurt bus companies. Negative publicity followed every incident in which black passengers were removed, shot, or beaten by drivers, police, or other passengers, or denied access to bus transportation. Black newspapers carefully documented every incident that violated black passengers' civil rights. As the civil rights movement became national news, mainstream papers such as the *New York Times* also reported on the failure of bus companies to protect black riders and the violent behavior of some bus drivers and white passengers.

The bus drivers themselves gained a reputation in the black community as surly at best and vicious, sadistic, and violent at worst. They might stop the bus and refuse to move unless black passengers obeyed their orders. Some drivers carried guns and handed out self-determined punishments that could involve the death penalty for violating Jim Crow laws when black passengers asserted their rights as citizens. In Montgomery, Alabama, the bus drivers felt empowered to be particularly nasty, referring to black women as "black bitches" or "whores" and ignoring African Americans waiting at bus stops on rainy days, believing that black people, when wet, emitted a stink.[7] Dozens of examples of these self-appointed vigilante enforcers appeared in African American newspapers and magazines, and the bus drivers' bad behavior was one factor contributing to the Montgomery bus boycott.

In Georgia in 1944, two soldiers, one white and one black, chose to sit together on a bus. The driver, John T. Rachols, drew his gun when the two informed him that they wished to stay where they were. Rachols started firing, sending them running for their lives.[8] A year earlier, a bus driver shoved Steve Edwards and his wife off a crowded bus. When they asked for the return of their fare, the driver shot Edwards twice. As he lay on the ground, a white passenger drew a gun and shot him again.[9] Clearly, sometimes the "good citizens" on the bus joined in to reinforce the supremacy of the white community and the criminalization of the free movement of African Americans. They felt confident in committing these acts of violence because the state rarely took notice of or enforced consequences for their actions. Dr. Amos Carnegie, a minister from Chattanooga returning home from a fundraising trip, refused to give up his bus seat so that a white man could sit. Two white men on the bus knocked him to the ground and proceeded to beat and kick him, while the bus driver paid no attention.[10] Despite the brutal tyranny of Jim Crow, hundreds of ordinary African American passengers, denied their civil rights on buses, were brave enough to challenge the slights they experienced on buses, trains, and other forms of public transportation by standing up to drivers or refusing to move. African Americans sitting in the white section of a bus or train intentionally delayed the white passengers as well as the driver, making the train or bus late in reaching its destination. Others filed lawsuits against bus companies.

There were plenty of resisters long before 1955, when Rosa Parks refused to give up her seat on a Montgomery bus. In 1940, Pauli Murray, the young attorney and civil rights activist, who later became the first female African American Episcopal priest, boarded a bus to Durham, North Carolina, to visit relatives for the Easter holiday with her friend Adelene McBean. Murray despised bus travel, describing it as "the public humiliation of black people to be carried out in the presence of privileged white spectators, who witnessed our shame in silence or indifference."[11] When the two women changed buses in Richmond, they found that the Greyhound's seats were broken, so they sat in one of the rows reserved for white passengers. The bus driver insisted that they move to the broken seats, and he called the police when they refused. Charged with disorderly conduct and fined forty-five dollars, they were ordered to jail by the judge when they could not afford to pay.[12]

In 1946, Irene Morgan, a woman in her late twenties, traveling through Virginia from her home in Baltimore, refused to give up her seat when the bus driver demanded that she relinquish it for a white passenger. Morgan informed the driver that because the bus was on an interstate trip, she was not required to observe intrastate segregation laws. After an unpleasant verbal exchange, the bus driver refused to continue on the trip and called the sheriff. With all of the other passengers watching, the sheriff and a deputy dragged Morgan from the bus and arrested her. She was jailed for violating Virginia's transit segregation law and also charged with resisting arrest for kicking and fighting back as the law officers physically removed her from the bus. The NAACP adopted her case and appealed her conviction all the way to the United States Supreme Court, arguing that Virginia's segregation laws violated the interstate commerce clause of the Constitution. Although the Court agreed, the case did not end segregation on public conveyances. That would come fourteen years later, in 1960. "Old Man

Jim Crow was rocked by a resounding right hook to the chin but was not down for the count," reported the *Chicago Defender* on *Morgan v. Virginia*. The southern states simply ignored the ruling and continued to segregate their buses.[13]

Murray's and Morgan's incidents were only two among the many complaints that poured into the NAACP about the various forms of bigotry preventing black travelers from mingling with white passengers on trains and buses. Struggling to keep all riders happy, railroad officials tried to mitigate the humiliation of Jim Crow travel. They mistakenly reasoned that separate cars might spare black passengers the indignity of being transferred to the colored car midjourney and might perhaps prevent dissatisfaction or, worse, legal action. In a letter to Thurgood Marshall, C. G. Pennington, the general passenger agent of the Pennsylvania Railroad, tried to justify the practice:

> Seats in coaches on the through streamlined trains between New York and points south of Washington are all reserved and in order that colored passengers destined to points south of Washington will not be disturbed, a car on such trains is reserved for their use.[14]

By the 1940s, many African Americans had the financial resources to travel for pleasure and for business. Often they even had the wherewithal to purchase tickets for the more expensive first-class Pullman train cars. Regularly demeaned, black passengers wrote on behalf of their race to redress assaults on their dignity, but they received little satisfaction from their letters. The NAACP counsel sent complaints to the offending bus, rail, or streetcar companies, but the often-patronizing replies indicate that nothing substantive was done. Hundreds of complaint letters resulted in no court cases and no concessions—only attempts to placate the writers. "I regret very much that you should have occasion to report difficulties experienced . . . ," the letters always began. "It is not our company policy to discriminate" and "The segregation law does present a most difficult problem" were the phrases they used to suggest that the segregation on public conveyances was not the company's problem. Rather, they implied, the bigotry associated with travel was society's problem to solve.

In the 1940s and 1950s, the NAACP invested significant time and energy responding to complaints from all over the country about unsettling encounters between blacks and whites on public conveyances. Ordinary African Americans regularly penned these missives to the NAACP to protest discriminatory acts and willingly offered their experiences as potential test cases for lawsuits. These selfless acts could easily result in the loss of their jobs or housing, jail, or even death, tactics used by white racists as deterrents to prevent such protests and eliminate the threat of court action.

COLLECTIVELY, BLACK passengers and service employees helped one another endure the indignities of life and travel in Jim Crow America. Madge Washington remembered the terrible rides she experienced in railroad cars before the 1930s, when electric and diesel engines began to take the place of the filthy coal-burning boilers. The railroads placed the "Negro car" directly behind the engine, and soot poured into the passenger compartment. While "the Pullman porters treated us so well," she remembered, "sometimes the black men in the car, frustrated by the conditions, would pull the emergency brake as a protest."[15]

On a train to Norfolk, Virginia, in 1948, a dining-car steward calmly protected two young black women from a disgusting breakfast. Vernell Allen and her girlfriend were on their way from New York to Virginia to visit her friend's family. Tired and hungry from traveling through the night, the two women found the separate dining rooms for black and white riders bothersome, but they were too famished to make an issue of it. After about ten minutes of waiting patiently, the black waiter, who was serving both the white dining room and the colored dining room, arrived to take their orders. "I told him I wanted bacon, and eggs, and ham," Vernell recounted. The waiter eyed them and looked around to see who might overhear their conversation. "You don't want that," the waiter whispered. "I'll bring you some orange juice and some coffee. Everything else," he whispered, "if I serve it to you—it's food that's been scraped off the white people's plates from the other room." Understanding that the women would be upset by this revelation, and that he was sending them back to their seats hungry, the waiter sweetened the message that accompanied his small act of defiance and kindness. "To make the day better for you," he said, "I'm gonna put some vodka in your orange juice."[16]

In her more than 700-page compendium, *States' Laws on Race and Color*, a 1950 book that includes all of the legislation passed in the United States designed to enforce segregation or require racial equality, attorney Pauli Murray recounted that fourteen

Vernell Allen in 1946. The recent high school graduate moved to Brooklyn, New York, ready to begin beauty school. Anxious to travel, she took short trips with friends to places like Norfolk, Virginia, and Atlantic City, New Jersey. Vernell encountered Jim Crow in both the North and the South. (*Photograph courtesy Vernell Allen.*)

states required segregated train facilities, eleven states segregated buses, eleven states kept streetcars and street railways separated by race, four states segregated steamboats and ferries, and nine states specified separate waiting rooms.[17] The emotional and psychological effects of continual racist encounters—day in and day out, on buses, trains, and other public conveyances—exerted an emotional toll that was both exhausting and long lasting. Poet and commentator Langston Hughes referred to the barrage of racist slights, name-calling, Jim Crow signs, and discrimination experienced by black travelers as "Jim Crow shock," or "segregation fatigue." Hughes saw it in the anger of soldiers returning from World War II who had faced air bombardment and heavy artillery fire abroad, only to be humiliated and scorned at home. They were fed up—"nerves taut to the breaking point."[18] Describing his own experiences traveling, club owner and entrepreneur Walter Edwards explained how the fear and uncertainty of travel-related racism made him feel: "So it was a stress. I think that some of the things that we're going through today is from that trauma. We're still traumatized from some of that, you know."[19]

African American newspapers were filled with stories of the random vile acts like those experienced by Vernell and her friend, and by Walter Edwards, as well as the nasty language, threats, and taunts hurled at black passengers. *The Chicago Defender* had a policy of publishing these incidents "experienced by Negroes" in a regular column titled "The People Report."[20] While black passengers did not necessarily face these unpleasant experiences every time they left their homes or used public transportation, they never knew when unwelcome insults or assaults might occur. A woman in Chicago reported that some white boys harassed her sixteen-year-old brother as he traveled to and from a job. In addition to physically abusing the boy, the teenage passengers opened the bus windows and "accused him of 'stinking up the bus.'" The bus driver then joined in, saying, "Get off this bus, you stinking nigger."[21] In 1947, the Contact Services Company fired two young black streetcar operators for talking back to passengers after enduring obnoxious remarks and obscene taunts by "people who resented their race."[22] A man named Banner Jackson wrote to the *Defender* that a friend faced a barrage of epithets, followed by a beating, while waiting for the Halsted Street bus on his way home from work in 1961. He added that the same thing had happened to him in the summer of 1957. "This goes on every summer and nothing is done about it," he reported. "It is useless to report it to the police. They know about it but don't care."[23] Such confrontations are emblematic of hundreds of other documented events. "From the time they leave home in the morning, enroute to school or work, to shopping or to visiting, until they return home at night, humiliation stalks them," testified Roy Wilkins, the NAACP executive secretary, before the Senate Commerce Committee. "The segregation laws harmed the physical body," Wilkins continued, "but always they strike at the root of the human spirit, at the very core of human dignity."[24]

This persistent humiliation can lead to feelings of hopelessness and psychological stress, and some psychologists refer to it as a form of post-traumatic stress.[25] For those who witnessed lynchings or other forms of physical violence and brutality, the emotional toll intensified and in many cases lasted for generations as a heightened sense of fear. In addition to physical symptoms, it can create distrust of white people, anxiety, and symptoms of panic.[26] Even today, some African Americans experience these physical and psychological symptoms as a result of viewing graphic videos of police violence following the shooting of an unarmed black person. The fear and distrust associated with feeling that those whom we empower to protect us are dangerous can be overwhelming.[27]

The psychological toll that racism took and continues to take on African Americans cannot be overstated. One approach to this stress was to completely ignore the ugly parts of the African American past, a common practice among some older black middle- and upper-middle-class Americans during the mid-twentieth century.

Historian Jonathan Scott Holloway explained this selective memory in his memoir *Jim Crow Wisdom*. He recounted a story of his great-aunt Maggie's stubborn refusal to share the family stories of slavery that she remembered hearing in her youth. Aunt Maggie chose to remain silent about the family's unpleasant history, ensuring that with her death the "histories of social degradation, violence, and importantly, survival disappeared forever." "With her silence, my grand-aunt was participating in a long-standing practice of editing her memory, an artful forgetting for the sake of affirming her family's social position," Holloway wrote. Similarly, try as I might, I could not get my own mother, Alvenia Sullivan, to describe any of her negative experiences growing up in Jim Crow Fayetteville, North Carolina, despite presenting her with evidence of the 1941 conflict at Fort Bragg, the identification of every black person by race in the local city directory, and other overt acts of discrimination about which she was certainly aware. I had heard the stories of the "good white people" that she knew and of her brother and sister putting her through college, the first in her family. She focused on the stories of the positive aspects of culture, education, and her family's triumph over adversity rather than the deprivation left by slavery or the practices of Jim Crow in her hometown, known nationally as Uncle Sam's Powder Keg. Many older family members, like my mother and Jonathan Holloway's Aunt Maggie, protected themselves emotionally and protected the class status they worked so hard to obtain with selective memory. They also controlled the image presented to white people. "They retained," as Holloway put it, "their positions as interpreters of blackness for the white community."[28]

As we will see, the purchase and ownership of the family automobile was one response to the stress and tribulations of public transportation by bus and rail—a means of avoiding the daily humiliations that resulted from being at the mercy of bus drivers and conductors, white passengers and policemen. Cars enabled unfettered travel without these continuous encounters with racism and provided some measure of both physical and psychological safety. Not surprisingly, beginning in the 1930s, African American families often took whatever resources they had or could muster to purchase a car, new or used. For black Americans, that car poked a finger in the eye of those who wanted to see the continuation of the separate, unequal public-transportation facilities. At least, that is how some black car owners saw their defiance of Jim Crow facilities. As one writer put it, "because of jimcrow [sic] on public transportation, he shows his resentment by owning his own facilities."[29] The automobile represented the ability to take charge of one's own destiny, to secure an aspect of life over which one had seemingly total control.

Chapter 3

AFRICAN AMERICANS AND THE AUTOMOBILE

My parents, Clyde and Alvenia (Wooten) Sullivan, moved north from Fayetteville, North Carolina, to Newark, New Jersey, in 1947, just after World War II. My father, recently discharged from the US Army, could not wait to leave the South. My mother, the first in her family to graduate from college, hoped for a job in a desegregated school system. Her bachelor's degree in elementary education from Fayetteville State College, the historically black college in her hometown, represented one of the few education options for a smart and ambitious southern Negro woman in the 1940s. The entire Wooten clan gathered to celebrate her graduation, according to the Norfolk Journal and Guide's *gossipy Fayetteville column. Like the white newspapers, the* Journal *had its own "society pages" that described daily events in the region's middle-class black community.*

Nell and Richard Wooten, Alvenia's two older siblings, never went to college. Instead, they attended trade schools and supported their baby sister at Fayetteville State. Nell learned to "do hair" and owned a beauty parlor. Uncle Richard expertly handcrafted orthopedic shoes to doctors' specifications. To the family, Wooten's Orthopedic Shoe shop, on the basement level of his Philadelphia row house, smelled of leather and glue. It is one of the smells I remember from my childhood. It was the smell of success.

My parents' romance began in 1941 with a game of checkers. After the altercation that claimed the lives of Ned Turman and Edwin Hargraves, Fort Bragg began hosting socials to bring young black women to the base to listen to music, dance, and play games with the colored soldiers to calm tensions. After the war, my parents "ran away to South Carolina to get married," and shortly thereafter Dad headed north, where a job awaited him as the Newark branch photographer for the Baltimore Afro-American *newspaper. The Seaboard Coast Line train, pejoratively known as the "Chicken Bone Express," brought my mother north within a month or so, and she secured a teaching position in the Newark public schools. By the time she arrived in Newark, my father had found an apartment, and a newly purchased used car stood in the driveway.*

Thousands of southern migrants flooded into Newark and nearby New York City, as well as other cities, seeking opportunities unavailable in the south after the war—part of a second wave of the Great Migration. The most fortunate found jobs, education, and housing open to them in certain parts of the state. My parents, after settling in and surveying the real estate market, purchased a two-family house—at 391 Badger Avenue in Newark—and rented half of it to another young family.

At night, my father attended the Newark College of Engineering with help from the G.I. Bill. The Model T was their lifeline. That car took them to work and took my father to college at night. They drove downtown to shop at Bamberger's on the weekends, to the Acme market for groceries every Friday, and to St. Mary's Episcopal Church on Sunday mornings. Sometimes they drove down to Atlantic City on Sunday afternoons, just to take a ride. My father loved driving. Each summer, when my mother took the train back to Fayetteville to visit the Wooten clan for a week or two, he drove down to pick her up. As with many other African American couples, the automobile held a special meaning, for they were no longer at the mercy of Jim Crow trains and buses. The car provided security, dignity, and opportunity and gave them the freedom to go anywhere—to have complete independence. It also represented their status as free Americans.

BETWEEN THE 1920S and the 1960s, automobile ownership changed African American life. You could not be asked to move to the back of the bus—or, worse, to get off and reenter through the back door—if you drove your own car. The horsepower of an automobile also gave African American drivers the ability to escape. Cars enabled motorists to move rapidly without being stopped or harassed by white citizens anxious to take the law into their own hands. There are instances of African Americans being dragged from their cars and beaten by angry mobs, but there are certainly far more cases of black people simply driving past whites without being detected or of outrunning a dangerous situation.[1] Getting behind the wheel became, at times, an equalizer.

Emily Post, the arbiter of white America's etiquette, expressed concerns that cars leveled the social playing field. She complained about the ordinary citizen who purchased a new car and "felt that he automatically became the equal of every owner of a similar car, and the superior of the owners of all cars of less importance." The car, Post feared, enabled the lower classes to feel equal to the middle classes. Post further lamented that "the man in moderate circumstances will stint himself in every way to buy a car actually beyond his means, thus to gratify his desire to go one better than his neighbor." Not only did cars make you more equal, she continued, but they could make you more confident and aggressive.[2] Post saw the automobile as an unfortunate invention for those, like herself, who wished to preserve the existing social order. Others, however, especially African Americans, viewed the automobile as the necessary invention of a democratic society.

W. E. B. Du Bois, editor of *The Crisis*, the magazine of the NAACP, traveled throughout his life for both business and pleasure. As a sociologist, civil rights activist, and speaker, he spent many hours on the road. Sometimes he traveled by Jim Crow train car, but, tellingly, he preferred his own automobile. Most African Americans who could afford cars purchased them. And many had a special relationship with their cars.

Du Bois clearly loved driving, especially in his old, reconditioned car. In 1932, he drove all the way from New York to the site of a contentious coal miners' strike in Harlan County, Kentucky.[3] "All over and everywhere the colored people are traveling in their automobiles," he wrote in a 1932 column in *The Crisis*. He seemed quite pleased with the increasing number of black car owners, noting that car ownership was a particular boon to businessmen—insurance agents, officials of fraternal and religious societies, and the like. With great satisfaction, he commented on the positive way that the automobile changed transportation for one member of the black elite, a prominent clergyman:

> I remember once that the venerable Bishop Turner stricken with paralysis, could for neither love nor money, hire a Pullman berth from Savannah to Atlanta. They fixed the old man up in the "Jim Crow" smoker across two seats. Yesterday I saw the A.M.E. Bishop of Florida. He was gliding along in his Cadillac car with a chauffeur on the way from Jacksonville to Atlanta. He looked extremely comfortable.[4]

Furthermore, Du Bois took great delight in the fact that car travel seemed to be putting a damper on certain businesses that supported the Jim Crow system. "[T]he only discrimination that we chanced upon was one at which we heartily laughed: a filling station on the Jacksonville–Daytona road had a sign 'For white trade only.' We passed it four times and saw no single car there. 'These crackers persist in being fools!' says my companion."[5]

W. E. B. Du Bois' first car. Du Bois, pictured here in the 1920s, loved traveling in this old car and often drove long distances to meetings, conferences, and sites of social injustice. (*Department of Special Collections and University Archives, W. E. B. Du Bois Library, University of Massachusetts, Amherst.*)

While all Americans—white and black—enjoyed the freedom and privacy that the automobile afforded, these advantages were far more profound for black Americans. "Of course Negroes ride in the Jim Crow coach here," commented a wealthy black man from North Carolina. "But I don't ride in it; I just don't ride trains now. I use my car and drive anywhere I want to go. That's one of the reasons I have a car."[6] Operating a motorcar proved to be a wonderful, liberating experience for citizens for whom the full rights of citizenship and mobility were denied. The automobile opened up the entire nation for exploration, emboldening black people to visit national parks and monuments, historic sites and museums, and to take vacations or just go for a drive. "We feel like Vikings," exulted Alfred Edgar Smith, an African American journalist and administrative assistant for the federal Works Progress

Administration.[7] "What if our craft is blunt of nose and limited of power and our sea is macadamized; . . . The nomad in the poorest and the mightiest of us, sends us behind the wheel, north, south, east, and west, in answer to the call of the road."[8]

Assuming the role of "Vikings" appealed to black travelers because of the many prohibitions on mobility, historical and contemporary. Drivers relied only on themselves when traveling by car. Willie Cooper, whose first car, "Old Betsy," was a key-lime 1956 Buick, refused to give up his driver's license at the age of seventy-five. "He wants to drive," said his daughter, *Detroit News* reporter Desiree Cooper, "because he has a right to—and he's earned it."[9]

Like Willie Cooper, most African Americans who drove cars found themselves more at ease than usual when behind the wheel. "The ever-growing national scope of modern business commands; pleasure suggests; and (in down right selfish frankness) it's mighty good to be the skipper for a change, and pilot our craft whither and when we will," wrote Alfred Edgar Smith.[10] Smith served as a bureau chief and writer for the *Chicago Defender* and as a member of Franklin D. Roosevelt's Federal Council on Negro Affairs, so he was often on the road traveling for work and to and from Washington, DC.

The newfound freedom offered by the automobile, however, also brought black Americans—as it did not for white Americans—into contact with new dangers. Black drivers could venture unwittingly into the wrong neighborhoods or stop at the wrong places. Despite these potential perils, families and business travelers continued to drive into unknown regions and across state lines. Black motorists encountered racist law-enforcement officers, racist gas-station attendants, bigoted automobile repairmen, threatening road signs, and restaurants that would only serve food to black patrons through a window slot in the back door. Sometimes black motorists even faced the anger of racist mobs. Driving a car through unfriendly and even hostile neighborhoods and all-white communities represented a small yet meaningful personal act of bravery—a statement of rebelliousness and refusal to accept the status quo or to give in to fear.

Cars allowed for these encounters not only because they permitted more freedom of movement but also because they offered a measure of safety to the driver and passengers. Parents traveling with children in a car could more adequately protect their offspring from the verbal and psychological battering that could accompany a ride on a public conveyance. Historian Spencer Crew reminisced about growing up in the 1950s: "[T]hat big old car was like a cocoon," he remembered. "We didn't know anything except what we saw out the side windows. We could hardly see over the back of the front seat. Our parents protected us from all the racist stuff along the road."[11] Children were able to grow up proud rather than ashamed of their identity, without the public assaults that could accompany bus and train travel. A car could move you from one African American neighborhood—or safe zone—to another, enclosed in your own rolling living room. It was "a racial shield."[12]

Like Du Bois, Booker T. Washington also viewed the automobile as essential to black life, but for very different reasons. "The most modern vehicle for transportation is the automobile," he proclaimed. For Washington, cars were a tool for attaining economic self-reliance. With car ownership came the ability to leave the South, to get a job as a chauffeur, a truck driver, a taxi driver, or perhaps even to start a business. "It is doing almost as much for the Negro as the mule has done," Washington believed.[13] While for Washington the automobile took on the role of a practical tool, other members of the black middle class[14] viewed their cars as weapons in the arsenal to push the cause of civil rights by refusing to accept what Du Bois called "color discrimination" in public accommodations. Cars enabled black drivers to participate in a solution instead of contributing to the segregation problem by accepting it. As one article put it, the Negro showed his rejection of

Marjorie Doneghy and Virginia Brooks stand beside David Brooks' 1957 Chevrolet Bel Air convertible with a continental kit, a decorative accessory that mounted the spare tire behind the trunk. The photograph displays the car as a proud status symbol, but it also suggests how the family car provided safety and protection for these little girls ready for church on Easter Sunday. (*Kentucky Historical Society, Frankfort.*)

Jim Crow transportation and his "resentment" simply by "owning his own facilities."[15]

In his study of African Americans in rural Georgia, ethnologist Arthur Rapier found that black travelers used their automobiles not only as a way to evade the "irritations of the unequal transportational [sic] facilities provided by train and bus and plane" but also as a method of resistance to a racist system.[16] Rapier's informants, and by extension black people elsewhere, understood that they could eschew the racist public transportation system and help starve it of money by using their cars. At the very least, they denied the operators of buses and trains fares to support racist practices.

W. E. B. Du Bois wrote a detailed description of a 1929 trip he made throughout the South to understand what it was like to travel the region as a black person. He traveled 1,399 miles—by Pullman car, Jim Crow car, and automobile. The trip illustrated the unpredictable nature of the conditions that African American travelers encountered. From Petersburg, Virginia, to Raleigh, North Carolina, he found the Negro coach "not as modern a coach as that of the white," but it was clean, and he noted that the conductor said, "Please." From Hamlet to Charlotte in North Carolina, however, a trip of seventy miles, he rode in "a miserably dirty car which any decent State Board of Health would have condemned." The number of African Americans driving automobiles, even at this early date, proved a total surprise to him, but a welcome one. Du Bois' anecdotal observations suggested that the automobile was having an effect on Jim Crow segregation, denying it funds. "My chief joy," he wrote, "in these 'Jim Crow' rides was those empty cars. The automobile is certainly bringing just retribution upon the silly profiteering of Jim Crow."[17] The car could also play a more direct role as a weapon against Jim Crow, as it did during the 1955–56 Montgomery bus boycott and similar acts of open defiance.

FROM THE end of World War II, the black community in Montgomery, Alabama, organized to try to end segregation on the city's buses. Jo Ann Robinson, a local college professor and activist in Montgomery and president of the Women's Political Council (WPC), headed a group that sent Mayor W. A. Gayle a letter detailing three requests:

1. A city law that would make it possible for Negroes to sit from back toward front, and whites from front toward back until all the seats are taken.
2. That Negroes not be asked or forced to pay fare at front and go to the rear of the bus to enter.
3. That buses stop at every corner in residential sections

Martin Luther King Jr. assists women supporting the Montgomery bus boycott into a volunteer's automobile. To force the bus company to desegregate city buses, volunteers used their cars as taxis to ferry people to work. The car became an effective tool to help defeat Jim Crow. (*Don Cravens photograph, Getty Images.*)

> occupied by Negroes as they do in communities where whites reside.

The letter also explained that twenty-five organizations had been mobilized to support a bus boycott if these changes were not made. Even after the letter, however, black passengers received disrespectful treatment on city buses, and some, like fifteen-year-old high schooler Claudette Colvin, were handcuffed and arrested for refusing to give up their seats to white riders. On December 1, 1955, Rosa Parks also refused when asked to stand so that a white man could have her seat.

Parks' refusal is famous, of course, but the role of the automobile in this protest is not so familiar. After her arrest, the African American community took action. Key to the success of the bus boycott was the purchase of a small fleet of station wagons that picked up anyone in need of a ride and drove them to their destinations. Black cab drivers picked up walkers and charged them only ten cents, the cost of a ride on the city buses. These "private taxis," along with the fleet of station wagons and anyone else who used their car to help but did not charge passengers any fee at all, starved the bus system of passengers and revenue until public officials relented and eliminated separate sections in the buses. The extent to which the boycott crippled the city's bus lines was not known until 2018, when a cache of documents and record books that had been tucked away in the attic of James H. Bagley, manager of the Montgomery City Lines Company, surfaced. The ledgers, found by Bagley's granddaughter, showed that income plummeted 69 percent between December 5, 1955, when black riders stopped using the buses, and December 20, 1956, when the boycott ended. Documents indicate that Bagley did everything he could to keep the buses running. He cut some bus routes and laid off drivers in an attempt to stanch the bleeding—a move that angered the drivers' union. Hundreds of people, afraid that this action on the part of southern blacks weakened Jim Crow, sent in letters of support with their unsolicited contributions. "Please, please don't let the niggers have their way about riding your cars," a North Carolina supporter wrote. "If you give into them the whole South will go black. I believe if you hold out they will all eventually come crawling back to the buses."[18] After the citizens of Montgomery proved that nonviolent direct action could be extremely effective, other cities adopted bus boycotts as a method of resistance.

The automobile proved to be essential for more than the boycotts. It helped make the civil rights movement possible in a segregated world in which the participants needed the ability to travel to different cities quickly and safely. Some African Americans viewed cars as the *foundation* to the success of the movement: "The key to the movement was a key to an automobile . . . the key to a

Florida A & M student Ruby Powell thumbs a ride during the 1956 boycott of segregated buses in Tallahassee, Florida. Powell is alerting black private automobile owners that she is a part of the protest. As in the Montgomery bus boycott, the use of private automobiles helped Negroes to defy Jim Crow laws. (*Associated Press.*)

damn good automobile," proclaimed the *Pittsburgh Courier*.[19] For instance, a problem often arose when African Americans flew into a city and tried to get from the airport to a hotel or meeting site. Strict rules governed cabs—whom they could transport and where they could go. White-owned cab companies held the franchises to transport customers to and from the airports. Hotel shuttles would not usually transport black passengers, or would force them to ride in the back, and only if there was extra room. Black cabbies were not permitted to pick up their passengers at the airports. Since the laws varied from state to state, it was never clear what might happen when a black person disembarked at a terminal. They could be stuck at the airport. This dilemma made the "Fly and Rent Club" an essential part of any civil rights action. As one article described it, you would "fly to the airport of your destination and rent a car from there." The rental car made transportation to and from the airport convenient and proved to be an important part of the travel experience for Dr. King, other civil rights leaders, and black corporate executives. "The first thing one did after booking a flight to a southern airport was to arrange for a U-Drive it car."[20]

African American cab companies were often prohibited from taking their passengers to and from airports. These laws not only gave white cab companies an unfair competitive advantage but also left black passengers stranded. In some cities, the cabbies could be arrested if they violated the law. This photograph is from Birmingham, Alabama, 1956. (*Danny Lyon photograph, Magnum Photos.*)

While cars fueled the civil rights movement, they were most often used to drive to work or for leisure, and social class affected car ownership for black Americans, just as it did for white Americans. Some white Americans saw their automobiles as symbols of their status in society, and cars served the same purpose for some African Americans. As early as 1916, C. W. Churchill, a writer for *Harper's Weekly*, knew that "[t]he motorcar has woven itself into the fabric of social life: it has become an intimate and necessary part of good living. The place it fills in our affairs is so conspicuous, and the association of the owner with his car is so noticeable, that public opinion does not fail to classify men and women according to the cars they select for their personal use. The owner is known by his car, whether he wishes to be or not."[21] This comment anticipates the importance the automobile would achieve by the 1950s as a status symbol for car owners, both black and white. Riding in an attractive or expensive car enhanced the prestige and self-worth of the driver and his passengers. (Most drivers in the first half of the century were men, although an increasing number of independent-minded women drove cars, more so toward mid-century.) African Americans had few opportunities to feel valuable and valued in American society. "In every city of any considerable size Negroes are to be found in possession of some of the finest cars made in America—and they are the original purchasers too," bragged Robert Russa Moton, describing African American car ownership in 1929. Moton was an educator, successor to Booker T. Washington as president of Tuskegee Institute, and a prolific writer on African American life.[22]

The growing black middle class shared many of the same hopes and values as the white middle class. They yearned to have well-paying jobs, to own the same consumer goods, to send their children to high-quality schools, and to take vacations during their leisure time. Successful black encounters with white Americans, they hoped, would change negative attitudes about race. Moton described his vision of the hopes and desires of black life almost entirely in material terms: "The thinking Negro wants for himself and his children the same things the white man wants for himself and his children."[23] For Moton, attaining material success was not about imitating white life. Rather, it was about providing a comfortable American life for black families and demonstrating the worth of black people as human beings. Moton expressed the views of many when he identified American values through the material possessions, modern conveniences, and educational and cultural events to which black families aspired. As he saw it, the Negro home should include:

> Books, paintings, sculpture, music, newspapers, magazines, all are common adjuncts of home life. There is the annual vacation for all the family, sometimes by train, sometimes by motorcar. Among them are club life for women as well as for men. Card parties, receptions, at-homes, dances are all a part of the social programme for visiting guests; and where conditions make it possible without humiliation, there are theatre parties also followed by suppers and dances, all of which reflects the genuine Americanism of the Negro. Along with these go literary, scientific, professional, and art societies and clubs whose members have qualified for degrees from recognized American institutions and have distinction in their respective fields. These are the finer flowers of Negro home life.[24]

In Moton's eyes, the quest for civil rights could be equated with the quest for economic equality. Becoming good consumers, he argued, would lead to the "genuine Americanism of the Negro." Full rights followed from economic success, economic freedom, and membership in the middle class. And among the visible indicators of such success were the motorcar and the annual family vaca-

This elegant Harlem couple in their 1930 Cadillac Series 452 proudly display their raccoon coats and their upper-middle-class status. The car, with its wide white-sidewall tires and brightly polished chrome, is particularly showy. At the time of purchase, it was worth about $6,900, considerably more than the median income of black or white families in that era. This is one of the most famous images associated with the Harlem Renaissance. (*Couple in Raccoon Coats, 1932, by James Van Der Zee © Donna Mussenden Van Der Zee.*)

tion, usually by automobile. Unfortunately, Moton's analysis did not address the significant barriers, both legal and customary, that locked black people out of the full rights of citizenship and economic attainment. His dream of middle-class success for all black Americans would be satisfied for some, but certainly not for all.

FIRST CAME a big question: What car to buy? Selecting that perfect car could be a challenge for every American family, but the calculus was different for African Americans. Black families in the South, or ones with southern connections, needed a car that would provide a safe and secure ride in a Jim Crow environment. Pontiacs offered "roomy" and "trouble-free performance." The greatest attribute of Studebakers, aside from their airplanelike appearance, was their durability. Ford claimed to offer the most affordable cars on the road, with "comfortable tweed interiors," generous seats, and fashionable new colors like sea-mist green and bay-view blue. Black magazines, newspapers, and travel guides like *The Negro Motorist Green Book* offered advice and periodic profiles of the latest automobile models to help their readers select the most serviceable makes and models. The choice could make the difference between a safe journey and a dangerous confrontation. Black buying power, vehicle selection, and even driving practices were all sharply determined by discrimination. Black families had specific criteria for selecting cars and very specific needs when they went out on the road.

Lewis Hanley posing in front of his 1932 Chevrolet Coupe, ca. 1935. (*Kentucky Historical Society, Frankfort, 1995ph2.34AAFRAA1.*)

For many drivers, safety surpassed all other measures. The terrible saga of the civil rights activist Medgar Evers offers a case in point. Evers hoped to become a lawyer, so, in the summer of 1954, with a bachelor's degree from Alcorn Agricultural and Mechanical College (now Alcorn State University), he applied for admission to the law school at the University of Mississippi. He received a rejection letter, because "Ole Miss" did not accept black students in the 1950s. Instead, Evers became the first field director for the NAACP in the state of Mississippi. This new job involved driving all over the state on back roads and in isolated rural places to gather evidence of arson, to investigate murders, and to examine other crimes committed against black residents that were ignored by the local police because of the victims' race. Evers knew well the dangers of the job and the hostile attitudes toward the NAACP held by many white Mississippians. They viewed him as a racial agitator, stirring up the accepted social order. Working for the NAACP could get you lynched or shot. Despite the precautions Evers took, white supremacist Byron De La Beckwith would murder him in his own driveway in 1963.

A black man—particularly a black man driving the back roads of Mississippi—had to think long and hard about which car to buy. Special concerns, such as how comfortable a car would be for sleeping or how easily it would allow a quick escape from an angry mob, generally did not concern white drivers. Evers selected a large and imposing Oldsmobile with a V-8 engine for his excursions around the state. The car's utilitarian body design belied the power under the hood. The engine—the Rocket 88—was a precursor of the muscle car that high school boys, with cigarettes rolled in their T-shirt sleeves, would covet in the late 1950s and 1960s, but for Evers it was a practical rather than an ostentatious choice. The Rocket 88 would not be pushed around or shoved from the road by a less powerful car or a pickup truck, and Evers' long frame could stretch out on the seat to sleep if need be.[25] Most important, when you pressed the accelerator, that "Olds" took off and could outrun an ambush.

This advertisement announces the new Oldsmobile Rocket 88. With its powerful engine, it was a good choice for African Americans who needed fast acceleration. (*Charles Clark III photograph, collection of the author.*)

Even for those black people whose jobs did not take them on back roads in Mississippi, specific factors played into their decisions when buying a car. Although black families were more likely overall than white families to purchase used cars, they preferred to buy larger, more expensive, and sturdier makes of automobiles than those favored by white car owners.[26] A larger car could hold plenty of necessary gear for long trips. It was perceived as safer than a lighter, smaller car in the event of an accident, and it was viewed as a more reliable method of transportation.

American capitalism responded to the rising black middle class. Black-owned newspapers in such major American cities as Los Angeles, Baltimore, Chicago, Philadelphia, and Washington conducted community readers' surveys to assess consumer clout and determine which products resonated with black purchasers. Where did black buyers put their money? By determining product preferences, the newspapers hoped to boost their own advertising revenue. They reasoned that if the companies producing Gold Medal flour, Esso gasoline, Buick automobiles, and Gerber baby food knew just how many black families used their merchandise, these major corporations might readily place ads in black newspapers. Professional marketing firms designed the surveys, a fascinating record of the buying habits of black Americans during the 1930s, 40s, and 50s—a time when black people remained largely invisible as American consumers. Among the details collected in the surveys were the makes of automobiles that black people purchased most frequently.

Newspaper readers answered questions about everything from their preferred brands of household laundry soap to the most frequently visited gas stations. In addition to gaining potential advertising, the newspapers hoped to dispel stereotypes about the black community. "Their lives are in effect invisible to most Americans, who rarely bother to look behind the Color Curtain at the Negroes' homes, their places of work or worship, or their spirit," observed a writer for *Time* magazine.[27] The newspaper surveys graphically demonstrated the economic power of the growing black middle class in American cities and highlighted the similarities between these upwardly mobile families pictured in the market reports and their white counterparts.

The families in the surveys owned tidy middle-class houses with clean stoops and striped awnings. Readers of the final report on Philadelphia observed a photograph of a perfectly coifed young family smiling back from the cover. *The New Philadelphia Story: A Survey of America's Third Largest Negro Market* identified "the characteristics of the Philadelphia Negro Market" in 1945.[28] Obviously designed to appeal to a white corporate audience, the family on the cover exuded respectability and a commitment to American values. The photograph suggested that since the African American family—prosperous, traditional, and very fair skinned (they were surely chosen for that reason)—looked just like any other

American family, there was nothing to fear. Black families dressed like your family and shared the same beliefs—except that they had slightly darker skin. Other pictures of nuclear families—husbands and wives sitting in modern living rooms reading newspapers while children dutifully did their homework—peppered the reports. These drawings, accompanied by charts and statistics, indicated to white business owners the importance black families placed on reading and education. Obviously these families had disposable income, and you might be able to get some of it by selling them your products. Statistics confirmed the black community's commitment to education in each report. The Baltimore report noted that 99.4 percent of the wives and 97.8 percent of the husbands had education averaging 7.7 years of school. And "81.7% of Baltimore's school age Negroes attend school."[29]

Automobiles and gasoline figured prominently in each of the marketing reports as indicators of the durable goods that defined what it meant to be an American consumer. In 1945, the *Baltimore Afro-American* newspaper surveyed its readership, touting the city as "America's 5th largest Negro Market." Baltimore, the report concluded, had a growing and increasingly affluent Negro population with significant purchasing potential. According to the report data, 77 percent of the working people in the city held positions "graded higher than semi-skilled or unskilled." More than half of these workers lived in Baltimore's "better class homes." The city's survey results reflected both wartime deprivation—most of the cars owned by Baltimore's residents had been purchased before the war, and new cars were not available during the war years—as well as postwar anticipation and hope. Many of the respondents answered that they anxiously awaited the opportunity to buy a new car once the war ended. Members of the black community in Washington, DC, also intended to buy new cars after World War II, "when they are again being built."[30]

The average income of Baltimore's black community matched the average of black communities in other major American cities—which meant it was far behind white Americans' income. For example, in 1946 only 25 percent of the urban black families surveyed earned more than $3,000 per year, and three-quarters of these families earned less; 44 percent of urban white families earned more than $3,000.[31] Still, Baltimore's large African American market had the wherewithal to acquire a considerable amount of consumer goods. Photographs offered proof of the report's claims. The pictures showed fashionably dressed African American women shopping in local grocery stores for such popular products as Free State Beer, Schindler's Peanut Butter, and Morton Salt. *The Baltimore Afro-American* encouraged white-run corporations to "Consider the moderate cost of cultivating the well-filled pocket-books of COLORED AMERICA." Some manufacturers already saw the value in cultivating black shoppers. Procter & Gamble, Colgate–Palmolive–Peet, Gerber baby food, Johnson & Johnson, and other companies regularly placed ads in black newspapers and magazines, and several of these firms hired black executives.[32]

The overall buying power of the new urban Negro showed tremendous growth in all areas of consumer goods, but particularly in the sales of automobiles. By the 1940s and 1950s, all of the studies indicated a significant increase in the number of black American households with a car parked out front or in the driveway. One study estimated that 475,000 black families owned at least one car, with half of these cars purchased new. "This year, Negroes will spend well over $200 million for new cars. And Wait! That's only in seventeen metropolitan areas with a total of 1,200,000 Negro families. With some four million Negro families in the United States, you can imagine the potential automobile buying power across the nation."[33] "Colored America is one-tenth of your national market. In the larger cities the percentages are much higher," claimed the *Baltimore Afro-American*.[34] The newspaper identified "a large . . . homogeneous body of consumers" in Washington, DC, and in every major American city "which is characteristically middle class."[35] According to these reports, if African Americans in the United States were a country, they would have the equivalent per capita income and buying power of the prosperous nations of Western Europe. "This country does exist," bragged one market survey. "It is the Negro market in the United States."[36]

These arguments—patronizing or worse by today's standards—sought to entice mainstream manufacturers to open their showrooms, dealerships, and stores to black America. Rather than directly confronting Jim Crow practices, they attempted to open these markets by stressing the economic gain that companies could expect. Money, the marketers reasoned, provided the power to dilute segregation and racism in the United States. Their appeal to consumerism was, after all, the American way, yet the advertisers had to be convinced that black Americans were actually people with buying habits like everyone else. In addition, the series of market studies also provided the most detailed picture of the brands of automobiles most popular with black consumers.

In Baltimore, the black community exhibited a fondness for large, roomy Buicks, the car choice for 18 percent of the black car owners. After that, 14.5 percent owned Dodges, 13.2 percent had Fords, and 11.9 percent drove Chevys. In Philadelphia, "America's Third Largest Market" for African Americans, the 1946 survey also showed that the sturdy and reliable Buick was the favorite. "Buick is first choice in automobiles, ranking over Ford, Chevrolet, and Plymouth, significant in that it shows the willingness to make a relatively heavy investment in a product which is a big factor in the opportunity it gives for family utility and recreation," claimed the report. A Buick was not inexpensive; at the time, in fact, it ranked among the most prestigious brands. In 1946, a Roadmaster, one of the costliest Buick models, had a list price of $2,110. That same year, a Cadillac could run as much as $4,000. African Americans preferred Buicks for their reliability and their size.

The *Pittsburgh Courier*, one of the most important and widely circulated African American newspapers in the country, surveyed its readers in 1950 and posted similar results. Pittsburgh's black con-

Clad in her fur coat, an African American woman discusses a fashionable Chevy Deluxe Sport Coupe with a black automobile salesman in 1949 or 1950. (*Courtesy of the Maryland Historical Society, Baltimore.*)

sumers purchased Buicks more often than other brands of cars.[37] In a nationwide survey, the New York–based Interstate United Newspapers organization identified Buick as the car of choice among African American buyers.[38] Later surveys showed different preferences, but clearly African American buyers always chose larger cars. "[S]ales figures show that compact cars do not have as much appeal to Negroes as they do in the general market," commented an article in the *Chicago Defender.*[39] The key finding of a study of the differences in automobile-buying behavior between black and white Americans was that African Americans, overall, tended to favor more expensive, heavier, and more powerful cars, regardless of income. The study concluded that generally automobiles seemed to be more important to African Americans.[40] Indeed, they were.

Still, many black families drove Fords or Chevys, the most economical choices. More black consumers bought one of these two cars than any other. But Buicks and other luxury cars were proportionately more popular with black drivers than with white drivers of similar income levels. "The Cadillac, Lincoln, Imperial, and Buick became the trademark for success from 125th Street in Harlem to Los Angeles," claimed an article in *Sepia* magazine.[41] More important, owners viewed them as more reliable and less prone to breakdown. Even Buick's advertising tagline, "When better cars are built, Buick will build them," gave consumers confidence in these solid, dependable vehicles.

Len Newsome, C. C. Poinsette, and Thomas Clemons of Pittsburgh pose proudly beside their Buick after a bear-hunting trip. A large, heavy Buick like this one was the most popular choice for African American drivers. (*Teenie Harris Archive/Carnegie Museum of Art, Getty Images.*)

Median Income by Race for Selected Cities, 1949

City	White	Negro	Other Races
Chicago	$2,644	$1,901	$2,153
Philadelphia	$2,419	$1,566	$1,717
New York	$2,517	$1,707	$1,863
Baltimore	$2,355	$1,368	n/a
Pittsburgh	$2,284	$1,529	n/a
Washington, DC	$2,830	$1,906	$2,348

In 1949, African Americans (referred to in the 1950 census as Negroes) earned an average of two-thirds of the income earned by white Americans. Despite their lower incomes, however, African Americans tended to prefer larger automobiles for a variety of reasons, including safety and protection, reliability, engine power, and sizes of the trunk and seats. Black motorists stranded without a black hotel might end up stretching out in their cars to sleep.

African American Car Ownership by Make of Automobile

Data Source: US Census of Population: 1950, detail table 87, income by state, city, and race. US Census Bureau, Suitland, MD.

City Surveyed	Buick	Ford	Chevrolet	Plymouth	Dodge	Olds	Pontiac	Cadillac
Philadelphia	18.7	11.3	10.7	10.0	8.7	8.7	8.0	3.3
Pittsburgh	19.4	13.7	9.7	9.1	n/a	9.1	5.7	3.4
Washington, DC	18.7	11.3	10.5	10.0	8.7	8.7	8.0	3.3

African American car ownership in three American cities between 1945 and 1951, based on surveys conducted by a variety of market-research firms for the *Philadelphia Afro-American*, the *Pittsburgh Courier*, and the *Washington Afro-American* newspapers. The *Pittsburgh Courier* did not include the Dodge in its listing. These data indicate the popularity of the larger, more powerful, and more expensive Buick among African American automobile buyers. The data also demonstrate that black drivers purchased Cadillacs in the same proportion that white drivers purchased them—a little more than 3 percent. (Note: The abbreviation *Olds*, above, is for Oldsmobile.)

Factory Prices of Cars by Make of Automobile, 1950

Make / Model	Price
Buick	
Special Series 40	$1,803–1,983
Super Series Series 50	$2,041–2,844
Roadmaster Series 70	$2,528–3,407
Ford	
Deluxe Six	$1,333–1,472
Deluxe V-8	$1,419–1,545
Custom Deluxe V-8	$1,590–2,107
Chevrolet	
Special Series Six	$1,329–1,450
Deluxe Series	$1,482–1,994
Plymouth	
Deluxe Six	$1,371–1,840
Special Deluxe Six	$1,603–2,372
Dodge	
Wayfarer	$1,611–1,738
Meadowbrook	$1,848
Coronet	$1,927–2,800
Oldsmobile	
Seventy-Six Series	$1,615–2,360
Eighty-Eight Series	$1,725–2,585
Ninety-Eight Series	$2,095–2,615
Pontiac	
Streamliner Series Six	$1,673–2,343
Streamliner Series Eight	$1,742–2,411
Chieftain Six	$1,571–2,122
Chieftain Eight	$1,763–2,190
Cadillac	
Series 61	$2,761–2,866
Series 62	$3,150–3,654
Series 75 (Fleetwood)	$4,770–4,959

Source: Ron Kowalke, Standard Catalog of American Cars 1946–1975, 4th ed. (Iola, Wisconsin: Krause Publications, Inc., 1997).

IT SEEMS self-evident that African Americans with higher incomes bought more expensive cars. In the District of Columbia, for example, 15 percent of black residents with rents above fifty dollars per month drove a Buick, usually regarded as an upper-middle-class car. Only 5.3 percent of workers with rents below thirty dollars per month bought Buicks.[42] But when choosing a family vehicle, income and purchase price were not the only determining factors. Important criteria for these car buyers included trunk space, safety, speed, performance, and reliability.

A large trunk stowed suitcases and other bags for annual vacations or business travel, but African Americans traveling by car needed to transport supplies that white travelers might never consider carrying unless they were on a camping trip. Black magazines and newspapers urged drivers to stock their cars liberally with provisions to make it possible to drive straight through to a destination without stopping, or only stopping as necessary for gasoline. Baskets overflowed with sandwiches and jugs of water and iced tea. What would happen if you needed a bathroom along the road and the gas stations barred you from their restrooms because of the color of your skin? A large old coffee can became a "pee can," a makeshift toilet in an emergency. I remember my grandmother always insisting that my father carry a pee can in the car for long trips, even in the 1960s. As a child, I assumed she just had a weak bladder.

For many African Americans, carrying these objects was routine—just one of the costs of being black in the United States. Historian Karen Fields' parents transformed the family car into a "self-contained capsule" containing food, water to fix a potential radiator leak, and lots of maps to outline the routes through the countryside and preclude the need to ask for directions.[43] Food, often packed in a shoebox, ensured a hearty, safe, and unadulterated meal. Civil rights activist Dorothy Height's memoir recounted a 1943 trip to Nashville where she was invited to share one of these carefully packed shoebox lunches. The feast inside included "boiled eggs, fried chicken, bread and butter, a piece of fruit, and a small can of juice." She also carried a can opener to open the juice.[44]

Valerie Cunningham, who grew up in New Hampshire, recalled that when she was a girl, her nervous father always brought a potty on trips, "in case I had to go to the bathroom, and toilet paper, and food." Even for short trips—"and we're talking about a one-hour trip to Boston"—the family patriarch wanted to avoid having to stop and ask to use the restroom at a service station, even in the North.[45] Jerry Hutchinson remembered that his family always packed a coffee can to use as a pee can. It was second nature. "My parents never addressed why we had to carry it. They didn't need to, because even as a child I already knew the answer to the unasked question. Ole Jim Crow didn't allow for us to use the restroom whenever we stopped for gas. That stop for fuel would be the only stop made. It just wasn't thought safe to do otherwise."[46]

All-star pitcher Jim "Mudcat" Grant remembered his family taking along their own picnic spread when they traveled, to avoid the shame of going around to the back door of a restaurant or the humiliation of having the food shoved through the "colored" food slot. Concerned about the quality of the meals sold to black tourists by white-owned establishments, the Grants prepared special meals for the road. They suspected that any restaurant willing to sell them a meal might use spoiled food, food taken from the trash, or worse—food laced with spit from the cook. "We carried ice in the car, we carried sandwiches in the car. We carried drinks in the car. . . . Some good old homemade lemonade was better than anything you could buy, anyway."[47] Of his days as a professional baseball player—for the Indians, Twins, and other major league teams—Mudcat remembered, "When we would stop to get food, the white players could go in the restaurant, but we couldn't. So . . . we would eat in the kitchen because they had black cooks in the kitchen. And, of course, we ate better in the kitchen than we would have [out front]." When he went on the road with the team, Mudcat found that he could not check into the same hotel as the white players. Like other black athletes, he was left to find a hotel in the black section of town.[48]

By the 1950s, historian Spencer Crew's family stopped at some of the national chain restaurants when they traveled—A&W Root Beer, Bob's Big Boy, and later McDonald's. "You could drive up and they would serve you in the car," recalled Crew.[49] You did not have to interact with the other customers. For the Grant, Fields, Cunningham, Hutchinson, and Crew families, their large cars served as completely outfitted family homes-away-from-home. To make up for their inability to find hotels, motels, and bathrooms along the way, the large, roomy car could become an extension of the bedroom, the living room, and the dining room. Limiting encounters with white strangers meant bringing along everything you could possibly need.

Black drivers, afraid of getting stuck on the side of the highway, selected cars they believed to be consistently dependable. An inferior car could strand you in a frightening town, as Lonnie Bunch learned in 1962, when he was ten years old. Now the fourteenth secretary of the Smithsonian Institution and formerly the founding director of the National Museum of African American History and Culture, Bunch and his father were driving through a Virginia town when their car broke down. Within just a few minutes, several cars of police officers swarmed around the two and proceeded to harass the older Bunch for stopping his car in an affluent white neighborhood. Bunch instructed his son to stay quiet as the officers pushed the two to get out of the area quickly and go to the local black hotel. The officers could not have been less concerned about the Bunch family car; they simply wanted them out of the white neighborhood—immediately. But unfortunately, they could not get the car started. "I've never been so frightened in all my life," Lonnie remembered.[50]

Purchasing a large car also made long hours behind the wheel less stressful and more comfortable. "I wanted a heavier car—a more comfortable car, because I was on the road constantly," said

New York engineer Henry Johnson of his robin's-egg-blue Buick.[51] "I think the enthusiasm for larger cars in the black community," noted Bill Gwaltney of his experiences traveling with his parents and his brother in the 1950s, "relates to the need to have a good place to sleep should you encounter trouble along the road or be unable to find the colored hotel."[52]

Prior to the popularity of bucket seats, the leather (or vinyl) upholstered front and back car benches functioned like firm, overstuffed sofas or mattresses. Sometimes no black hotel could be found for miles, and there was no place to sleep except in the car by the side of the road. Some performers and others who traveled regularly drove all through the night, rather than risk sleeping by the roadside. This practice, however, could prove perilous. Harlem businessman Walter Edwards described his memory of late-night driving:

> Most of us had to travel by night, because the people see you during the days, they may attack you. So they couldn't tell who was in the vehicles at night. It wasn't all that light on the highways in those days. So you traveled by night, and you stayed at a relative's or friend's home up and down your route.[53]

To avoid sleeping by the roadside, drivers sometimes took turns at the wheel and hoped they could stay awake while others in the group slept. Black performers usually had little trouble finding venues for performing throughout the country, but overnight accommodations could not always be found so easily.

Gospel singer Mahalia Jackson rarely even bothered to find a room, knowing how difficult it might be. She preferred instead to use her car as a rolling hotel and to travel to her next gig late each night after an exhausting performance. In her autobiography, she described her grueling singing schedule, the frenetic nature of travel, the difficulty of finding food and lodging while on the

Musicians traveled frequently by automobile and often late at night because they could not find lodgings in the communities in which they performed. In this photograph, two musicians ride in the rear of a large sedan, possibly a Buick Limited or a Cadillac Series 75. Such large vehicles carried all of the gear that music groups and other travelers needed, but they also enabled the occupants to sleep comfortably, if necessary. (*Musicians Playing Accordion and Washboard near New Iberia, Louisiana, ca. 1938, Russell Lee photograph, Library of Congress Collection, Farm Security Administration.*)

road, and her preference for big vehicles. She found travel a nerve-racking necessity: "To turn off the main highway and find a place to eat and sleep in a colored neighborhood meant losing so much time that we finally were driving hundreds of extra miles each day to get to the next city in which I was to sing," she wrote. "It got so we were living on bags of fresh fruit during the day and driving half the night and I was so exhausted by the time I was supposed to sing I was almost dizzy."[54] Jackson could afford a big, heavy car, and that is what she drove. In white mythology, black Americans bought large cars to show off or to imitate white behavior, but for black travelers a roomy interior and performance trumped other considerations in most cases.

Black laborers commonly drove trucks, an expected and accepted sight on any street in the country. Americans naturally approved of black men working in service occupations, as chauffeurs driving fancy automobiles for rich families or businesses, and could often mistake the owner of such a car as the driver for a wealthy white family. Black men also drove taxicabs, again a service, but many cab companies were segregated. On the whole, whites often saw black owners of private automobiles usurping white privilege by overstepping their "place" in American society.

While practical reasons guided African American consumers' choices of larger cars, many white Americans viewed a black man with a big, expensive car as a source of irritation and a challenge to the social order. According to a 1929 study, whites often reasoned that black people had no right to drive nice cars. A separate study documented instances of white drivers in cheap cars intentionally damaging better-quality vehicles driven by blacks—just to be malicious and in a misguided attempt to protect their own perceived social status.[55] "Sometimes I think the only one who doesn't resent us owning a Cadillac," joked comedian Dick Gregory, "is General Motors."[56]

Negative popular attitudes about African Americans driving Cadillacs in the mid-twentieth century are reminiscent of earlier stereotypes of big-lipped so-called coons dressed in fancy clothes. These cartoonish prints, ubiquitous in the nineteenth century and well into the twentieth century, appeared in children's books, sheet music, books, magazines, and framed parlor art. They mocked black people as pretentious and flamboyant for trying to adopt the behaviors that supposedly were reserved for whites alone. Some Americans believed themselves justified in assuming the role of vigilantes and condoned violence to enforce their views about who should and who should not own a particular brand of car. Black motorists driving through the wrong white neighborhood or owning a car deemed too fancy for Negroes might even be dragged from the car into the street. The argument was moral as well as economic. Why should a people perceived of as childlike, lower class, and inferior—who worked primarily in service to whites—own expensive cars? Black people driving luxury cars contradicted popular notions of white supremacy.

Mahalia Jackson could easily afford a Cadillac, but, unlike white

Images like this turn-of-the-twentieth-century sheet music portrayed African Americans as uppity imitators of white behavior and not worthy of fine material goods. The stereotyped characters seen here display their ineptitude with over-the-top evening attire that features extreme patterns, exaggerated leg-o'-mutton sleeves, and pretentious accessories like walking sticks and pince-nez. In the Motor Age, African Americans purchasing fine cars were considered by many whites as similarly pretentious. (*John Hay Library, Brown University.*)

performers, who engaged in far more extravagant purchases, Jackson constantly found it necessary to justify her choice of such an expensive car. At least four times in her autobiography, she found it necessary to explain why she bought a Cadillac, noting that her extensive travel schedule, the need for comfort while constantly on the road, and the one-night performances in towns far from airfields and train stations made a high-quality car a necessity:

> The one-night-stand concert artist has to be stronger than a Mississippi mule. You finish singing about eleven o'clock at night. You're too keyed up by the evening to go to bed but you're in a strange town and by that time even chatting with the nicest visitors is a strain. . . . Most of the time you can't make a good train or plane connection that will carry you anywhere near where they have booked you to sing the next night. The best thing to do is to get in a good car and go. It has to be a big, fast-driving easy-riding car so that you can get your rest. Sometimes we leave town right after a concert and sometimes we sleep and get out after an early breakfast, but we spend most of the time between concerts on the road.

While African Americans preferred larger cars for practical reasons, the vast majority of black car buyers purchased cars other than Cadillacs. Yet so ingrained in American culture were racist notions of black people striving beyond their station (as perceived by white people) that whites and some blacks believed the popular folklore that more Negroes than whites owned Cadillacs. "Check that cat. He's pushing a Caddy and his old lady's pushing a broom," went a popular self-deprecating view of blacks who owned fancy cars.[57] "Blaxploitation" movies of the 1970s also played with this stereotype, portraying pimps in souped-up vehicles.

So prevalent was the mistaken impression that all Negroes drove Cadillacs that some black publications continued to offer justifications for supposed extensive Cadillac ownership. "Just as to white

Americans the Cadillac is a sign of wealth and standing," noted editor John H. Johnson in *Ebony* magazine in 1949, "so to Negro Americans the Cadillac is an indication of ability to compete successfully with whites, to maintain the very highest standard of living in this nation."[58] Johnson believed that Cadillac ownership furthered economic equality. To him, it was a tool: "The fact is, that basically a Cadillac is an instrument of aggression, a solid and substantial symbol for many a Negro that he is as good as any white man."[59]

Several other publications justified, on supposedly reliable grounds, the erroneous notion that luxury cars predominated in black neighborhoods. The *Negro Digest*, also published by John H. Johnson, commented that African Americans preferred to buy Cadillacs, and it both justified and condemned the practice in an article on the black vacation market. "With other avenues of expenditure closed to them, Negroes have been inclined to put their extra cash into big cars and expensive clothes," the author commented derisively. "Says one Harlem Negro, fish-tail Cadillacs are almost bumper to bumper along Lenox Avenue."[60] A black man from St. Louis, noting the city's poor housing conditions for some black residents, observed: "A flashy car becomes their living room."[61] An African American businessman told *Time* magazine: "Negroes are driven to spend their earnings in showy ways because they still cannot get the more ordinary things a white man with a similar income would buy." An article in *Ebony* pointed out that many black people lacked access to housing, leisure pursuits, and the other good things that a white American might buy with discretionary income: "Long ago they found out that they could not live in the best neighborhoods or hotels, eat in the best restaurants, go to the best resorts because of racial discrimination."[62] *Our World* magazine conducted an extensive study in seventeen American cities with large black neighborhoods and discovered that "the chances are ten to one that if you went out to buy yourself a new car, your choice would not be a Cadillac at all, but a Buick or a

Chevrolet: maybe a Ford or Mercury. This is the brand preference, one, two, three of the Negro market."[63]

Despite the anecdotal sightings of black drivers in Cadillacs, these cars actually accounted for only 322 of the 9,644 black-owned cars in Philadelphia in 1946. In Baltimore that year, only 154 African American households owned Cadillacs, placing these vehicles near the bottom of the preferred list—above DeSotos and below the substantial but clunky Hudsons in popularity.[64] A 1969 study concluded that only 1 percent of black people in the country purchased Cadillacs and thus the belief that Negroes bought flashy cars was an invidious stereotype.[65] In the end, it is clear that many white Americans simply did not believe that black people had a right to buy expensive cars.

At the same time, black people had good reason to spend their money on cars: They were frequently prevented from spending it on houses. Racist laws and practices often shut them completely out of the housing market. Collusion between realtors and banks redlined entire communities. This discriminatory and illegal practice involved drawing a red line, either literally or figuratively, around residential blocks for the purpose of limiting those who could get a mortgage within the drawn borders. Duplicitous banks refused to grant mortgages to qualified black families, preventing them from owning houses in certain areas and "protecting" all-white neighborhoods—keeping "white spaces" white. Many African Americans could neither buy houses in white neighborhoods nor get mortgages in black neighborhoods. Even federal lenders identified African American neighborhoods as being high risk for mortgages. Attorneys and realtors often placed restrictive racial covenants on housing deeds to ensure that the owners could not sell to black families or to Jewish families, although restrictions on black buyers were more pervasive.[66] It may be that during the Depression, federal agencies such as the Home Owners' Loan Corporation (HOLC) and other New Deal programs actually contributed to discrimination by incorporating racial bias into their calculations of financial risk. If a bank designated a neighborhood as "too risky," it would not issue mortgages there. Insurance companies joined in the deceit by refusing to sell homeowner policies to black buyers.

Automobile dealers, albeit sometimes reluctantly, sold cars to black customers, and in the 1950s and 1960s a growing number of African Americans were able to purchase automobile franchises and open their own dealerships, making purchasing a car considerably easier than buying a house.[67] A 1959 study of African American automobile ownership by prominent economist Marcus Alexis, plus several subsequent studies of black consumerism based on Bureau of Labor Statistics data, provided quantitative evidence that black Americans' ability to purchase such expensive goods as automobiles stemmed from their inability to make such other large purchases as houses. While Alexis' research indicated no significant differences in leisure spending habits between black and white buyers in comparable economic classes, the black middle class demonstrated a strong willingness to scrimp and save so that they could purchase cars.[68]

Fearful of the often-inferior merchandise dumped in black neighborhoods, black buyers carefully scrutinized the quality of every type of merchandise, from automobiles to pancake flour. These consumers wanted to make sure they did not get stuck with junk just because they were black.[69] "A long history of exploitation makes him [the Negro] wary of cheap, shoddy goods. . . . [A] Negro will spend more of his salary on high priced goods than a white man," commented an article by Sherwin Badger in the *Negro History Bulletin*, citing research done by *Time* magazine.[70] Surveys of black Americans indicated preferences for Pepsi and Coca-Cola over store brands of soda, and black people, no matter what their income levels, purchased well-known brand names of baby food, hot cereal, and toiletries over generic varieties. Most consumers, black or white, preferred name brands to generics, but black consumers, unlike whites, distrusted the low-end and generic brands and even believed they could be tainted. Viewing with suspicion claims made by white salespeople, these consumers wanted to buy brands they knew they could trust. Would shop clerks tell a black buyer the truth, or would they try to unload inferior or potentially dangerous merchandise onto black customers? If white consumers purchased and trusted name brands, these products had to be safe, many black shoppers reasoned. "The Negro is sensitive and is constantly on guard against deception," concluded one market survey.[71] Tired of inferior food and other shoddy consumer goods, black women in Harlem joined together to establish the Consumer Protection Committee in 1947. "It's not enough that we are forced to pay exorbitant prices for what we buy," Mrs. Wilson, one of the leaders of the group, told reporters. "We must pay these prices for goods that are definitely inferior quality."[72] The problem had not gotten any better by the 1960s, when labor leader Joseph Overton reported that many merchants would say, "Why throw out defective and inferior merchandise when it can be sent to Harlem?"[73]

The information about high-quality consumer products did not simply come from advertising, but through word of mouth. African American domestics, for example, learned about specific consumer goods by using them in the homes of their employers. They then chose these brands when making their own purchases, assuming that they were of good quality and could be trusted as safe. A Baltimore market study reported that "many colored public service and domestic service workers buy almost identical brands and measure value by the same yardstick as their employers."[74] They were not mimicking white behavior; rather, they believed that they were protecting their families from goods that might be adulterated and sold to black people to harm them.

Although African American consumers preferred name brands to generic brands, they did not simply purchase these products blindly; they frequently patronized companies that supported the black community economically. They actively worked to encourage businesses in cities across the country to hire qualified black employees in skilled and professional positions, not simply menial jobs. Companies that refused to hire black workers might even be subject to boycotts. The most effective program to pressure corporations to expand their hiring occurred in Philadelphia. Called the Selective Patronage Movement, the collaboration among more than 460 black ministers and their churches successfully influenced the management executives at thirty corporations. The Philadelphia Selective Patronage project of the 1960s, similar to the "Don't Buy Where You Can't Work" movement of the 1930s, used handbills, posters, word of mouth, and Philadelphia's pulpits to launch boycotts. Tastykake baked goods piled up on the shelves of Philadelphia markets because of the company's policy prohibiting blacks from being hired as salesmen, office workers, and skilled workers. The Tastykake bakery boycott ended with African Americans in ten skilled and sales positions. Selective Patronage then targeted the Pepsi-Cola bottling plant, Breyers ice cream, and Gulf Oil companies.[75] African Americans of all classes, but more pervasively the middle class (which had more disposable income in the first place, of course), used the power of boycotts and protests to break Jim Crow hiring practices and ensure the availability of name-brand products for black consumers.

Likewise, when it came to buying fuel for their cars, African Americans preferred nationally advertised brands of gasoline; in exchange for their patronage, they expected oil companies to respond to their needs. Black consumers chose gas stations that emphasized courtesy and cleanliness over lower price.[76] To ensure a more positive experience at the gas pump, black purchasers sometimes drove across town to find a station that treated them well.[77] During one of many trips between Maine and Florida in the early 1960s, Morris Johnson and his wife, Doris, stopped at a gas station. As the attendant filled the tank, Morris asked the location of the restroom. When told it was for whites only, Johnson calmly instructed the attendant to stop pumping the gas and paid the bill. The couple then drove across the street to the Esso station that sold higher-priced gas, inquired about their bathroom policy, liked what they heard, and filled up. After this experience, the Johnsons always chose Esso gasoline, even if the gas was a bit more expensive or the location was a bit out of the way.[78] Other African Americans found similar reasons to purchase Esso gasoline. While most oil companies ignored the African American market, Esso placed advertisements in the black media, welcoming patrons to their gas stations and offering the use of their clean restrooms. "Esso's consistently strong showing in the Negro markets," commented the *Philadelphia Afro-American* survey, "is due to its advertising and special promotion to this market."[79] Still, not every Esso station

Most gas stations sold gasoline and oil to African American drivers, but few, with the exception of Esso, permitted travelers to use the restrooms. Esso's nondiscrimination policy made it the preferred brand of many black families. James and Royal Sultan owned this full-service Esso gas station in Orangeburg, South Carolina, pictured here in 1958. One of the most successful independently owned black businesses in the area, it was also one of a small number of black-owned gas stations in the nation. James and Royal were early supporters of the civil rights movement. (*Cecil Williams photograph, Getty Images.*)

welcomed black customers with open arms. Each station's franchise owner made the final decision, despite company encouragement, whether or not to discriminate.

BY THE late 1960s, the overall demand in the United States for large, heavy cars diminished. In 1969, a Louis Harris poll indicated that both black and white automobile buyers preferred Chevrolets, Fords, and Pontiacs rather than Buicks or other large, heavy automobiles. Perhaps this change in tastes indicates that black consumers no longer needed cars wide enough for sleeping or large enough to carry a trunk full of supplies. Beginning in the 1950s and into the 1960s, an increasing number of overnight accommodations, restaurants, and gas stations became available to African Americans. "Conditions have improved greatly . . . in the south and throughout America for Negroes who travel the highways," observed an *Ebony* magazine writer.[80] Black Americans gradually became more comfortable traveling across the United States, in large part because of the sweeping civil rights legislation finally passed under President Lyndon Johnson, after decades of black activism. The Civil Rights Act of 1964 invalidated the Jim Crow laws, accelerated the process of integrating public accommodations, and eased, but did not eliminate, the difficulty of travel for black motorists.[81] A clutch of black-owned hotels and motels, primarily in urban areas, had grown to hundreds of establishments across the country that ranged from simple and unpretentious guesthouses to resort complexes with air-conditioning, televisions, swimming pools, and restaurants. A small number of white hotel owners—some who believed in integration, others who were anxious to take advantage of a new market—began to receive black patrons.

Overall, the automobile was a boon to African Americans, despite the inherent dangers they faced on the road. By contrast, white Americans were more skeptical about the way that cars would change the nation. From the dawn of the automobile age, the mainstream press periodically warned the public that the automobile would affect American life in dangerous and negative ways. They cautioned against the perils of speed, the potential for the dissolution of rural families and communities, and the possibility that long-held traditions would be no more. Black people generally ignored these warnings.[82] They hoped the speed of the automobile would mean that they no longer had to abide wagon and carriage etiquette, which required black deference. And to many black people, preserving "tradition" meant preserving white supremacy—the sooner it was dismantled, the better. The car meant not only increased freedom and safety, in most cases, but also opportunities to challenge racism in American society. Ironically, despite the individual freedom that most drivers perceived and celebrated, the automobile and the laws that followed its invention created a web of regulatory practices that included driver testing, licenses, automobile registrations, police stops, checkpoints, and speed limits, among a host of other restrictions designed to protect the public and maintain control over vehicles.[83] For African American drivers, some of these restrictions would be used as ways to continue to control their mobility.

Chapter 4

"THROUGH THE WINDSHIELD"

> It's mighty good to be the skipper for a change, and pilot our craft whither and when we will. We feel like Vikings. What if our craft is blunt of nose and limited of power and our sea is macadamized; it's good for the spirit to just give the old railroad Jim Crow the laugh.
>
> —Alfred Edgar Smith,
> "Through the Windshield," *Opportunity*, 1933

Even though my family lived in the city, almost every house on the block had a garage and every family owned at least one car. My parents owned two, because they went in different directions to work each morning. One was an old Willys Jeep that offered a bone-pounding ride and so little heat in the winter that it left our teeth chattering. The other was the typical American family car: a Ford station wagon with "genuine" faux wood grain on the side.

Our house was in a quiet, integrated residential neighborhood in Newark, New Jersey. Tucked away between two busier avenues, the street was only two blocks long, so few cars interrupted our kickball games in the street. Although I didn't really think about it at the time, we could have operated a miniature United Nations on the block, for Beverly Street was like a microcosm of the world. A couple of African American families, in addition to my own, lived nearby, as did a recently arrived immigrant family from Israel. I remember sitting with their son in the back of our third grade classroom using crayons to help him practice the names of colors in English. A Russian family and a couple from Poland lived down the block and an Indian family lived next door; delicious and unfamiliar smells wafted from their kitchen window on summer afternoons. In an apartment around the corner, an Italian American family with four kids became fast friends with whom we played on endless summer days until it got dark. In the heyday of Chef Boyardee, we tasted real Italian "gravy" made from scratch.

A large cherry tree shaded our backyard, and the above-ground pool that my father installed transformed our yard into a neighborhood hangout for the local children. We climbed that tree, picked the cherries, and stuffed ourselves. Dark black cherries still evoke memories of my childhood and climbing that tree. My best friend, Harriet Kahn, lived around the corner, and we walked to school together. My mother worked at Monmouth Street School, a few miles away, and many of her colleagues—mostly Jewish women in the teachers' union—were also family friends. I thought everyone ate lox, bagels, and cream cheese for Sunday breakfast. The Newark where I grew up was a cocoon, a fact I did not realize until we moved to the suburbs and I discovered what it was like to be the black girl at school. By the time I was ten, I had been to several bar mitzvahs, and I remember the Kahn family sitting shiva when Harriet's mother died, and she moved away. It was the greatest sadness of my childhood.

We drove everywhere. On Sundays we attended a progressive and integrated Episcopal Church—St. Andrews. The Episcopal Diocese of Newark stood at the vanguard of "radical" thinking in the church, and my parents spoke of their support for black and female clergy and black empowerment activities. We spent many weekends at the main branch of the public library downtown and the nearby Newark Museum, a great art collection that included the works by African American artists that no other museum was then collecting, although I was unaware of that fact at the time. Upstairs, to our great delight, we found aquaria of living frogs and snakes.

Many black families who reached Newark in this era—the 1960s—when it was already in decline, found no jobs and no opportunities. I remember my mother bringing food and our old, too-small winter coats to kids at her school who needed warm clothing. Newark had a reputation as a dangerous city, but in my personal experience it was far from it. My family moved easily between our integrated neighborhood and safe black spaces when we went to visit family in the South or on vacation. Although my brother and I were unaware, our parents were all too familiar with the reality that there were places they could not go and that were not safe for us as an African American family, even in the North. African Americans still needed to plan carefully before entering white spaces.

GEOGRAPHER KARL RAITZ has described the American roadside as a physical place, but also a social construction shaped by business imperatives and local mores. Although the highway itself—the macadam—was a public space presumably open to all, the roadside represented private interests.[1] The roadside "enabled travel along the road," as Raitz points out. The businesses along the road made it possible for travelers to go great distances in short amounts of time. The roadside represented local attitudes not always friendly to travelers with darker skin.

The new independence that the automobile provided was circumscribed somewhat for African Americans and other motorists of color as they looked out across a landscape dotted with hostile signs and segregated establishments, although their enthusiasm for their cars was not diminished. Magazine articles reported the concerns that black people felt about taking vacations. "Travel for Negroes inside the borders of the United States," noted the *Saturday Review* in 1950, "can become an experience so fraught with humiliation and unpleasantness that most colored people simply never think of a vacation in the same terms as the rest of America."[2]

When stopping at gas stations, restrooms, hotels, and restaurants, African Americans often encountered embarrassing rejections. Black parents sheltered their children by stopping as infrequently as possible until they reached a physically and emotionally "safe" destination. Black motorists often preferred to drive directly to their journey's end, which might be a welcoming black community or one of the limited number of African American resorts across the country, like American Beach in Florida, Oak Bluffs on Martha's Vineyard, Idlewild in northwestern Michigan, or Val Verde near Los Angeles (known as the "black Palm Springs"). They loved the road and the wonderful destinations that awaited at its end, but they distrusted the racialized roadside.

In our naiveté, my brother and I did not realize it, but our parents certainly understood that each time we left the safety of our comfortable, middle-class neighborhood in Newark, where we felt accepted and protected, we embarked on a potentially perilous adventure. Travel and vacations could offer risky experiences into the unknown. But the automobile itself, the speed at which it traveled, and the materials of which it was constructed—metal and glass—created a sense of security that persuaded many families to take chances and traverse potentially hostile spaces. A growing number of black families took summer vacations as the century wore on, striking out across the country to see its natural beauty as well as visiting family and friends. The steadily increasing crop of black executives in American corporations found that they too needed to travel for business purposes. As Esso executive James Avery wrote, "While the formidable task of proving oneself capable of doing a job as well as anyone else was a demanding one, traveling as a Black representative in sales promotion, public relations, and marketing in the '40s and '50s and, in fact, before the passage of the Civil Rights Act of 1964, was a real challenge."[3]

As many writers have shown, race is an organizing factor of place in the United States.[4] In addition to long-established customs and traditions of de facto segregation in the northern states, a confusing maze of laws created legal segregation in the southern states.[5] The variety of customs and laws made travel across state lines and even within one's own state extremely confusing. This legal and social patchwork separated people into racial categories and divided places into white spaces and black spaces. Prior to the 1960s, relatively few spaces outside of a small number of residential neighborhoods were integrated.[6] A considerable number of white Americans believed inaccurately that keeping geographic spaces entirely white enabled them to maintain good schools, high property values, low crime rates, cleanliness, and high social status. The assumption that the presence of African Americans would depress property values helped to maintain residential segregation—even though, in fact, African Americans were often willing to purchase property at premium rates.[7]

Idealized white settings—resorts, golf courses, country clubs, hotels, beaches, and restaurants—maintained their elite nature, to some extent, through the exclusion of black people, who were the perceived source of many social problems. Ironically, many white exclusive clubs also hired uniformed black maids, waiters, servers, or personal attendants as a way to emphasize their authority.[8]

Keeping white spaces white, according to this rationale, not only protected white people physically from black people; it also protected their social status. Segregation prevented any fraternization that could lead to interracial relationships or "race mixing," as it was called. "You wouldn't want your daughter or son to consort with a Negro and perhaps to fall in love and marry, would you?" Keeping white spaces white helped to keep the fictional purity of the white "race."

DURING THE Jim Crow era, white Americans generally prohibited black Americans from mingling with them in most social situations or in designated white spaces. Not only exclusive clubs, but also any public accommodations constituted a white space. Motels, movie theaters, bowling alleys, libraries, even phone booths—wherever people gathered or whatever whites touched—offered opportunities for potentially unpleasant encounters because black travelers also needed the services of these places. No matter how well dressed or respectable they appeared, African Americans found themselves unwelcome in most white spaces and only tolerated in others.

Historian Robert Weyeneth has categorized the two methods for keeping black people and white people apart as "segregated spaces" and "partitioned spaces." Segregated spaces provided separate and usually unequal places designed to ensure that blacks and whites would not have intimate contacts within the public sphere. Parks, restaurants, swimming pools, and country clubs that totally excluded one race or the other in an attempt to prevent all contact are examples of segregated spaces. Partitioned spaces used walls, ropes, or signs to keep blacks and whites apart within a single environment. Divided or partitioned spaces—waiting rooms separated by a wall or a rope, for instance, or movie houses with the balcony set aside for black moviegoers—were less-costly alternatives to building duplicate structures.[9] Even those environments that could be considered shared spaces—such as city streets or highways, department stores, motor camps, or even national parks—might be divided by race, depending on where in the country they were located, the inclination of the owners of private roadside or community businesses, and the attitudes of local residents. North and South, East and West, many white Americans viewed a black American in their neighborhood or on their streets as suspicious, or even dangerous, and therefore worthy of being harassed, arrested, or, at the very least, removed.

From the 1930s to the 1960s, the vast majority of America's space was white space, reflecting the feelings of the dominant culture that mixing people with light skin and people with dark skin was not good for American society. Despite the long history of coerced "race mixing" that existed between white slave masters and their black female slaves, many Americans viewed the practice of even permitting black people to live in their communities as dangerous. A survey undertaken at Fisk University in 1938 by sociologist Charles S. Johnson confirmed the depth of belief in the color line.[10] Johnson found that the traditions of racial segregation in the United States in the early part of the twentieth century constituted "a dynamic racial orthodoxy or ideology which rationalizes the race system and provides a philosophical bulwark for it."[11]

Both methods of segregation—partition and separation—depended on a person's appearance, and the way observers perceived skin color, hair texture, or facial features. If someone thought

Tuesday at the Memphis Zoo. The segregated Memphis Zoo was open exclusively to white people every day except Tuesday, when only black people could visit. (*© Dr. Earnest Withers Sr., courtesy of the Withers Family Trust.*)

you looked like a Negro, you might be identified as a Negro. As W. E. B. Du Bois commented in *The Souls of Black Folk*, the totally arbitrary fiction of the color line enforced white supremacy. How you looked affected your ability to travel safely and to gain admission to public accommodations and white spaces. Your race—or, perhaps more accurately, your color and your countenance, assessed through the lens of a stranger's biases—determined where it was appropriate, safe, and possible for you to go. Simply by looking at you, a merchant, a service station attendant, a hotel receptionist, or a lifeguard could decide your worthiness to enter a white space and use its services.

If a question about one's identity arose, African Americans endured the indignity of being asked to confirm their race so that they could be properly segregated. Dark skin might be tolerated if a well-tanned white man walked on the beach, but not when the skin belonged to an American Negro. One evening after a concert, a puzzled hotel desk clerk asked famed opera star Marian Anderson, "Are you a Negro?" to be sure that he could justifiably deny her a room at the hotel. A similar experience greeted a leading "Negro educator" invited to eat in the dining room of the United States Congress. A congressman from the South, unsure of the man's identity, took it upon himself to question the stranger: "Sir, are you a colored man?" When the man answered in the affirmative, the congressman said, "Then you can't eat here."[12]

South Carolina and other southern states found another solution to identifying people by race. Anxious to make sure that black travelers were not accidentally given the civil rights accorded to white people, the state granted white people special legal "powers," a practice akin to deputizing them as "race police." Any person attempting to sit in the white section of a bus, waiting room, train car, or other public space and looking suspiciously like an African American could be challenged to provide evidence that they were indeed white. No data exist to confirm how many times citizens exerted their race-police powers, but the policy demonstrates the lengths to which the state of South Carolina was willing to go to keep its population divided racially.[13]

Although many white Americans believed the color line to be extremely clearly defined, it was actually quite permeable. Early in the twentieth century, an article on race published in *The American Israelite* made clear the difficulty of determining racial identity just by looking at an individual. It also highlighted the potential repercussions of being branded a Negro. The article reported on a railway company that empowered its employees to push black passengers into the "colored" train car. Overzealous workers made mistakes, and a court ordered the company to pay damages to a Jewish woman inadvertently forced into the Jim Crow car by a conductor who had decided that she was "a mulatto."[14]

Some fair-skinned African Americans regularly flouted the system by "passing," which could mean either being seen as white or actively pretending to be white. Passing enabled light-skinned African Americans to enter white spaces without being challenged. Harry Murphy, for example, integrated the University of Mississippi years before James Meredith forced the doors of the school to open to black students. "They're fighting a battle they don't know they lost years ago," Murphy later told the press. In 1945, when Murphy enlisted in the US Army, the enlistment officer checked the "W" box without asking him about his "race." As a member of an officer-candidate training program, Murphy started taking classes at "Ole Miss." Mistaken for white because of his wavy hair and light skin, he took advantage of and enjoyed all of the attendant social and financial benefits of this quintessential white space.[15] Quite by accident, Murphy fell into passing and then exploited the situation to make his life easier. That was certainly the case in New Orleans, where a considerable number of black people had fair skin. Passing enabled them to enjoy white privilege in public accommodations. Leah Chase, co-owner of Dooky Chase's Restaurant, a fixture in the city's black community, laughed when she remembered how some of her colleagues pulled the wool over the eyes of unsuspecting white residents. "So those people of color—and there're many of them, honey, who were blond, blue eyes and big mixture. You would maybe see them in the line at the movies. They would be in the white line—you would be in the black line. If they got on the bus, you would be behind the little screen, and they would be in front. But you didn't say anything. You just let that go."[16]

Other African Americans used passing not only as a way to gain white privilege but also to play practical jokes on unsuspecting white folks and to mock the system of segregation. One person reported: "My father has sixteen brothers and sisters and . . . a lot of them used to pass as white. . . . I mean it's easier if you can go to any movie theater you want. . . . [A] few of my aunts told me about a place they used to go to and eat all the time that was 'whites only.' . . . [T]hey did it as a joke . . . they did it because they wanted to show how stupid [segregation] was."[17]

Walter F. White, the fair-skinned, blue-eyed director of the NAACP from 1929 to 1955, intentionally posed as a white man to uncover the truth about the lynching of sharecropper Jim McIlherron. Feigning interest in buying the farmer's land, White used his light skin color to gain the trust of the good citizens of Estill Springs, Tennessee, where McIlherron lived. Although at first he avoided asking directly about the lynching, the proud members of the mob could not resist recounting their deeds around the stove in the town's general store. Jim McIlherron owned a desirable plot of land coveted by the local white folks. But they complained that what really set them off was McIlherron's disrespect for his white neighbors. He had the audacity to strike a white man. The lynchers decided to exact the ultimate penalty for this infraction, and they slowly burned him to death. Walter White knew that if his ruse had been discovered, he would have been "subjected to even greater fury for the sin of 'passing' as a white man" and entering white space than McIlherron faced for owning a desirable piece of land.[18]

Of course, not everyone agreed with segregation laws, and many whites as well as blacks saw them as ridiculous, including those white musicians who toured with black musicians, as perilous as that could be. Sometimes pretending to be black even proved useful for whites, a way to protect themselves from zealous law officers or angry mobs bent on punishing "race mixing." Musician Joe Wilder played in a large mixed-race band and remembered with humor an incident with the Charleston, South Carolina, police. The local sheriff and a deputy pulled up shortly after the band arrived at the hall. "I'm just here to tell you there's not going to be any mixed-race bands playing down here in Charleston," barked the sheriff. Lucky Millinder, one of the members of the group, assured the officer that this was not a mixed-race group, even though it was obvious that some of the musicians had blond hair and blue eyes, and he went down the line asking each member, "Are you colored?" Each man answered, "Yes." When he got to the end of the line, the first trombonist, Porky Cohen, who had a pronounced lisp, answered, "Why thertainly." We had to "chew on our tongues," laughed Wilder, "trying not to break up because it was so ludicrous. . . . And they got in the car and drove off."[19]

Similarly, white blues musician Johnny Otis moved back and forth across the color line as necessity demanded. He "passed for Negro" when spending time with black musician friends. Following his marriage to a black woman, posing as a black man proved more convenient and safer. But, when he and an African American friend wanted to spend the night in a segregated hotel, he again assumed his white privilege, with his friend posing as a personal valet.[20]

Black drivers and those who traveled with them never knew when or where the rules of segregation might be enforced or what

Bandleader Johnny Otis, a white Greek American, sometimes passed for black to pacify segregationists who refused to permit mixed-race bands to play in certain venues. (*Charlie Gillett Collection, Getty Images.*)

practices and traditions might predominate in a given locale. One service-station attendant might be perfectly willing to serve African Americans; another might refuse service. One store clerk could be cordial and another hostile. In many stores, black patrons were not permitted to try on clothing, although they could purchase it. While some restaurants placed Jim Crow signs in their windows, others simply did not serve African Americans—or they only allowed them to purchase food through a window around the back. How one might be received depended on the region of the country, the attitudes of the community, and the personal predilections of the hotel, restaurant, or business owner. As African American travelers used the interstates to go outside of their familiar home communities, they found white businessmen along the roadside often anxious to take their cash but equally anxious to maintain the color line. An African American student recounted buying a soda in Norfolk, Virginia. The soda jerk served him but did not allow him to sit down to enjoy his drink. Once the student finished, the seemingly pleasant clerk demonstrated his disdain for his customer by intentionally smashing the glass.[21] The unpredictability of such behavior highlights the potential of the roadside to be both an illogical and a humiliating world.

The results of a 1950 survey conducted in restaurants in Washington, DC, reinforce the fickle and unpredictable nature of the environment that black travelers faced. In 1949, civil rights activist Mary Church Terrell and two of her colleagues established Washington's Coordinating Committee for the Enforcement of the DC Anti-Discrimination Laws. One of the first African American women to earn a college degree, she went on to be a founding member of the NAACP and a founder of the National Association of Colored Women's Clubs.[22] At the age of eighty-five, Terrell led the charge to desegregate restaurants in the nation's capital and force them to serve black patrons as well as white ones. She and her colleagues assembled 145 volunteers, both white and black, to visit ninety-nine different eating establishments in the downtown area. The committee went beyond identifying segregated facilities and designed a survey that would also gauge Washington's tolerance for integration. Business owners argued that they would lose white patronage if forced to accept an integrated clientele. Terrell's committee wanted to learn how white patrons would actually respond when faced with groups of black diners or with integrated groups of black and white diners.

The volunteers avoided civil disobedience, behaved in a "quiet, orderly" manner, and always presented themselves as "neat in appearance." Seating themselves peacefully at different types of restaurants and lunch counters in polite groups of two, three, or four, they ordered from the menus. Sometimes all-black groups and sometimes integrated groups conducted the tests. If the restaurant served the group, they ate and left. If they were refused, they politely asked to see the manager and informed him of Washington's 1872 and 1873 antidiscrimination laws. Of 316 restaurant visits, thirty-eight restaurants refused to serve the diners on every visit. Thirty-three served the groups without a problem, but some changed their minds and refused service on subsequent visits. Other restaurants that initially refused service seemed willing occasionally to serve black patrons. Overall, it became evident that African American visitors to the nation's capital could rarely predict the reception they would receive when looking for a place to eat. Terrell, Essie Thompson, Arthur Elmer, and Clark King filed a lawsuit against the Thompson Restaurant. In 1953, the court found the segregated restaurants in Washington, DC, to be unconstitutional.[23]

A SIMILAR mix of responses characterized the roadside. Instructional signs informed drivers of speed limits and road conditions and when to yield or stop. Route signs identified the specific highway numbers or names. Local business owners used privately erected roadside signs to alert tourists to their hotels, local attractions, and restaurants. Gas stations and other automobile-related concerns competed to attract consumers with signs in ever-increasing sizes and heights. Billboards advertised consumer products for the split second of attention a driver and passengers could give as they whizzed by. In addition to providing directional information, many of these markers also contributed to the definition of the land as white space and as off-limits, unfriendly, or hostile to black motorists.

Before the 1920s, little thought went into the placement of road signs or the length of their messages; by the 1920s and 1930s, however, advertisers and road designers alike knew that size, message, and strategic placement mattered. All of these things determined a sign's effectiveness. "Scientific" sign designers determined precisely how much motorists could read as they moved through the countryside and how large signs should be to attract attention. A perfect example of scientific sign design, the Burma-Shave signs, popular in the 1920s, consisted of six small, brightly colored signs along the right-hand edge of the road. Using humor, rhythm, and rhyme, the signs would be read sequentially by drivers. *If man bites doggie—That is news—If face—Scares doggie—Better use—Burma-Shave.* Spaced for ease of reading at precisely eighteen seconds apart for a car traveling at the typical speed of thirty-five miles per hour, the placards used clever verses and sometimes driver safety messages to convince readers to buy Burma-Shave shaving cream and later Burma-Vita Tooth Powder.[24]

Most highway and many advertising signs, like Burma-Shave, offered race-neutral, informational messages. Some were simple: *Route 66*. Others just stated the name of a town or city—*NEWARK*, for example. But some signs displayed messages that intimidated black travelers, and some reinforced the prevailing Jim Crow racial code of etiquette and social distance. Others threatened physical violence to discourage black people from stopping or even passing through particular places.

One of the most famous and well-traveled highways in the country bore a name that served as a constant reminder to black travelers of the oppression of slavery and the nation's view of the Confederacy as an idyllic era. Built to unite the South and the Midwest, the Dixie Highway extended south to Florida and north to Canada. African American families who had migrated to the North in the Great Migration often used the Dixie Highway as they went south to visit relatives. Construction crews completed the two main routes of the Dixie in 1927. That same year, federal legislation assigned a system of numbers to replace highway names. The Dixie Highway did not fit into the numbering system, because it already included multiple routes and route numbers. Well established in the popular imagination, roads like the Dixie thus retained their quaint, old-fashioned names.[25] The originator of the road's name saw it as a sort of peace offering that represented the coming-together of the North and the South after the "big war." For white northerners, the name *Dixie* came to represent the South after reunification; but for white southerners, the road represented the persistence in the modern world of their idealized antebellum glory.

African Americans saw the Dixie Highway quite differently: There was nothing romantic about it. The road's name reminded them of the terrifying and disgraceful period in American history when they were enslaved. Like the Confederate national anthem, the name of the Dixie Highway both humiliated and frightened black people.[26] Just thinking about the Dixie Highway and what its name meant frightened journalist John Williams during a car

This roadside sign was one of many marking the Dixie Highway, which ran from Florida almost to the Canadian border. (*Reproduced by permission of Berea College, Appalachian Center, Appalachian Studies Teaching Collection.*)

trip around the country. "Ominously all directions to Nashville were via the Dixie Highway," he wrote. "Where did it end, the Dixie Highway—in a cotton patch surmounted by a Confederate flag and an a capella choir of White Citizens' Council members singing *Dixie*?"[27]

Roadside signs constituted the most obvious and arbitrary form of racial intimidation on the new landscape along the nation's highways. Each state, municipality, and town erected its own roadside signs. Sometimes simple and hand-lettered, they were posted by an individual, a business, or a religious group. At times, the community or some local organization or club sanctioned the sentiments on the sign. In Greenville, Texas, the town slogan, *The Blackest Land, The Whitest People*, appeared on a banner across Main Street with the mantra repeated in paint on the water tower. The slogan also appeared as a neon sign and on a 1940s souvenir postcard depicting an automobile-lined downtown street. At least as early as 1892, the phrase *The Blackest Land* referred to the dark soil in the region that supported cotton farming, considered one of the richest blackland counties. The addition of *The Whitest People* to the slogan may have come in the early twentieth century with the unwanted immigration of Mexicans into the area and the Depression-fueled increase in the number of poor whites and tenant farmers—groups who certainly were considered undesirable and less white.

Whatever its origin—and even though the local white residents did not believe the sign to be offensive—African Americans found it both startling and terrifying. One traveler to Greenville during her childhood found the experience of the banner one of the worst memories of her young life: "I grew up in Texas during Jim Crow," explained law professor Vernellia Randall. "During that time going on long distance road trips had a distinct flavor for Blacks and I remember it vividly—the packing enough food for the entire trip (no restaurants), the using the bathroom on the side of the road (no gas station bathrooms), the sleeping in the car on the side of the road (no motels). But my most vivid memory of my road trips in Texas was the sign I read every time we went through Greenville, Texas—The Blackest Land, The Whitest People."[28]

The sign, seen by black travelers like the Randall family in the 1940s and 1950s, confirmed African American views about Greenville as a place to avoid. The town also had a dark history. In 1908, the white community accused an African American man of raping a white woman and summarily burned him to death in the town square. The banner's words were a grim reminder of the town's reputation as a site of mob violence and lawlessness. Its words contributed to the perception that nothing had changed, even as late as the 1960s.[29]

Jim Crow signs—signs that designated space by race for the purpose of keeping black people segregated from white people—

This banner across the Main Street in Greenville, Texas, frightened many African American travelers. (*Curt Teich Archives, Newberry Library, Chicago.*)

appeared on buildings, in train cars, on water fountains, at beaches, and in just about every public gathering space. While the vast majority of these signs existed below the Mason–Dixon Line, black travelers often came across them in other regions, too. Anywhere across the country, in fact, these signs cropped up, even though some states outlawed them. African Americans traveling on the Pennsylvania Railroad in the 1930s complained that "white" and "colored" signs could be found in train cars in New York. Western towns such as Cheyenne, Wyoming, adopted *No Colored Allowed* signs in the 1940s, when GIs arrived in town during World War II. And local controversies ensued in both Iowa and Nebraska when the NAACP took issue with Jim Crow signs and practices.[30] The Rock Island Railroad Company Large Car Shop in Iowa posted signs on the doors of their locker rooms, lavatories, and washrooms. Goldie Steele, a World War II veteran and master mechanic, incensed at the appearance of the signs in his workplace, tore them down and stamped them under his feet. "I was born in Iowa dirt: my father and mother sleep on the banks of the Cedar River here," Goldie told the *Chicago Defender*. "I went to France as an American soldier from Iowa and by God I'll not stand for my state nor any of her free citizens to be insulted by any KuKlux ignorant 'peckerwoods' from Arkansas and Oklahoma." Goldie's protest resulted in his firing for insubordination.[31]

A 1941 issue of the *New York Amsterdam Star-News* exposed the Jim Crow signs that cropped up even in Harlem, the capital of black America. The article's author, Sam Slaymaker, identified many landlords throughout the neighborhood who advertised for "white tenants only," with signs hung prominently on the exteriors of their premises. To capture the attention of potential white renters, the signs usually noted that apartments were modern and up-to-date to assure interested parties that although Harlem was a black neighborhood, white tenants could secure apartments of

Jim Crow signs came in a wide variety of forms—from this homemade version to others created professionally by sign painters. Large corporations like bus and railroad companies used mass-produced printed-paper signs. Professional signs produced by corporations to keep their business establishments white were proof that Jim Crow signs did not simply represent the racist ideas of a few "good ole boys in the back woods," but rather institutionalized American racism. (*National Museum of American History, Smithsonian Institution Archives.*)

In Nebraska, Lincoln Telephone and Telegraph even segregated the company's phone booths. Each state made its own determination about what should be segregated. (*Nebraska State Historical Society, Lincoln.*)

superior quality. "Why should I worry about the South when I am Jim Crowed right here?" asked the article's author.[32]

In some of these buildings, landlords charged rents according to the tenant's color—higher prices applied if you happened to be black. "Harlemites don't have to wait for complaints to come in from Georgia or Alabama," noted Slaymaker. "There are plenty of instances in which we're actually barred from enjoying citizenship rights in the heart of the world's largest all-colored community."[33] In Ohio, Illinois, Nebraska, and Oklahoma, as well as in every southern state—indeed, anywhere in the United States—a black person might encounter dozens of offensive Jim Crow signs any day of the week.

A few of these signs started to come down after 1956, in response to an Interstate Commerce Commission ruling against segregation in interstate travel, but some politicians and policemen continued to enforce discrimination even without them. Police Commissioner Clyde Sellers of Montgomery, Alabama, refused to protect the rights of black travelers and enforced segregation even after removal of the city's signs.[34] So ingrained were fear and attitudes of inferiority that removal of the signs in some cases made no difference. A black newspaper reported on some black southerners who could not bring themselves to defy Jim Crow traditions, even after the "white" and "colored" signs had been removed from the waiting rooms in Birmingham and Montgomery railroad stations. "Some Negroes act like the signs are still there," the reporter noted.[35] The removal of signs could not so easily change deeply entrenched traditions and decades of psychological intimidation. After a lifetime of subjugation and abuse, many African Americans simply did not know how to be equal citizens. Segregation was, for many, a way of life—one that was almost impossible to break.

On the highway, the most intimidating and frightening signs were ominous *Keep Out* threats, warning African Americans to stay out of a particular town or away from a particular place after

Farm Security Administration photographer Ben Shahn snapped this photograph of a Jim Crow sign painted on a restaurant window in Lancaster, Ohio, in 1938. The use of the word *cater* suggests that the establishment considered its service high class, and the rest of the sign explicitly states that such high-class service is suitable only for whites. (*Library of Congress, Prints and Photograph Division, FSA/OWI Collection [reproduction number, e.g., LC-USF34-9058-C].*)

sundown. Typical language read, *Nigger, don't let the sun set with you in this town*. Some signs underscored intimidation with mockery and racism, such as, *Run, nigger. If you can't read, run anyway*. Two African American men encountered such a sign as they attempted to attend the 1940 nomination announcement of their candidate for president, Wendell Willkie, in his hometown of Elwood, Indiana. The pair clearly understood the message and decided against attending.[36]

Sundown towns—jurisdictions that intentionally kept African Americans out by ordinance, custom, or violence, or all three—existed throughout the country. Indeed, dozens of communities—suburbs, tiny hamlets, and small cities—barred black people from entering their jurisdictions or allowed entrance into the community by day as long as the black people left by sundown. In his 2005 book *Sundown Towns*, historian James Loewen found evidence of more than 150 sundown towns in thirty-one states.[37] Of course, not all towns without minority populations were actual sundown towns. Sundown towns were places actively engaged in practices to control the coming and going of black people—towns that let potential visitors know the residents' racial preferences and worked subtly or overtly to prevent people of color from moving in. Particularly common in the Midwest, sundown towns included such places as Sheboygan, Manitowoc, and Appleton, Wisconsin; Utica, Ohio; the suburbs ringing the Chicago metropolitan area; and even Darien, Connecticut. Villa Grove, Illinois, mounted a siren on the town's water tower that sounded each day at 6 p.m. The custom, which continued until 1998, warned African Americans within the town's borders that it was time to leave.[38]

Some of these communities permitted black people to work as maids, handymen, cooks, or in other service professions as long as they left before the sun set. Even as a middle-aged lawyer in the early 1960s, Supreme Court Justice Thurgood Marshall faced the demand to get out of town before sundown. "[A] white man came up beside me in plain clothes with a great big pistol on his hip," Marshall remembered. "And he said, 'Nigger boy, what are you doing here?' And I said, 'Well, I'm waiting for the train to Shreveport.' And he said, 'There's only one more train comes through here, and that's at 4 o'clock, and you'd better be on it because the sun is never going down on a live nigger in this town."[39]

AFRICAN AMERICANS could not buy property in sundown towns, and they were expelled or intimidated if they tried. Often, nasty signs posted at the town borders warned black travelers of the possible consequences of entering forbidden all-white spaces. In addition to signs, and protective covenants on properties, local police immediately hustled offenders out of town or into jail.

Sometimes, "mysterious" acts of violence reinforced a community's attitudes toward people of color. Depending on the region of the country, sundown towns might also exclude people of Chinese descent, Mexicans, Native Americans, Jews, or even Roman Catholics. Some sundown-town signs lasted well into the 1970s. Many sundown communities continue to have little or no black population.[40]

Vidor, Texas, proud of its all-white population and determined to keep it that way, maintained a sundown-town sign well into the 1960s. Five different KKK groups in Vidor generated enough business to support a small Klan bookstore on Main Street, making it a particularly intimidating place to visit or to drive through (which could happen accidentally).[41] A sign on the outskirts of Tuscaloosa, Alabama, read, *Welcome to Tuscaloosa, The United*

This linoleum print, by artists Tony Perez and Lin Shi Khan, documents the sundown-town signs erected along American highways. It appeared in a 1935 collection of prints developed in response to the crisis of lynching in the United States. Nothing is known about the artists.

Klans of America. Other billboards urged motorists to join and support the local Klavern. Klan signs surely encouraged black drivers to put these towns in their rearview mirrors as quickly as possible.[42] Sylvester Hollis remembered seeing a variety of offensive signs along the road and in various establishments in Cullman, Alabama, when he was a boy in the 1950s. Like many sundown towns, Cullman's reputation as a place that African Americans should bypass was well known by local black residents. Hollis also recalled a particularly painful memory of the local CITGO station with its sign that read, *No niggers allowed in this service station or bathroom*.[43]

The Klan commonly chose to announce their presence in signage: *Welcome to Klan Country*, or *You Are in the Heart of Klan Country*. In Palo Alto in 1946, California's Klan painted

This highway sign at the entrance to Tuscaloosa, Alabama, "welcomed" travelers to town in the 1960s. Such signs of course intimidated black motorists, though some white Americans in the 1950s and 1960s perceived of the Ku Klux Klan as a respectable community club rather than the supporters of and participants in numerous lynchings and horrendous murders. (*Associated Press*.)

KKK in red letters three feet high on the road at the intersection of Homer Avenue and Ramona Street, to make sure motorists saw it.[44] As drivers entered the state of North Carolina in the 1960s, a billboard announced, *Welcome to North Carolina, You Are in the Heart of Klan Country.* So common was the state's association with white hoods that it was nicknamed Klansville, USA.[45] The Klan used their signs as a way to solicit converts to their cause and to convince citizens of their civic virtue. But the primary motivation for such signs was to frighten and intimidate African Americans and perhaps also the state's other enemies—Mexicans and Native Americans—in order to claim these spaces as white.

Founded in 1865 in the aftermath of the Civil War, the Ku Klux Klan had been terrorizing African Americans for decades by the time the Motor Age arrived. In 1915, the organization was reinvigorated as a result of white nativist fears about the large numbers of immigrants entering the country. The twentieth-century Klan flourished across the North and the Midwest as well as the South. Travelers' accounts of motoring through the countryside in the 1920s and 1930s mention encountering outdoor Klan rallies, meetings, and social events that lit up the night skies with burning crosses.

Throughout New Jersey during this period, angry men and women, often bringing their children, gathered periodically in dark cornfields and beside lonely roads to protest the presence of immigrants in the state. In Pompton Plains, near Paterson, a group armed with clubs and pistols met in May 1923 to initiate new recruits. Arranging their automobiles to form a large, open square, headlamps blazing, the Klansmen lit a forty-foot-tall cross, wrapped in burlap and soaked in accelerant, while the Grand Cyclops led the group in a straight-armed salute to the American flag and a pledge to "maintain peace and harmony." Earlier that same month, five hundred automobiles—with white ribbons hung on their radiators to identify their owners as members of the Klan faithful—went to New Brunswick, New Jersey, to condemn race mixing. That November, they burned thirteen crosses on the lawns of houses and businesses in and around Newark. At the height of their popularity in the 1920s, more than sixty thousand people considered themselves members of New Jersey's Klaverns.[46] One historian, George Chester Moore, referred to the state as the "Mississippi of the North" because of the second-class status of its African American residents and the lingering segregated school system in the southern half of the state. Southern migrants during the Great Migration likened the state more to Georgia than Mississippi—the Georgia of the North. The legacy of Klan meetings and cross burnings in New Jersey added to these dubious distinctions and to the state's standing as a dangerous place for black people.[47]

African American travelers might encounter hooded Americans in almost every state. Why would members ride a ferris wheel wearing their robes and hoods, as in this 1926 photo? Klan disguises created solidarity among members of the group, increased their visibility, and intimidated almost everyone else. (*Royal Gorge Regional Museum & History Center, Cañon City, Colorado.*)

The Klan's reputation for violence and intimidation among African Americans gave their road signs and rumors of Klan presence a heavy psychological punch among travelers throughout the country. Spencer Crew's father refused to take his family to visit relatives in New Jersey because of the state's reputation as a Klan stronghold.[48] In the 1940s, Vernell Allen observed that everyone in her safe Brooklyn community knew of New Jersey's reputation as "a Klan state" and regularly passed that information along to friends and travelers. When Vernell and her friends decided to drive to Atlantic City for a weekend in 1947 or 1948, they worried about stopping along the way and did so very cautiously as they traveled through what they believed to be dangerous white space to get to the shore. The group of friends carefully watched the expressions of everyone who looked in their direction. Vernell remembered the trip to the seashore:

> When we went to Atlantic City we drove there. We got some fellows to drive us down. It was one of the girls' boyfriends. They said to us, when we were driving out of Brooklyn—take food with you, water, whatever you want because we're not going to stop in Jersey because it's a Jim Crow state. . . . The Ku Klux Klan was in that area . . . the KKKs. . . . They didn't want you stopping. They didn't want to wait on you, and they would call you a nigger. We did have to stop. We found one place that looked sort of friendly. The guys had to get some gas or something. . . . We looked at the people's faces. We scoped them out. Before we went into the store we looked the area over and looked the people over.[49]

Many towns lacking the ominous *Welcome to Klan Country* roadside signs nonetheless acquired reputations as Klan towns. Black travelers needed no signs to identify such communities, because they usually had been forewarned. Black communities

Vernell Allen's friends snapped this picture during their trip to Atlantic City, New Jersey. Going from Brooklyn to Atlantic City in the 1940s, they feared traveling through New Jersey because of its reputation as a Klan state. Once they arrived in the resort, though, they enjoyed the vibrant African American community and its black beach. (*Courtesy Vernell Allen.*)

passed stories back and forth about the intimidation wrought by the Invisible Empire and what occurred to this or that family member when he happened to pass through a particular town. By sharing a tale, the storyteller was distributing valuable information that the mainstream media would not bother to report.[50]

Many other negative messages reached black drivers and their passengers as they sped along the highways. African Americans' lack of representation in advertising during the first seventy-five years of the twentieth century (excluding, of course, the black press) has been well documented. In the context of the American roadside, this exclusion contributed to the feeling of unease among black travelers when driving into unfamiliar territory.[51] The absence of black faces on billboards indicated the invisibility of African Americans to their fellow citizens. But, while they were simply ignored by advertisers, their depictions as comic buffoons or subservient slaves reflected the dominant culture's negative attitudes about black people as nonhumans and also supported notions of inferiority that black parents did not wish their children to experience.

Advertisers erected most billboards near city centers or near the entrances to population centers. To be viewed clearly by automobile drivers and passengers at highway speeds, billboards typically depicted large graphic images, rather than words. These visual messages convinced viewers to buy detergent, beer, automobiles, cigarettes, and any number of other popular consumer products. Any words that appeared on billboards needed to be large and very brief.

The billboards that included images of African Americans portrayed them as counterpoints to successful whites—the white person of superior status, the black person of inferior status. Paired with an affluent middle-class housewife, a smiling mammy peddled Oxydol detergent. Wearing the characteristic head wrap and proudly lifting high a basket of freshly washed laundry, the mammy spoke deferentially to her "mistress" in southern dialect. "Yes, ma'am, jes' a little" Oxydol makes the clothes bright and clean, the mammy character declared. The black woman thus assumed the role she had during slavery, pleasing the lady of the house and (from the white perspective) taking pride in doing menial work in support of the white household. The content and docile black mammy on the billboard re-created a comforting world in which blacks and whites knew their places and gladly assumed them.

For white Americans who no longer had servants, black mammies represented a social class lower than their own—a reassuring image indicating that they were not at the bottom of the ladder. In another popular billboard, the scantily dressed Gold Dust twins—the signature image for a brand of scouring cleanser and laundry detergent popular in the first half of the twentieth century—appeared as tiny African caricatures beside the larger-than-life Teddy Roosevelt, the archetypal white man, arriving back in America after a heroic African safari. On the billboard,

Uncle Sam greeted Roosevelt as a pitch to sell Gold Dust washing powder. *Teddy Roosevelt scoured Africa, the Gold Dust Twins scour America.* The tagline proclaimed, *Let the Gold Dust twins do your work.* The coal-black twins assumed the role of servants, carrying Teddy Roosevelt's suitcases while balancing boxes of Fairbank's Gold Dust washing powder on their heads. The billboard suggested that even without "help," any household could put these little African savages to work for them—and it unquestionably reinforced the idea of black people as uncivilized.

Roadside billboards rarely if ever depicted white Americans and African Americans as coworkers or equals, or black people as consumers or positive contributors. Manufacturers and business owners feared that white buyers would not purchase their products or use their services if black models appeared in their ads as positive images. They particularly feared the loss of all of their southern customers.[52] Such products as Chocolate Eyes chocolate milk, Two Coons Axle Grease, and Hendler's Picaninny Freeze ice cream used shabbily dressed black children for comic purposes on billboards and signs that promoted the natural inferiority of the black child from birth.[53] Smiling back at white travelers, the African American stereotypes in these roadside billboards assured viewers that black people not only held deferential roles in society but also were content to do so.

The NAM (National Association of Manufacturers) billboard captured on film by FSA (Farm Security Administration, a New Deal agency) photographer Margaret Bourke-White dramatically illustrated the differences between black lives and the depiction of white lives during the first half of the twentieth century. The advertisement portrayed an idealized American family—the NAM's version of the American dream. This perfect family included a white, well-dressed, smiling mother and father with two children and a dog (also white) riding in the family automobile. The billboard was one in a series that also included an image of a white family enjoying a picnic and a white family of homeowners replete with all the essentials of successful American life—a house, a car, leisure time, and the ability to travel. The middle-class family, attractive and well fed, appears completely unaffected by the Depression. Below this happy white family stands a sober line of real people—African American flood-relief victims displaced in January 1937 when the Ohio River rose and flooded Louisville, Kentucky. The larger-than-life billboard image defined automobile ownership as one of the joys and privileges of American family life and proclaimed in a written message, *There's no way like the American Way.* The American way encompassed "the world's highest standard of living" depicted as a scene of family leisure travel.

Margaret Bourke-White's famous 1937 photograph, *At the Time of the Louisville Flood*, illustrates starkly the dichotomy between the idealized American life ("the world's highest standard of living") and the reality of life for many black citizens. (*Margaret Bourke-White photograph, Getty Images.*)

Beneath the billboard, the photo focused on actual black citizens of Louisville queuing for public assistance. As in real life, the white family on the billboard appears oblivious to the local tragedy affecting the African Americans waiting patiently for Red Cross packages after the devastating flood, which killed nearly four hundred people. Bourke-White's stunning photograph demonstrates the clear differences, expressed in racial and economic terms, between the haves and the have-nots, and it juxtaposes American advertising "ideals" with black reality.

ASIDE FROM signage, businesses along roads and highways shaped the experience of travel for African Americans. Since purchasing gasoline often posed a problem, there was at least one exception. Esso actively supported the rising prosperity among black Americans through the corporation's willingness to sell franchises to black entrepreneurs when few others would do so. Standard Oil and later Humble Oil, acquired by the company in 1959, contributed to black financial success and bolstered the black middle class through their financial support. "Here are some of the nearly Two Hundred Esso Stations operated by Negro managers and owners," proudly commented the 1953 edition of *The Negro Motorist Green Book*. Mrs. Crane of North Carolina, for example, explained how ownership of her Esso station helped her to educate two sons and build a beautiful house across the street from her business.[54]

Standard Oil's Esso gas stations owned by African Americans or by willing white franchise owners distributed free copies of *The Green Book* to their black customers. Some stations personalized the back cover of the book with the name and address of the station, making it a promotional piece and the perfect companion to the free road maps that Esso also distributed. *The Green Book*'s preference for Standard Oil's Esso gasoline suggests that black motorists were always welcome at their service stations, but in fact hospitality varied widely across the country and reflected the racial attitudes of station owners and state customs. Many African Americans perceived Esso as being less discriminatory than other companies. Anecdotal evidence suggests that Esso stations that sold gasoline to black patrons and repaired their cars also permitted them to use the restrooms. Morris Johnson remembered stopping at various Esso stations and finding them welcoming. "I guess we started stopping there and you know, everything was quite friendly. . . . Matter of fact, we could use the bathroom."[55] When Sylvester Hollis' family traveled, they had very specific personal guidelines, based on their vacation experiences in the 1950s and 1960s. At home, they frequented a Texaco station owned by "a black guy in our neighborhood," but they didn't use Texaco gas when traveling, because the stations were not welcoming. CITGO stations would not permit African Americans in their bathrooms, according to Hollis, and they hung Jim Crow signs on the doors. He remembered a Phillips 66 station that would sell you gas, but "then you put the money on a table. They wouldn't take it from your hand. They wouldn't touch you. But, they would touch your money after you left." Hollis found Esso stations the most welcoming and preferred to stop there. National market-research surveys support the anecdotal evidence and indicate a preference for Esso gasoline, particularly in the East, where Standard Oil was headquartered. In northern New Jersey, almost 67 percent of African American drivers preferred Esso gas; in Boston, 50 percent of black drivers stopped at Esso stations. *The Green Book* included many photographs of gas stations that welcomed black customers; many of these sold Esso gasoline. Black New Yorkers frequented a larger variety of oil-company franchises, but the greatest number of drivers still preferred to stop at Esso stations.[56] Although not all of the gas stations listed in *The Green Book* were affiliated with Standard Oil, many photographs proudly included the company's Esso logo in their display advertisements.

To make themselves visible to hungry travelers along the highways, restaurants created large road signs, some of which depicted negative stereotypes of African Americans. Black marketers were quick to inform white advertisers when offense was given. "Negroes don't like to be labeled as a race specializing in a huge consumption of chicken, gin, pork chops, or watermelons. Many of them don't like any of the four—just as many whites don't like them."[57] Nevertheless, eating establishments and other businesses throughout the country used exaggerated and cartoonish images of black people to promise good food and antebellum hospitality.

Roadside restaurants created romanticized images of African Americans that reinforced nineteenth-century stereotypes. The "nationally famous" Coon Chicken Inn, an eatery founded in Salt Lake City in the 1920s, grew into a chain of profitable West Coast restaurants. Operating well into the 1950s, the Coon Chicken Inn used a logo featuring the large bald head of a grotesquely caricatured African American man with swollen red lips and a round bellhop hat. The grinning, comic "coon" winked at restaurant patrons, suggesting that they shared a joke. Diners entered the restaurant through the huge, toothy mouth, an idea that the founder, Maxon Lester Graham, thought would delight and attract children. The bellhop hat, symbol of a menial service job, matched the red lips in color and made the character look even more subservient. The menu featured "coon chicken and coon fried steak," among other "coon" favorites. The restaurant's owner claimed that he did not see the caricature as offensive or insulting, or even as a racial stereotype, despite the use of the derogatory word *coon*—often used to demean black men. Graham's preference for African American waiters, waitresses, and cooks, whenever possible, added force to the feeling of southern authenticity and clearly belied his claims that the "coon" was not racially motivated.[58]

In addition to "coon chicken," the traveling public also encountered Sambo's fast food along the road. The original restaurant

Traveling along the highways, African American motorists faced visual assaults from such logos as the giant grinning "coon" in the bellhop hat. This chain of restaurants operated from the 1920s to the 1950s. (*Collection of the author.*)

opened in Santa Barbara, California, in 1957. Its founders combined their names, Sam Battistone and Floyd Newell Bohnett (nicknamed Bo), to create Sambo, despite the association of that name with the banjo-plucking, watermelon-eating stereotype of the loyal, contented slave embedded in American history since the nineteenth century. Using the children's book *Little Black Sambo* as a theme for a fast-food restaurant outraged the black community in the 1960s and 1970s, even though the original book illustrations depicted a child in India. At the height of the restaurant's popularity, there were more than twelve hundred Sambo's franchises across the country. In the eyes of the African American public, each of these establishments represented support of the Sambo stereotype and a reminder that many white Americans viewed African Americans as perpetual and helpless children.

Hundreds of individually owned restaurants and other private businesses over the years used similar stereotypes of contented Aunt Jemimas, compliant Uncle Toms, and grinning minstrel-show caricatures along the roadside to attract diners and sell products. Mammy was the type of Negro whom white people loved—a good cook, subservient, disinterested in her own family, and uninterested in civil rights. The use of the stereotype went far beyond the Oxydol advertisements. In the *Nashville Banner* in 1931, an article lauded the quintessential mammy—Mammy Victoria Lipscomb, who served one Tennessee family for fifty years as a maid and nanny and remembered the days of slavery with fondness. At the age of seventy, "Mammy Vic" noted, "my white children treat me so well I'll go on until I'm one hundred." Harking back to the good old days, the article attributed this to "that true expression of understanding and love which existed between the two races in the old south."[59]

Dozens of family eateries appropriated the mammy image to hawk their food to travelers. The children's menu for the popular Mammy's Shanty restaurant in Atlanta featured an Aunt Jemima–like character ringing a dinner bell beside a dilapidated slave cabin. For some Americans (African Americans not included), mammy represented a comfortable figure who signified home, good service, and selfless care for her white family. Overweight, sexless, and sometimes offering comic wisdom, mammy provided the idealized view of black women that appeared in popular media from television to movies, literature and advertising. In the foreground, a watermelon-eating black child reminded visitors of the gracious living of the plantation. Mammy's Shanty's "Pickaninny Coffee Shop" exploited the popular stereotype of the feckless black child who lacked purpose and ambition. The popular PickaRib joint in Clarksville, Tennessee, used a cartoonish black chef to sell its main attraction—southern spare ribs. A black male chef in a bright white toque served as the restaurant's mascot.

Roadside restaurants in the South held no monopoly on the use of the slave stereotype to represent good service and good eating.

Topsy's Restaurant in Baldwin, Long Island, expanded to three home-style eateries specializing in—what else?—chicken. Popular from the 1930s to the 1950s, Topsy's Plantation used an image of a young and stereotypically overweight black mammy in an apron and headscarf. Named for Topsy, the wild slave-child character in Harriet Beecher Stowe's popular novel *Uncle Tom's Cabin*, the restaurant's tagline, "Eat with your fingers," informed diners that their usual middle-class manners could be suspended when eating in this "Negro-inspired" establishment. Topsy, the restaurant's namesake, no longer an unkempt child, has grown into black wom-

Topsy's Restaurant, with a young mammy figure as its symbol, represented several establishments in New York state. Similar eateries throughout the country had logos with stereotypes of black slave women—images that helped to maintain the place of African Americans in American culture. Black travelers constantly encountered these negative images. Topsy was the wild slave-child "friend" of the angelic Little Eva in the Civil War–era novel *Uncle Tom's Cabin*. Here, she has grown from a child to a young mammy. (*Collection of the author.*)

anhood and become a mammy and good cook—her unkempt pigtails tamed with the familiar headscarf.

Perhaps the ultimate roadside mammy could be found towering over Route 61 outside of Natchez, Mississippi. The almost-thirty-foot-tall building in the shape of a black woman in slave dress greeted tourists vacationing along the Gulf of Mexico, as well as residents of the region. Mammy's Cupboard, erected about 1940, became a popular roadside attraction. Novelty buildings shaped like a giant mammy, a derby hat, a brown drake duck, an elephant, or a tepee sprang up during the mid-twentieth century to induce motorists to stop along the highway. Visitors hungry for a meal entered mammy through her billowing, bright-red skirt.

With the growth of automobile travel came the popularity of a host of drive-ins and fast-food restaurants that used African American stereotypes to hawk their food, but some white

Mammy's Cupboard, a popular 1950s roadside stop in Natchez, Mississippi. (*Library of Congress, Prints & Photographs Division, photograph by John Margolies [reproduction number, e.g., LC-MA05-1].*)

The picture postcard for the Plantation Inn shows African American waiters and a waitress dressed as slaves to re-create the old South. Diners assumed the romantic and imaginary roles of masters and mistresses for the evening as they reveled in antebellum grandeur. (*Collection of the author.*)

travelers preferred a somewhat more elegant dining experience. The dining room at the popular Lake Shore Plantation Inn in Lake Wales, Florida, hired only black waiters and waitresses and dressed them in eighteenth-century slaves' garb. The Plantation Inn's widely circulated souvenir postcards described the experience. "[T]he Inn radiates contentment and hospitality," noted the description on the back of the postcard. Like actors on a stage, the workers in these establishments re-created slave roles—the men in breeches and waistcoats and the women dressed as mammies in bandannas—to enable white diners, for the evening, to bolster their class status.

Black as well as white Americans clearly disagreed about the meanings of these stereotypes and the ideas that they perpetuated. (I barely knew how to respond when, as a young museum director in northern Virginia in the late 1970s, a colleague my own age told me about her "dear mammy, Eleanor," who was "just like one of the family." I was quietly aghast.) A souvenir cookbook from Fredericksburg, Virginia, offered a dominant cultural perspective on the black-mammy stereotype as a "positive" image: "The very name 'Southern Cooking,' seems to conjure up the vision of the old mammy, head tied with a red bandanna, a jovial, stoutish, wholesome personage . . . a wizard in the art of creating savory, appetizing dishes from plain everyday ingredients."[60] The mammy was, to this way of thinking, the queen of the southern kitchen and a credit to black women. Sincere in their belief that they showed affection for the important role that their former mammies played in the lives of white southern children, the United Daughters of the Confederacy (UDC) insisted that Congress erect a national monument in Washington, DC, honoring the southern mammy. "The traveler, as he passes by, will recall that epoch of southern civilization" when "fidelity and loyalty" prevailed, noted a southern congressman. Even as the Dyer Anti-Lynching Bill gained no traction in Congress, the Senate of the United States approved the UDC request in 1923. Fortunately, irate protests from African American groups nationwide prevented the final monument from going up. "If you want to do something to honor us," fumed one article, "don't lynch our boys."[61]

African Americans despised these images and hated the underlying message—the association of black people with watermelon, chicken, pork, "good southern cooking," and, most of all, subservience. From an African American perspective, these images did not reflect black identity but rather the very limited idea of black women only as service workers. David Sullivan, a well-known African American market researcher in the 1940s, explained the feelings shared by his constituents: "Don't picture colored women as buxom, broad-faced, grinning mammies and Aunt Jemimas. Negroes have no monopoly on size. Neither are they all laundresses, cooks and domestic servants."[62]

Like all of the signs and symbols along the roadside in the era of Jim Crow, the mammy stereotype reflected the popular American view of African Americans as a serving class, a breed apart—worthy of working for white people but not worthy of the full rights of citizens. While one might speak positively and kindly of African Americans' abilities as cooks or chauffeurs, laundresses or maids, the images and messages offered along the roadside indicated that they were foreigners in their own country. The American landscape bombarded travelers with images of ol' Jim Crow in all of his manifestations—coons and mammies, pickaninnies and slaves—images that constantly reinforced notions of inferiority. Many white Americans only understood African Americans through these caricatures. Driving across the country reinforced these stereotypes and, for black Americans, reinforced the importance of alternative messages and the need for way stations—places of rest along the way.

Chapter 5

DRIVING WHILE BLACK

Traveling across the country in Air Force One is a bit different from driving across the country in a black skin.[1]

—Ernest Dunbar, *Look* senior editor, 1968

As in other southern cities and towns, Fayetteville's black population, which included a substantial number of middle-class citizens, knew their places. They knew they could not use most of the public accommodations in the city—hotels and restaurants, pool halls, clubs, and bars. In July 1941, the Colony Theater opened downtown on Hay Street, with separate entrances for black and white moviegoers. African Americans, who paid the same thirty-three cents for matinees, and forty-four cents for evening performances, that white citizens did, could sit only in the balcony. Two "colored" lunchrooms served the black neighborhood—The College Grill and the Corner Cafe on Hillsboro Street. The city's Christians separated themselves into twenty-eight white churches and eighteen labeled colored. *As Martin Luther King observed, "Eleven o'clock on Sunday morning was the most segregated hour in the nation."[2] Fayetteville's city directories assigned a tiny "c" to designate each resident and business that was "colored." Three local hospitals cared for the town's white residents, but black residents had to travel all the way to Raleigh to St. Agnes, the region's only decent hospital serving African Americans. Most black peo-*

ple simply stayed at home when they were sick and were nursed by family members.

My grandfather, Abel Wooten, who died in North Carolina the year after my parents moved to New Jersey and several years before my birth, was a skilled plasterer. His wife, my grandmother Fannie, took care of frail and sick elderly white folks and was known for her skill as a home nurse and a cook. (One of her specialties was a deep-dish apple pie that I have yet to be able to duplicate.) She was much in demand. Devoted to the Baptist Church (which meant no dancing or cardplaying on Sunday) and to the black community, Abel and Fannie Wooten participated actively in Fayetteville's black middle class, so their names appeared periodically in the Norfolk Journal and Guide, *the Virginia newspaper that regularly included a column on the comings and goings in Fayetteville's black community. "Miss Nellie Wooten of New York and Mrs. Eris Dawson Wooten of Wilson, N.C. are guests of Mr. and Mrs. Abel Wooten of Frink Street," read one such notice. They were in town to attend the graduation exercises at Fayetteville State Teachers College. "Their sister, Miss Alvenia Wooten, was a member of the class." In 1942, "The Junior League of the First Baptist Church met at the home of Miss Alvenia Wooten," the paper reported. "Mrs. Elizabeth Thompson (nurse) gave an interesting talk on defense."*

In early 1948, Abel came down with a serious case of pneumonia. In February, Nell, my mother's sister, called late in the day to tell my mother that she needed to come home. My parents prepared to drive straight through the night, hoping to make it home in time to say good-bye. But halfway to my mother's childhood home, the electrical system in their old car "went haywire," my father later recalled. The lights flickered and flashed erratically, and then went dark. The young black couple was stranded on a dark road in Virginia. They waited nervously, deciding not to call a tow truck or a garage and were uneasy about knocking on the door of a nearby house. As they sat there on the side of the road, pondering what to do, whatever had "seized" the electrical system miraculously "let go." My parents did not have to search for a black neighborhood. They did not need to find the black garage, or a hotel that might have rejected them. They continued their solemn journey, arriving in Fayetteville early the next morning.

Sadly, though, Abel died before my mother and father arrived. I have long wondered whether he might have lived longer, or even survived the illness, if there had been a local hospital that would have admitted him.

As in most southern cities, Jim Crow signs throughout Fayetteville, North Carolina, proclaimed the color line. Jazz musicians Tyree Glenn and Leon "Chu" Berry discover one of the few restaurants available to Fayetteville's black community. This photo, taken sometime in 1940, is one of the last images of Chu, who died tragically in an automobile accident in October 1941. (*Photograph by Milt Hinton, © Milton J. Hinton Photographic Collection.*)

THE FEAR my parents felt that night in rural Virginia was a common experience that united black drivers in the twentieth century. Fear shaped where they went, how they drove, and how they responded to events along the road. Even as the automobile enabled African Americans to avoid some forms of discrimination, it also opened up new ways for white Americans to discriminate, harass, and attack black Americans.

Black drivers on the roads and highways encountered white law-enforcement officers, representing white communities, who often attempted to control black mobility. Even prominent African Americans might find themselves stopped for driving while black. Dr. James Mackin, a white colleague of mine, remembered one experience in particular, when he was working as an academic administrator for Stillman College in Tuscaloosa, Alabama, a historically black institution:

> Dr. McNealey [the president of the college] and I would often travel together to conferences and off-campus meetings by car. The College vehicle was a Cadillac and, because Dr. McNealey was narcoleptic, we had a chauffeur, who was an older African American man. The picture of two African American men sitting in the front seats of a Cadillac was apparently too much for the state police, and we would almost always be stopped on trips of any significant length. We never got a ticket, but we were warned many times about speeding (although we weren't actually speeding).[3]

White drivers and community members might also be hostile and willingly join in the enforcement of segregation. While not every American community was a hotbed of racist activity, it was not always easy to identify the ones that were. In magazine and newspaper articles and in memoirs, African Americans wrote of the joys brought by the freedom of the road, but their enthusiasm was always tempered by concern for possible racial encounters. Some black drivers found driving profoundly nerve-racking. Worry about the safety of their families could prove overwhelming.

African Americans' fears were not limited to those living or working in the South. Valerie Cunningham, who grew up in Portsmouth, New Hampshire, remembered every car trip, no matter how brief, as stressful, in large part due to her father's obvious anxiety. He hated driving and he feared being outside of their neighborhood. Mr. Cunningham started guzzling water when he was nervous, and during any car trip he drank constantly from the old mayonnaise jar he used as a mug. "My father . . . I don't think he ever really got comfortable driving in the car, you know. Just driving fifty or sixty miles up to the White Mountains was an ordeal for him. It made him nervous. Driving fifty miles to Boston was an ordeal." Valerie's father so feared the dangers of driving while black that he never took his wife and child to visit their relatives in the South. Mrs. Cunningham's fair complexion, as contrasted with Mr. Cunningham's darker skin, intensified his concern. "If someone mistook her for a white woman, there would be hell to pay," Valerie mused. "[Y]ou had to be prepared, you know, for whatever might happen on the road."[4] Walter Edwards also feared going out in his car with his girlfriend, on the chance that someone who disapproved might take the law into their own hands. "I used to date a girl up in Connecticut, and she was very light-skinned. When I would drive her home, she had to put a scarf over her head and everything, because they would have thought I had a white woman in the car. You know, this was in Connecticut."[5]

Historian Spencer Crew's family shared the Cunninghams' fear and never drove more than two hours from their home, and then only to visit relatives. Most of the family's travels were in familiar terrain in their home state of Ohio. They avoided the standard vacation spots popular with white Americans, such as the beach or the national parks. Even though they only took short trips, Crew's parents spent time planning each one, making sure they knew exactly how to get to their destinations. His father owned and loved his light-blue Thunderbird, but he found it much more relaxing just to stay home and wax it in the driveway. Traveling just created too much stress.[6]

Gospel singer Mahalia Jackson succinctly explained the panic that she and her musicians felt when leaving an evening's performance to face the late-night drive to the next town where she would perform. As soon as she left the concert hall, she felt as if she had "stepped back into the jungle." They never knew where to find gasoline and oil, or where they could use restrooms. Despite the singer's wealth and broad popularity, with both black and white fans, she was "just another Negro" when she was on the road:

> My accompanist Mildred Falls and I were traveling in my car, a Cadillac. My cousin, John Stevens, a young actor and drama teacher from Chicago, was doing the driving. From Virginia to Florida it was a nightmare. There was no place for us to eat or sleep on the main highways. Restaurants wouldn't serve us. Teen-age white girls who were serving as car hops would come bouncing out to the car and stop dead when they saw we were Negroes, spin around without a word and walk away. . . . The looks of anger at the sight of us colored folks sitting in a nice car were frightening to see.[7]

Driving into a new town created a particular kind of dread. Black drivers in a white neighborhood often invited undue interest and, at times, violence. African American magazines and newspapers, as well as progressive publications such as *The Christian Century*, regularly published stories of chance encounters along the roadways that cost African Americans their lives.

In 1936, a minor collision in Birmingham between a white truck driver and a car driven by an African American teacher turned deadly. As the occupants of the two vehicles stood discussing the accident, a passing car filled with white men took issue with what they perceived as an interracial conversation. In addition to a vicious verbal attack, the men hurled bricks at the black driver, striking him in the head. He was not treated at the local hospital but was simply "patched up," perhaps analogous to my grandfather's treatment at home for pneumonia. The teacher, his skull fractured, died that night. "It might never occur to anyone to take a Negro to a hospital," an article describing the incident noted sarcastically.[8]

In Detroit in the summer of 1943, an altercation between black and white youth on the bridge to Belle Isle led to a riot that included random acts of violence against black citizens, particularly motorists. According to NAACP Director Walter White, after a series of "dangerous rumors" took flight, mobs of angry white men roamed the streets, turning over cars and pulling black motorists out onto the streets and beating them.[9] The *New York Times* described the violence: "White aggressiveness was confined largely to attacks on Negroes found in white sections and attacks on the automobiles of Negroes driving in these sections."[10] In the end, twenty-five African Americans were killed, most of them by the police.[11]

Unlucky families, out for a drive, also could find themselves in the wrong place at the wrong time. In 1956, *Life* magazine photographer Robert Kelley captured an image of a terrified black family that happened to be passing Clinton High School in Tennessee when they encountered an angry white mob. Men and women alike set upon the victims, rocked the car, and roughed up its occupants. Law enforcement often looked the other way, not wanting to arrest the "good citizens" of the community. Sometimes the police even joined in.

African American drivers faced a variety of perils on the highway. In this 1956 photograph, a young white man, Billy Middlebrooks, tried to dissuade a mob attempting to haul a black motorist, who was simply passing through town, from his car. African American drivers viewed automobiles as a protective environment, but sometimes even a powerful engine was not enough to help them get away. (*Library of Congress, Prints and Photographs Division, Visual Materials from the NAACP Records [reproduction number, e.g., LC-USZ62-90145].*)

Some of the most dangerous threats faced by black drivers occurred during or in reaction to civil rights marches, or the attempted integration of schools, hotels, parks, or other public accommodations. On January 23, 1957, when Willie Edwards stopped to buy a soft drink before going home, Henry Alexander and three other white men, all members of the Klan, approached his Winn-Dixie truck. They were searching, they said later, for a black man whom they suspected of insulting a white waitress. Recently hired as a driver for a chain of grocery stores, Edwards was at the end of his first delivery run. It would also be his last. The men forced him, at gunpoint, out of the truck and into their car.

They drove him to the Tyler–Goodwin Bridge, spanning the Alabama River near Montgomery, and ordered him to jump or be shot. Edwards died in the cold, rapidly moving water fifty feet below the bridge. Three months later, fishermen dragged his corpse from the river. Until then, his distraught wife had no idea what happened to him, and the local authorities declined to help her.

Alexander admitted that he, like many other white men he knew, also engaged in routine harassment and violence against black drivers and their passengers in retaliation for the bus boycott and other changes to the southern racial order. His acts of racist terrorism included flipping lighted cigarettes into drivers' cars, throwing rocks at the newly integrated buses, and even shooting a pregnant black woman who was riding the bus.[12] Although prosecutors tried several times to bring to justice the perpetrators in the Willie Edwards case, none of the men ever saw the inside of a prison cell. Before he died of lung cancer in 1992, Alexander confessed his role in the Edwards murder to his wife, who then apologized to the Edwards family.[13]

Nine-year-old Joseph Holloway endured a similarly harrowing experience, although he lived to tell the tale. In 1961, the Holloway family left their home in Los Angeles to visit Joseph's dying grandmother in Louisiana. Joseph's Uncle Gus Holloway drove a new Chrysler, but he did not know the roads very well, and neither he nor his wife could read. The couple depended on young Joseph for help deciphering the road signs.

Like most black families, the Holloways wanted to stay on the main highways, but they made a wrong turn somewhere near Waco, Texas, and got lost on back roads. Winding up in an unfamiliar town just as the sun set, they were stunned to find themselves driving slowly into the middle of a lynching. The crowd's racist frenzy rose to a climax as they lit the black victim on fire. The man screamed in agony, his body contorted, and the smell of his burning flesh filled the air.

When the lynchers spotted the Holloways' Chrysler creeping along, its passengers' faces pressed against the car windows in horror, the rioters shouted and ran for their own vehicles, hoping to catch the Holloways and add them to the pyre. Turning around, as quickly as the large car would allow, Uncle Gus pushed the accelerator to the floor and raced out of town with the lynch mob in hot pursuit. Uncle Gus saved the family by running with the headlights off and hiding silently for hours on a country lane as both police cars and the mob prowled the dark roads hunting for them. Everyone in the car trembled with fear.

When the family returned to Los Angeles, Holloway's aunt immediately enrolled in literacy classes, as she attributed the wrong turn to her inability to read the road signs, and she was determined that another such life-threatening mistake would never happen again. Most automobile trips, of course, were uneventful and did not result in the kind of terrifying encounter experienced by the Holloways, yet African American drivers understood the potential for danger every time they got into their cars.[14]

BLACK DRIVERS often were more fearful of the authorities than of the possibility of a run-in with an angry mob—and that fear wasn't limited to the police. Black travelers sometimes disappeared after encounters with police, never to be seen again. Fear of the police and stories of police harassment and violence circulated widely in black magazines and newspapers and were passed along through word of mouth. Although no studies exist of racial profiling in the 1930s or 1940s, hundreds of anecdotal stories from across the country indicate that black drivers perceived themselves as targeted by police road patrols simply for being black while behind the wheel of a car. "First of all you have to watch *how* you drive," Ernest Dunbar, senior editor for *Look* magazine, wrote in an open letter to President Lyndon Johnson. "If the posted limit is 50 miles per hour, you have to deduct 10 miles per hour off that for being black. So you go 40 mph. There are all those cops just lying in wait for whom you'd be a welcome haul."[15]

A police officer dragged this African American man from this car during the unrest in Harlem in 1944. There is a long history of tension, fear, and mistrust between African Americans and police in the United States. (*Bettmann, Getty Images.*)

Black motorists could face particularly perilous consequences if they were involved in traffic accidents. Police officers tended to favor white drivers over black drivers in determining fault, regardless of the circumstances of the accident. Natchez, Mississippi, electrician Willie Wallace recalled an accident in which he was involved as a young driver and the unfair treatment he received from the responding policeman. "I remember one night a [white] lady coming around the corner, ran into me. She was drunk." When the policeman arrived, he sent the woman home so that he could take care of her "problem"—in other words, Willie. "Of course I got the bulk of it," remembered Willie, "because they were saying that we both hit each other, when I never did anything. But that's the way the policeman wrote it up, to protect this lady."[16]

Some black travelers believed that the best way to resolve a traffic accident safely was simply to admit fault, exchange information, and leave the scene as quickly as possible. With a little luck, the responding officer would let you go. Major-league baseball pitcher Jim "Mudcat" Grant advised that the best course of action was to stay in your car and away from the driver of the other vehicle, if possible: "If the person was white that the accident was against, you stayed away from them, because you didn't want anything to happen. So, when the police showed up, you had all your credentials and made sure that everything was proper."[17]

The police were not the only authorities black motorists had reason to fear. They also knew that if they were injured in a car accident, treatment would likely be delayed, inadequate, and segregated—if they received any aid at all. When Danny Earl Clay and his ambulance partner drove out to the scene of an accident near Chunky River, Mississippi, they encountered a Harris Ambulance Company vehicle—a white ambulance—on its way back the fifteen miles into Meridian to the hospital. "Harris had two-way radios and we didn't," noted Clay. The police or the ambulance service waited until the white victims had been removed from the scene before even calling the black ambulance. A person's chances of survival from a traumatic injury in a car accident are greatest if they receive care quickly. Clay remembered that two of the black people involved in the crash died that night. "There was definitely a lapse of time there," said Clay, "perhaps as much as thirty minutes" before the ambulance could even get to the victims.[18]

The nature of hospital and ambulance care for black Americans profoundly affected many motorists, their passengers, and

Automobile accidents posed some of the greatest threats to African Americans traveling along the nation's highways, particularly in the South. Often they had no access to emergency health care if injured while on the road. (*Teenie Harris Archive/Carnegie Museum of Art, Getty Images.*)

even pedestrians crossing the road. Dozens of stories document the unnecessary injuries and deaths of African Americans in accidents as a result of neglect and hospital segregation under Jim Crow.

One particularly disturbing example occurred in 1931, in Atlanta. Headed home from a visit with his daughter Olive, George White stepped off the curb and was hit by an automobile trying to beat a red light. George had very light skin and could easily be mistaken for white. (His son, the fair-skinned, blue-eyed Walter White, was then executive secretary of the NAACP.) The car that hit him was driven by a doctor at the Henry W. Grady City Hospital, the main section of which was for whites only. The man loaded White into his car and sped off to Grady Hospital, where the city's best doctors worked frantically to save him. When bystanders who observed the accident notified the White family, George's son-in-law, a man with rich brown skin, rushed to the colored hospital, only to be told that his father-in-law could not be found. Then, thinking that George might have been misidentified as a white man and taken to Grady, he checked the white wards. When the doctors and nurses discovered their mistake—that they had "put a nigger in the white ward"—the staff could not remove him fast enough. Walter White described his father being "snatched from the examination table lest he contaminate the 'white' air." Still unconscious, he was put out of the Henry W. Grady white ward in the pouring rain, despite his serious injuries, and carried to the Negro ward across the street.[19]

Vermin and cockroaches infested the hospital's Negro ward. As the family kept vigil at White's bedside, they had to keep elevating their feet to avoid the rats. Unfortunately, nothing could be done for George White's injuries; the attending nurses could only make him comfortable. The vigil lasted sixteen days as the family observed an overworked staff attempting to keep clean a dingy, dilapidated, and overcrowded ward. Atlanta's black population was then about ninety thousand, yet Grady Hospital's filthy and inadequate Negro ward and a private black sanatorium with a dozen beds had to serve that entire community.[20]

Separate but unequal hospital facilities existed in the North, too. In 1937, Composer W. C. Handy, the arranger of Negro spirituals and the "Father of the Blues," took his wife, Elizabeth, to New York's Knickerbocker Hospital for treatment of a cerebral hemorrhage. The hospital kept her waiting in the ambulance for an hour while her doctor argued with the staff about admitting the critically ill woman. They had no facilities for Negroes, he was told, and she died shortly thereafter. In a 1950 incident, an ambulance carried a group of men involved in a car accident to Breckenridge County Hospital in Kentucky. Because the hospital lacked a Negro ward, the men were left for hours on the floor of the emergency room, untreated, although they received some morphine for pain. One of the men died.[21]

Some colleges even refused to send their students to athletic competitions for fear that the athletes might not return to campus alive if they happened to be in an accident while traveling. "Negro players have experienced the greatest difficulties in securing medical care and hospitalization," reported the *Atlanta Daily World.* The paper cited three "inexcusable deaths" that could have been prevented. In 1947, when six members of the track team and the coach from Clark College (now consolidated with Atlanta University as Clark Atlanta University) were seriously injured in an automobile accident, an ambulance transported them fourteen miles to a hospital in Manchester, Tennessee. Refused admission on the pretext that the hospital was at capacity, the ambulance conveyed the two most seriously injured students thirty miles farther to the University of the South Hospital in Sewanee, Tennessee, which offered first aid but then sent them on their way. Finally, Donelson, a private African American hospital in Nashville, fifty miles from the site of the accident, provided the necessary treatment.[22] At this point, four hours had passed, and student Jeffrey Jennings died soon after arrival. In the end, most of the students were relatively fortunate and survived; in many parts of the country, it was impossible to find a hospital that would accept even the most seriously injured black patients. And, in this case, white motorists helped the less seriously injured students get to Donelson Hospital.[23]

The 1930s saw a shift from privately funded hospitals to increasingly professional public hospitals, and the trend accelerated after World War II. In 1932, only one hospital bed existed for every 999 African American citizens. For white Americans, by contrast, the ratio was one for every 110 patients. Eighty-two percent of the hospitals in the United States admitted some black patients to segregated wards by the 1950s, but quotas determined the number of beds available to them.[24] In the South, few hospitals accepted any black patients.[25] In Nashville, for example, only Hubbard Hospital, a Negro facility with just thirty beds, struggled to provide care for the sixty-five thousand black residents of the city, while two church-affiliated hospitals and two general hospitals refused to admit any African Americans.[26]

In 1941, my mother was fortunate enough to be able to go to Raleigh, North Carolina, for a needed hospital stay. "Miss Alvenia Wooten has returned home from St. Agnes Hospital," noted a newspaper's social column. Then twenty-four years old, she traveled more than sixty-four miles to the hospital because no decent black hospital existed in Fayetteville. St. Agnes was considered the only well-equipped hospital for African Americans between Washington, DC, and New Orleans, a distance of more than 1,087 miles. In addition to excellent patient care, St. Agnes provided much-needed training for black nurses and sponsored a residency program for black doctors, a rarity in the United States.

Prior to the 1960s, the health-care establishment generally divided inpatient spaces by race, in three ways. A very small number of progressive communities had fully integrated hospitals that admitted anyone who needed care to whatever beds might be available, whether in a ward or in a semiprivate or private room. Another group of hospitals created separate segregated spaces for black and white patients. A separate wing—or, more commonly, an attic or basement ward designated "for Negroes"—kept black patients in distinctly inferior accommodations. Peeling paint, unsanitary conditions, inadequate treatment options, and insufficient nursing care were common in these partitioned wards. White patients in the same hospitals might recuperate in air-conditioned comfort in well-kept and fully staffed rooms. Often, a black patient requiring hospital admission was told that no Negro beds were available because the hospital's small quota had been filled. White hospitals also refused to grant admitting privileges to black doctors and refused to hire black nurses, so black doctors and nurses often could not care for their own patients, even in the Negro wards of hospitals.[27] Of course, many communities only had white hospitals. Some had both white and black hospitals, but this was rare. So confusing were these situations that ambulance drivers had to be familiar with the specific policies on treating African Americans at each facility, and the availability of beds, so that patients would not be turned away from one hospital after another when in need of critical care.[28]

Several black hospitals, including Newark's Community Hospital (1927–1953) and Detroit's Mercy General Hospital (1917–1976), provided excellent care but struggled for survival. Howard University Medical School in Washington (founded as Freedman's Hospital in 1862) and Meharry Medical School in Nashville (1876) offered high-quality care, but they could only serve people in their regions. Most black hospitals did not have the diagnostic equipment or laboratory facilities found in the large urban facilities that treated white patients. Although black hospitals received some philanthropic support, their patient bases were not large enough or wealthy enough to allow them to purchase the necessary top-of-the-line equipment.

Black motorists might find themselves having to navigate the complexities of American hospitals if they were injured in a crash, but the scarcity of black hospitals also produced a kind of Jim Crow medical tourism. For a serious illness, black citizens might need to travel hundreds of miles, typically by car or ambulance, to the nearest available inpatient facility. Some people were so wary of segregated facilities—knowing them to be poorly funded, poorly staffed, and lacking equipment and outpatient facilities—that they would go on extended road trips to find alternatives. Mortician and ambulance driver Danny Earl Clay, who lived in Meridian, Mississippi, remembered driving patients to hospitals as far away as Cleveland in the 1950s and 1960s in search of better care. "If a family member up north had access to good health care, we might be asked to drive the patient up there to get to a better hospital," he recalled.[29]

African American physicians and nurses did not believe in this segregated system of care, but they felt that they had no choice. Black hospitals, where they existed, offered at least a modicum of treatment, even if most did not have trauma facilities. "We don't wish anyone to get the idea that we condone these discriminations, which will some day be corrected," wrote John A. Kenney, the medical director of Newark's Community Hospital in 1939, "but what are we to do while this slow evolutionary process is developing?"[30]

Segregated ambulance services further complicated the problems black Americans encountered after automobile accidents. Ambulances for white hospitals often refused to transport black patients, a situation that led black funeral homes to use their hearses as ambulances.

Segregated ambulances and hearses lasted, in some places, well beyond the 1960s. As a result, many communities, white and black, relied on a vehicle called a "combination coach," which converted from a hearse to an ambulance with a bed that moved up

The combination coach made it possible to convert a hearse into an ambulance. Segregated ambulances, often owned and operated by funeral homes, transported the sick and dying from automobile accidents to whatever hospitals would accept them.

or down, depending on whether the occupant lay on a stretcher or in a casket. The 1964 white Cadillac hearse that carried President John F. Kennedy's body to the airport for the trip from Dallas back to Washington after his assassination was a combination coach. Jackie Kennedy sat beside the casket in one of the seats provided for ambulance attendants. Danny Earl Clay drove a combination coach built on a Cadillac base for the Berry and Gardner Funeral Home in Meridian, Mississippi, and used it for both accidents and funerals.

For African American auto-accident victims, the availability of an ambulance might depend on whether or not the ambulance driver happened to be heading to a cemetery at the time of the emergency call. A funeral in progress could delay the conversion of a hearse into an ambulance. Many black funeral directors also worried about the long distances they might have to drive to find a hospital that would accept black accident victims, as too long spent on an ambulance call could lead to a loss of business. In one high-profile case that gained national publicity in the black press, a young college student broke his neck when the car in which he was riding had a blowout and overturned on a gravel road. Two hospitals turned away the injured young man. It took a long time to find a funeral director/ambulance driver who could be persuaded to drive the injured student thirty-five miles to the nearest hospital that would accept him. The delay, unfortunately, ensured his death.[31]

In 1931, W. E. B. Du Bois wrote about the plight of black travelers injured in accidents, devoting one of his columns in *The Crisis* magazine to the tragic, untimely deaths of his good friend Juliette Derricotte, dean of women at Fisk University, and her student, Nina Johnson, an undergraduate in her senior year. Pained and outraged by the poor treatment the women received following a serious car accident, Du Bois dispassionately presented every detail of their ordeal.

A group of four women decided to drive from Nashville, the home of Fisk, to Dalton, Georgia, "to avoid the Jim-crow cars of the South, and the difficulty in getting meals and other transportation." The details of the crash mattered little, but the pattern of discrimination and inhumanity was clear. Some local white bystanders tried to help the injured as much as they could, but Hamilton Memorial, the local hospital, accepted no black patients. At first, no ambulance responded to the call for help. The black funeral director finally arrived with his hearse and transported the women to a local white physician, and then another and then another. Although the women had suffered severe injuries, the doctors felt no compulsion to provide more than first aid. The women did not receive treatment, nor were they taken to the modern hospital in the city. Instead, the hearse bumped along over back roads until it reached the home of a black woman with a reputation for caring for the sick and injured, although she had no training as either a doctor or a nurse. She treated the women to the best of her ability, but with no success. Other witnesses at the scene of the accident noted that the woman's house was filthy. Nothing could

Juliette Derricotte, the popular and talented dean of women at Nashville's Fisk University, died at the age of thirty-four after an automobile accident in which she and a student were thrown from the vehicle. (*Fisk University, John Hope and Aurelia E. Franklin Library, Special Collections, Fisk Photograph Collection, Nashville.*)

be done, at that point, to save the lives of Derricotte and Johnson or to alleviate their terrible suffering.

It must have been a macabre scene, as their desperate friends rode with them in the ambulance/hearse—a vehicle that presaged their fate—urging the funeral director/ambulance driver to rush them from place to place in a futile attempt to save their lives. After being carried throughout much of the Georgia countryside, the two women lingered for hours before dying. "In the light of this," Du Bois asked, "what shall be said of the civilization of Dalton, Georgia?"[32] The oft-repeated story of Dean Juliette Derricotte and Nina Mae Johnson became a cautionary tale for African Americans of the dangers of the road.[33]

In that era, when the authorities were first notified of an accident, the race of those injured was often the first question that dispatchers asked. In 1960, Columbia University historian Kenneth Jackson witnessed a terrible automobile accident in Memphis. "The fire hydrant was sheared off," Jackson remembered, "and was spewing water everywhere. There was an Oldsmobile upside down. People were badly hurt. I called the emergency number—the equivalent of 911 at that time—the first question they asked me was, were the people black or white? The most important question when people were dying was what race are they!"[34]

"Where should a Negro get hurt?" mused writer Esther Balderston Jones sarcastically in 1932, bemoaning the treatment received by black patients at many of the nation's hospitals and clinics. In Tennessee, African Americans might have a chance of getting a hospital bed. "You would not have to drive more than a hundred miles to a hospital if you located your accident wisely in Tennessee! But there might be problems if your car accident occurred in Chicago or Birmingham. "Best have your accident near Charleston," if at all in South Carolina, she argued, since at least a good number of hospital beds were there for Negroes. But there was not a single hospital bed for Negroes in forty-two of that state's hundred counties. Overall, Jones found emergency care for African Americans woefully inadequate everywhere in the United States. "Until kindness can over step color lines we have not met the plain duty of pagan humanity, let alone Christian." She concluded: "It is really best for the Negro not to get hurt at all anywhere."[35]

THE HIGHWAY took its greatest toll on those who traveled regularly for their work. "Many Negro casualties are among show people," observed an article in *Our World*. Traveling late at night, and often tired from a performance and anxious to reach another city in order to get some sleep before the next show, singers, band members, and nightclub performers and their support staffs were more likely to be involved in automobile accidents. Alcohol may also have played a role in some car wrecks, since it was so prevalent in—and so central to the culture of—nightclubs and performance spaces.

Earl Bostic was involved in a crash in 1951. Traveling at four a.m. toward Jacksonville, Florida, Bostic's Fleetwood Cadillac plowed into the rear of a gasoline truck, pinning its occupants. After performing into the wee hours of the morning, Bostic, an alto saxophone player, was drowsy. Fortunately, he and his band members, who were traveling with singer Dinah Washington, did not die that night.[36] Many others were not as lucky. Singer Ruth Brown, nicknamed the "Queen of Rhythm and Blues," Tommy Gaither of the Orioles, tenor saxophone player Chu Berry, and vocal musician Trevor Bacon were among the black entertainers who died during the first half of the twentieth century in car wrecks. Some died instantly; others were injured and had to face the challenge of finding decent hospital care.

In 1937, the great blues singer Bessie Smith, her arm nearly severed in the impact, died after a late-night traffic accident. The tragedy immediately raised questions about the circumstances surrounding her death, and stories circulated that Jim Crow practices had killed her. Some reports erroneously noted that she bled to death while being driven by ambulance to multiple hospitals, her companions searching frantically for one that would admit her. Others reported that slightly injured white victims of a nearby fender bender needed medics' attention before they could attend to the critically injured Smith. It is far more likely that a black ambulance transported her to the regional black hospital, where surgeons amputated her arm in a doomed attempt to save her life.

Yet so suspicious was the black community about deaths following automobile accidents that even when racism and neglect could not directly be blamed, many people refused to believe the reports. Rumors surrounding the deaths of well-known black personalities in car accidents raced through African American communities. Dr. Charles Drew, the brilliant young surgeon who conducted pioneering research in blood storage and blood transfusions and saved countless lives during World War II, died in a car accident in North Carolina in 1950. Leaving Washington late one March night, Drew set out with three other physicians in a Buick roadster for a medical conference in Tuskegee, Alabama. Because of the usual difficulty of finding a hotel, the group planned to drive through the night. While his companions napped, Drew apparently fell asleep at the wheel. The car veered onto the shoulder and overturned. An ambulance took Drew to Alamance General Hospital in Burlington, North Carolina, where the white doctors worked feverishly to save him, recognizing him as not just any Negro but as a renowned physician. Although the hospital had few beds available for Negro patients, they did not send him away. Tragically, however, Charles Drew died of his injuries.

To this day, the belief persists that the father of modern blood banking bled to death at the hands of heartless racists. Historian Spencie Love postulates that the strength of the Drew legend illustrates the incredibly destructive psychological trauma that racism causes. African Americans saw, in Drew's death, an ironic and instructive tale of the dangers of the highway. The message was clear: On the road, even the smartest, most important black man was just another nigger.[37]

Another black man died that same year, and in the same county, after a car accident, and his death helps explain black suspicions about post-crash deaths. In December 1950, twenty-four-year-old World War II veteran and North Carolina A&T college student Maltheus Avery was driving his Pontiac when he hit a furniture truck on Route 70, about thirty miles outside of Greensboro, North Carolina. The ambulance took him to Alamance General Hospital, the segregated facility where Charles Drew died. Alamance's

Charles Drew in the lab at Howard University, 1942. Dr. Drew developed a method for the long-term preservation of blood that saved countless lives during World War II. When his automobile turned over on April 1, 1950, an ambulance took Drew to Alamance Hospital, a segregated facility in Virginia. Immediately recognizing the famous physician, the doctors worked desperately to save him. He died from massive injuries, but African Americans all over the country believed that he had not received adequate care because of his race, as had occurred to countless other African Americans. (*Scurlock Studio Records, Archives Center, National Museum of American History, Smithsonian Institution.*)

Negro ward had only five beds in the basement. Avery had a traumatic head injury, so Alamance's emergency-room doctor quickly transferred him to the larger and better-equipped Duke University Hospital, which had more beds for Negroes.

Duke was thirty-five miles away, and when Avery's ambulance arrived there, his handlers found that all fifteen of Duke's Negro beds were full. The hospital staff, which later claimed to have given Avery "supportive measures" during his ten-minute stay in their emergency room, sent him, now dying, to Lincoln, the nearby black hospital, where Avery, the married father of a young child, died within minutes, never regaining consciousness. It is possible that his injuries would have resulted in his death even if he had been admitted to Alamance or Duke.[38] But more timely treatment certainly would have given him a better chance of survival.

IF THE automobile age opened up new possibilities for black Americans while imperiling them in new ways, it also changed the casual everyday interactions between black people and white people. The automobile required a new code of driver etiquette that was different from the etiquette of the horse-and-wagon era. Black people driving their own cars altered the accepted rules of racial conduct. Although etiquette varied by region, white people generally expected black people to be obsequious and deferential in every situation. Particularly in the southern states, black citizens were expected to move from the sidewalk to the gutter when whites walked by, or to step into an alley or against a store wall to permit white citizens to pass. White people owned the sidewalk. Black people averted their eyes, bowed their heads, removed their hats in the presence of white women, and generally made themselves as invisible as possible on public streets. During the day, blacks might do menial work for whites—as porters or maids, laundresses or laborers, sometimes assisting them in such highly personal tasks as dressing or shaving. At night, they were expected to return to their own communities and stay there. When they were not being useful as servants or performers, they were expected to be out of sight. Any behavior that challenged these customs threatened the accepted social order.

The automobile helped change racial etiquette by empowering Negro motorists to ignore these rules and be more aggressive in encounters with white motorists. For instance, they could disregard expectations for deference because white drivers could not always tell who was behind the wheel.[39] Cars placed more distance between travelers than did open wagons or crowded train cars. As African Americans traveled throughout the country, the rapid and anonymous nature of automobile travel continued to disrupt customary behaviors. Enclosed vehicles moving at high speeds on highways made it more difficult, although not impossible, for white Americans to practice discrimination with a glance and force personal deferential behavior from behind the wheel—as they had on the train, the bus, or even walking down the street.

In 1938, lamenting the loss of the face-to-face contact and proper manners occasioned by the passing of the buggy and the advent of the automobile, an *Atlantic Monthly* author wrote wistfully, "I realize that motorists in fast-moving glass-enclosed cars cannot exchange the gracious greetings or the gallant gestures of the horse-and-buggy era."[40] White motorists could not expect black drivers to pull to the side of the road to let them by or to give them the right-of-way at every intersection—protocols that might have been expected with carriages, where all occupants were clearly visible. People walking down the same sidewalk could demand that black citizens step into the street or move aside, but those same acts of obsequiousness could hardly be required at highway speeds. Maintaining racial etiquette required that one's identity be known and clearly visible. Was that light-skinned driver white or merely a light-skinned Negro? Perhaps he was Jewish or Italian, or Portuguese.

In *Etiquette: The Blue Book of Social Usage*, published in 1949, Emily Post referred to the automobile age as the "beginning of an entirely new era of social behavior." Etiquette mavens sold new editions of their manuals by offering advice on how to negotiate the confusing new manners required on the road. In some southern communities, white drivers assumed that they *always* had the right of way and could justifiably pull out in front of a black driver at any time. The "Safe Driving Rules" in *The Negro Motorist Green Book* subtly warned black drivers to watch for this dangerous behavior: "[W]hen the other car passes you, watch out that he doesn't cut in on you."[41] Expressing his concerns about those who tried to maintain the old racial propriety from behind the wheel of a car, one black driver commented:

> These white women act like they think these brakes is colored too and just naturally stop dead still when they sees a white woman bursting into an open highway without stopping. They look up and sees you colored and keep going like it's a disgrace to stop at a sign to let a nigger pass.[42]

The danger posed by the speed of the automobile made concerns about safety take precedence over race, gender, or class etiquette, and states enacted standardized traffic laws to safeguard all concerned. Emily Post reflected these concerns in her well-known *Blue Book*. She explained that, for the protection of everyone on the road, no distinctions should be made between men and women in motoring manners. Safety, not decorum, had to be the primary concern. Her comments revealed that she saw "women drivers" as a different breed, but she still supported standardization of road rules. "While gallantry is expected of all gentlemen, on the highway women drivers lose the ready identity of their sex and simply become 'another driver.'"[43] Certainly this became true of black drivers as well.

Black motorists became adept at self-preservation on the road, doing their best to avoid contact with white drivers, especially the police, and they used every precaution to avoid being pulled over. Having a nice car (but perhaps not too nice) also helped. They tried to stay out of the way and below the speed limit. For long trips, driving late at night was another strategy to avoid other drivers.

Black men in particular needed to be careful to avoid being caught in an incident with a white woman driver whose innocence would automatically be believed. A black motorist in Arkansas warned other drivers:

> You have to be pretty careful driving on the streets here in town. They [whites] drive so wild and crazy here that you have to be on your toes. I drive naturally and watch out. The white women drivers are not as careful as they might be, so I keep close watch out for them. You know how far you would get with them in any kind of argument about right and wrong. The best thing I know is to stay on the right side, and as far out of the way as possible.[44]

In the 1950s and 1960s, at the start of the summer travel season, African American magazines and newspapers ran articles full of useful driving tips to inform black motorists about how to protect themselves from unpleasant, embarrassing, and dangerous encounters while driving. The *Pittsburgh Courier* urged drivers to research and learn the different driving regulations for the states they would pass through in order to prevent being stopped by the police for a moving violation. Black motorists frequently relied on these articles to help them map the safest routes and to avoid sundown towns and other places of potential violence. They were advised on the importance of heeding all speed and road signs and carefully changing lanes to avoid police stops.

Journalist John Williams' travel diary, published in 1964, offered driving advice for black motorists based on his personal experiences while reporting from across the country. He suggested stopping to buy gas only in large cities, and he encouraged black drivers to be vigilant in watching for hidden speed zones and speed traps. Some of the towns that he drove through, he wrote, did not post speed limits until it was too late. "You've had it," he declared, if a law enforcement officer stopped your car:

> They'll pull you back into town to appear before the judge, but the judge won't be there. They'll tell you that you have to post a bond of fifty, seventy-five, or a hundred dollars, in order to be free to go on your way. If you post the bond, they'll tell you when to come back and appear before the judge. You never come back; who in hell wants to come back to Georgia? And they *know* that all you want to do is get away. Watch your step, keep your tongue inside your head, and *remember where you are*.[45]

Jim "Mudcat" Grant traveled with seven different major-league teams over the course of his baseball career from 1958 to 1971. When out on the road, he recommended always driving at well below the speed limit. "There were a ton of rules in those days. If you were black driving . . . you couldn't go two miles over the speed limit 'cause that gave a white police officer a chance to give you a ticket."[46] Other drivers urged motorists to gas up close to home the night before a trip, and to stick, where possible, to the boring but safer interstate highways to avoid accidental encounters with angry mobs in small towns. *The Amsterdam News* presented rules for "black driving," including carefully planning each trip in advance, doing a complete safety check on the car to make sure it would not fail mechanically, and avoiding driving while fatigued.[47] Some drivers even carried a chauffeur's cap in the car so that they could pretend to be the driver of a white man's vehicle, rather than the owner, if necessary.

AS EVER, the fear of harassment, violence, and even death lay behind these precautions. Indeed, black motorists were the victims of one of this nation's most notorious instances of vigilante violence. In the summer of 1946, on Moore's Ford Bridge, in Walton County, Georgia, a group of white citizens stopped an automobile carrying two young African American couples, Roger and Dorothy Malcom, and George and Mae Murray Dorsey. George Dorsey had recently returned home from distinguished service in World War II and was suspected of stabbing a white man accused of having an affair with Dorothy. After the white men stopped the car, they pulled the couples out, riddled their bodies with more than sixty bullets, and lynched them. Seven months pregnant, Dorothy Malcom's belly was slashed open and her unborn baby ripped from her womb. Although everyone in the white community knew who had committed the appalling murders, they closed ranks and kept the

The families of the couples murdered at the Moore's Ford lynching gather at their fresh gravesites. (*1946,* Atlanta Journal-Constitution *via AP.*)

perpetrators' terrible secret. The murders enraged President Truman, who ordered the FBI to investigate. A grand jury convened and heard testimony for sixteen days, but no one was ever prosecuted for the brutal Moore's Ford lynchings. In 2019, the US Court of Appeals for the Eleventh Circuit ordered that the 1946 grand jury testimony be opened, a move that may finally bring closure to the case.[48]

This egregious act of domestic terrorism, along with other similar acts, had the desired effect: intimidation. Black people knew that they too could encounter white terrorists who valued neither African American life nor the law—nor even basic human decency. They also knew that they could commit their crimes with impunity. Driving while black could not be avoided, but African Americans took whatever precautions they could to protect themselves and their families.

The automobile expanded the freedom of movement and the opportunity to travel throughout the country for all Americans, but this freedom often meant something different—and often, simply more—to blacks than to whites. At the same time, every black driver knew the potential dangers and the rules to follow to stay as safe as possible. Even though they traveled with detailed maps and itineraries and followed the available signs as best they could, the challenge of identifying welcoming towns, hotels, and gas stations required something else. As we will see, the ideal trip companion was a detailed travel guidebook designed specifically for black travelers. Such a travel guide could literally be a lifesaver.

Chapter 6

TRAVEL GUIDES FOR EVERYONE

> The white traveler for years has had no difficulty in getting accommodations, but with the Negro it has been different.
>
> —*The Negro Motorist Green Book*

Sitting at the dining-room table, my father plotted and carefully marked the route to Niagara Falls on an Esso map from the local gas station: Garden State Parkway to the New York State Thruway; Thruway to Niagara Falls. The trip was our first family vacation by car other than the annual drives south to my grandmother's house in Fayetteville, North Carolina—which my father detested. We rose before dawn and left Newark on the major highways. The first night, we stayed with some family friends on a farm near a tiny hamlet in western New York. The tidy white farmhouse had chickens in the yard, puffy down comforters on the beds, and fresh milk for breakfast in the morning. For the second night of our trip, my father had reserved a room in advance in Niagara Falls. In the 1950s and 1960s, vacationers often drove until they found a motor hotel that looked appealing and had a vacancy sign out front, but making a reservation provided the best possibility of securing a room successfully.

When we reached Niagara Falls, we found the motor hotel easily. My father, whose anxiety was apparent, went in to secure the reservation. My brother and I, sitting in the back seat, did not know that there was a chance we could be sent away by the estab-

lishment. But our father returned smiling. He need not have worried; with fair skin and wavy hair, his racial identity was quite ambiguous. The modest hotel room, decorated with kitschy figurines of Latin dancers hanging over the beds, was clean and roomy. My father's careful planning and my mother's skills as a navigator had paid off. Like so many other African American parents, they worked hard to shield us from the trials and perils of the road.

FOR BLACK AMERICANS, securing a decent hotel or motel room took planning, knowledge, and a bit of luck. Organizing a cross-country family vacation might take weeks and could involve mailing out inquiries and making many phone calls. The automobile age witnessed an explosion of travel-guide literature, as more and more Americans took to the road and drove to parts of the country that had previously been beyond their reach. Yet these guides, by and large, were aimed at white Americans. Most guides, brochures, and magazine articles did not specify which hotels accommodated black travelers. Before the late 1960s, African American travelers could never rely on mainstream guides and information when planning their journeys.

"Prior to 1945, the number of hotels, restaurants, motels, and such establishments that solicited or welcomed Negro patronage outside the south was infinitesimal," reported George Schuyler, weekly columnist for the *Pittsburgh Courier.* Citing a survey of 2,500 citizens conducted by the Washington, DC, firm of Andrew F. Jackson and Associates, Schuyler said that Negro travelers found a welcoming environment "in not more than 6 per cent [sic] of the nation's better hotels and motels."[1] In another article, he wrote: "There are probably fewer than twenty cities in the country where Negroes are not completely barred from white-owned restaurants. . . . Refusal is usually bold and callous; even where civil-rights laws exist, restaurant owners know that custom is with them." African American travelers typically had difficulty gaining entrance to beaches, amusement parks, theaters, swimming pools, bowling alleys, and just about every other place of public gathering and entertainment.[2]

Some of the new travel literature quite explicitly supported segregation and ideas of difference. In 1928, Jan and Cora Gordon wrote a popular memoir of their car trip from Maine to Georgia. The two automobile adventurers saw themselves as sophisticated white anthropologists observing (in their view) "simple indigenous peoples"—Chinese, German, and Albanian immigrants—with quaint, primitive customs. The Gordons described the foreign accents they heard as "dialect." The "otherness" of southern "Negroes" fascinated them. During a sojourn on the Sea Islands, off the coast of Georgia, the two focused on the role of white women in helping the black "natives" test "their capacity for social development." Revealing the women's beliefs of black men as predators and rapists who preyed on "pure" white women, the Gordons commiserated with Mrs. Puckett, a southern white traveler who feared for her safety. She believed that a black man on the island might revert to his base natural instincts and attack her. "I tell you we white women hereabouts don't dare go out alone at all," Mrs. Puckett grumbled angrily, "even though we manage to keep them niggers in order by lynching one now and again."[3]

Claudia Cranston, a travel writer for *Publishers Weekly,* found evidence in 1936 of what she called "the end of Depression travel inertia." She noted a spike in steamship bookings and a dramatic increase in the number of travel books, booklets, and travel magazines being published and purchased. Brentano's, one of New York's largest bookstores, anecdotally reported that travel-book sales jumped "somewhere between 50% and 100%" in the mid-1930s, and Cranston wrote of seeing customers even coming to blows over the travel books at Macy's during the Christmas rush.[4] The *New York Times,* a more reliable indicator of middle- and upper-class reading habits, regularly ran reviews of the numerous travel books and guides appearing on the market during this era.[5]

The popularity of mainstream Depression-era and post-Depression travel books may have been, to some extent, the result of the opportunity to "see" and enjoy other places from one's armchair—to escape hard times through vicarious experience. "As everyone knows," noted an article in the *New York Times*, "almost all good travel books can be read in two ways: for quiet enjoyment amid the static comforts of home—escape literature; or for suggestions, which may or may not take the form of practical usefulness for personal travel of your own—pursuit in a peculiar but literal sense."[6] Among the travel books available in the 1930s, the most popular ones served as light entertainment.[7] Like journals or travelogues, these books provided personal reflections based on an author's meanderings through the American countryside or overseas by car, train, steamship, or plane. Other travel narratives, with alluring titles such as *Romantic and Historic Florida* and *Trailing Cortez Through Mexico* (both published in 1935), carried readers to distant and wondrous places that they would probably never have the chance to visit. For Jewish readers, books about travel to Israel, Russia, and Egypt described the Jewish world and introduced foreign customs and religious practices. All of these books provided vicarious delights, whisking weary Americans away from dreary diets and economic deprivation.

In addition to the books recounting personal travel experiences, travel guidebooks provided tourists with specific advice and directions about how to see America. Baedeker, the old standby of mass-produced guides, earned its reputation in nineteenth-century Europe. But the guides were not well suited to American geography. *The American Baedeker*, first published in 1893, was, like its European parent publication, aimed at travelers making their way around large, old city centers. Designed for walking or train travel, it soon enough was obsolete, a relic of the nineteenth century in a country now based on streetcars, subways, and then the automobile. It sold chiefly to foreign tourists, and, as one observer remarked, was as obsolete as "the Oregon Trail by the 1930s."

There were other reasons that an American Baedeker did not make sense in a society built around automobiles and highways. Motorists needed up-to-date information about roadside motels, route numbers, street signs, and markers, which were not included in Baedeker guides. In any event, the size and diversity of the United States made producing a single national guidebook a quixotic endeavor. The wide variety of terrain, cultures, and cuisines, as well as endless sights from Maine to California, would have required a heavy, unwieldy book the size of a dictionary, which few travelers would purchase. "The size and complexity of the country have made difficult the production of an adequate, one-volume guide for the United States as a whole," wrote travel writer Elizabeth Platt in 1939.[8]

Instead, a wide variety of specialty and regional guides appeared. Despite their varied subjects, they shared one characteristic. More than simple manuals to places and highways, these books assumed an audience of white readers seeking to vacation with people like themselves. Appealing to middle-class values, the books highlighted prestigious hotels and accommodations that excluded people of color, and they promoted leisure pursuits for people who could travel anywhere in the country without hindrance. While African Americans, Jews, and Native Americans provided entertainment as performers at nightclubs and tourist attractions at certain resort destinations, many white Americans did not want to find themselves elbow-to-elbow with these individuals in the hotels and restaurants they visited while on vacation.[9]

When traveling, white Americans encountered African Americans primarily as providers of services. The presence of black waiters and chambermaids contributed to the luxury of restaurants, hotels, and resorts. In travel books, they appeared as background characters, often as a means of emphasizing the pastoral nature of some tourist regions.[10] The historical stereotypes of the faithful slave or unctuous servant, the compliant chauffeur or obedient maid—as well as the seedy characters from the wrong side of town—made cities and towns sound more exotic, and even a little bit dangerous, for adventurous travelers. African Americans never appeared in these volumes as citizens, family vacationers, or even businessmen or women on an equal footing with whites. They were not tourists, but tourist attractions.

In contrast to the travel guides, the federal government's promotion of tourism reflected both the divisions in the country between black and white Americans and the government's desire to please multiple constituencies. The Department of the Interior waded into the automobile travel guide business with *Travel USA*, a magazine-style publication designed to boost the economy during the Depression. The office of the United States Travel Bureau, a little-known New Deal program, used *Travel USA* to encourage any and all Americans to travel the country, increase their spending, and thus help the nation's recovery.[11] During its brief run, the magazine never pointed out which accommodations were segregated, nor did it offer suggestions for black travel agents. Segregation was never mentioned. It was understood.

Although *Travel USA* ignored the difficulties of traveling in Jim Crow America, the United States Travel Bureau actively promoted African American tourism in a publication geared specifically to black Americans. The bureau recognized the spending potential of the growing black middle class, whose disposable income and interest in travel could help to stimulate the economy. The US Travel Bureau created and circulated a simple publication—it was little more than a list, and it had a simple, all-type cover—of a small number of segregated Negro hotels, guesthouses, and YMCAs for African American vacationers.

UNITED STATES TRAVEL BUREAU

NEGRO HOTELS AND GUEST HOUSES

1941

UNITED STATES
DEPARTMENT OF THE INTERIOR

The United States Travel Bureau created a government-sponsored listing of hotels and guesthouses for African American travelers to promote tourism after the Depression. (*Library of Congress.*)

Another New Deal program, the Federal Writers' Project, produced travel guides that attempted, although with limited success, to bridge the racial divide by including sections on various ethnic and racial groups. The Works Progress Administration (WPA) state guidebooks, called *The American Guide Series*, had even loftier goals for readers.[12] Not merely travel guides, these books—one for each state—included political and social commentary. Ideally, writing the books would put writers back to work, but as historian Christine Bold has emphasized, they also attempted to create a shared national identity. The WPA guides mapped a cultural landscape ravaged by suffering and economic collapse, and they constructed an ordered and patriotic image of the United States that appealed to popular needs of the time. Written and priced for the middle class, the guides illustrated the unique aspects of the geography and history of each region of the country, while also highlighting the shared American experience.[13]

Each guide included accounts of the state's largest cities; sections on history, geology, art, and architecture; descriptions of important sites; and a route guide for motorists. The WPA guides offered modern, if bureaucratic, support of an increasingly important national commodity—tourism. But despite the rhetoric about national unity, some groups still did not fit into the vision of a "shared" experience created by these guides.[14]

Many of the guides included independent sections on black life, reflecting the separate world in which African Americans lived. The *WPA Guide to 1930s New Jersey*, for example, described Negroes and foreign-born whites as members of one-dimensional folk cultures, separate from the mainstream. Germans and Poles appeared as musical people who enjoyed singing societies and orchestras. New Jersey's Italian immigrants cultivated peppers, artichokes, and eggplants. The state's Negroes fared the worst. Assigned no redeeming characteristics, they were classified as apathetic and impoverished.

The people of Gouldtown, a mixed-race community in southern New Jersey, came in for derision because of their race mixing and their refusal to accept their Negro status. The guide indicated that they could not be considered whites.[15] Ignoring Atlantic City's vibrant black community and nightlife, the New Jersey guide reinforced the role of African Americans in the city only to service white tourists. The book noted that on the boardwalk a visitor could find a "procession in rolling chairs, propelled mostly by Negroes, who are not paid for waiting time but only for every hour they push."[16]

The writers of the New Jersey guide failed to recognize or chose to ignore the hundreds of middle-class black tourists who annually visited Atlantic City's guesthouses and tourist homes and its popular, segregated "Chicken Bone Beach." (Joe Louis, Josephine Baker, and Sammy Davis Jr., among other famous personalities, visited the black beach.) Instead, the guide warned: "North of Atlantic Avenue the city deteriorates into a dingy section, somewhat improved by recent slum clearance and street repairing. This is the Northside home of Atlantic City's Negro inhabitants—23 percent of the total population and, next to that of Newark, the most important Negro population of the State. They form a reservoir of cheap labor for the hotels, amusement piers, restaurants, riding academies, and private homes."[17]

In an attempt to recognize African Americans as an important part of American cultural life, Henry Alsberg, the head of the Federal Writers' Project and editor of the series, hired poet and Howard University English professor Sterling Brown as the National Negro Affairs editor. A prominent Jewish intellectual, Alsberg, who wrote for publications like *The Nation*, passionately supported social justice causes. He charged Brown with addressing African Americans' absence from state guides and developing new sections, written by black writers, for later editions. The insulting language in the earliest editions that sparked criticism from black readers also posed a challenge for Brown. He hired approximately thirty writers, including novelists Ralph Ellison, Richard Wright, and Claude McKay, and novelist and anthropologist Zora Neale Hurston.[18] Hurston wrote the "Negro section" of the Florida volume. Viewing folk culture as the nation's unifier, the book matter-of-factly attributed the richness of Florida's heritage to four distinct groups: the "cracker, the Negro, the Latin-American, and the Seminole." Other volumes incorporated stories of accomplished black heroes. Hurston introduced her readers to journalist and newspaper publisher T. Thomas Fortune, founder of the *New York Age*, whose career began in Florida, and she discussed Harlem Renaissance writer and native son, lawyer, and activist James Weldon Johnson.[19]

The "Negro Harlem" section of the New York City guide, written primarily by Richard Wright, offered a textured and varied portrait of a black community that encompassed working-class, middle-class, and poor people not overly optimistic and cognizant of urban problems. The statewide guide described black nationalist Marcus Garvey, NAACP editor W. E. B. Du Bois, and a host of community organizations from labor unions to artists' groups. But, even with these portraits, the books managed to project a picture of "the Negro" as different, exotic, unlike the rest of America—a people with a rich culture impaired by discrimination, a problem to be solved. The black writers attempted to represent a black perspective on the places they described, but they had no control over what the editors actually included, and the entire project existed within the context of a racially divided America with certain assumptions about "the Negro." The New York City guide noted: "It has been said that the Negro embodies the 'romance of American life'; if that is true, the romance is one whose glamour is overlaid with shadows of tragic premonition."[20]

The WPA guides, although more sophisticated than other travel guides of the time, offered both "positive" and negative stereotypes of, for instance, "Negroes"—as good musicians but naïve and childlike. The later volumes often put information about black life and culture in separate, segregated sections. Even after the hiring of Sterling Brown, when the WPA guides attempted to embrace African Americans as a part of the cultural life of the nation, the books still presented black people as a separate underclass. The WPA guides to the southern states emphasized the latter more than the former. These volumes reflected the prevailing southern racial attitudes (attitudes that seem to have been tolerated by or even acceptable to the rest of the country). A 1929 article in *Travel* magazine, for instance, described the "Happy-Go-Lucky" nature of Birmingham's "sepia settlement." The article portrayed the black residents as idle, loud, and flamboyantly dressed—in a city where hucksters, voodoo doctors, and trinket salesmen loitered in streets strewn with watermelon rinds. The descriptions of the lively street scene conjured up a foreign place within the United States for white tourists looking for an exciting experience. Thrill seekers could immerse themselves in a "faraway locale" where black people were the natives—supposedly offering an opportunity to mingle with primitive people without leaving the country. "The stroller who plunges into the dusky crowds on Saturday," the magazine commented, "is caught up in a carnival gaiety."[21] Such astonishing depictions offered nonconfrontational and nonthreatening amusements for whites—at the huge expense of blacks.

More than twenty years later, some travel writers continued to portray African Americans as though they still lived in a pre–Civil War plantation culture, by focusing on historic sites and stories that reinforced the "positive attributes" of slavery in American history. These writers praised the Confederacy and celebrated the lives of slaveowners. A travel guide to North Carolina proudly informed visitors that the state contributed more "heavily in men to the Confederate armies than any other." After the war, the guide reported, the "State went through a disastrous period called 'Reconstruction.' "[22] According to the guide, this "disastrous period" included temporary military occupation by African American troops and passage of the Fourteenth Amendment, giving full citizenship to the newly freed slaves—a development the writer clearly did not see as positive. Another guide—the 1937 *Southeastern Travel Guide*, a series of regional paperbacks published by the American Automobile Association (AAA)—encouraged tourists to visit the Hermitage in Tennessee to see the home of President and Mrs. Andrew Jackson, to visit their tombs, and to see the gravesite of one of their slaves, "faithful Uncle Alfred," buried near them in the garden.[23]

It got worse from there. Claiming that it was written for New Yorkers visiting Washington and the southern states, the *Southeastern Travel Guide* included the popular route for black migrants returning to visit families in the South, but with no details on segregation. Like most publications, particularly those written for northerners and for broad public distribution, it avoided overt Jim Crow language, because the authors recognized such language as antithetical to the positive image of national unity that many tourism brochures hoped to promote. But its sympathies were clear. In telling the story of Mississippi, for example, the travel guide noted the return of white supremacy—"finally"—after the unpleasantness of Reconstruction: "The enfranchisement of the negroes, under the leadership of white republicans and the election of many of them to important state offices," the author commented, "caused years of conflict and bitterness." The book matter-of-factly condoned voting restrictions as well as the poll tests that would be declared illegal by the Voting Rights Act of 1965. "The racial problem remained acute until 1890, when suffrage was restricted to those who could read a section of the Constitution or interpret a section, if read aloud, as this effectively returned political government to the white race."[24] With the exception of the Tuskegee Normal and Industrial School in Alabama, described as "a coeducational school founded and conducted for negroes by negroes," no sites related to African American history appeared in the guide. The Washington, DC, home of abolitionist Frederick Douglass, for example, a popular site for black tourists, received no mention, even though Congress chartered the site in 1900.

The omission of hotel listings for blacks was another notable failing of the *Southeastern Travel Guide*. The hotel descriptions included no information about racial exclusion or inclusion, making them useless to African American travelers.

NONE OF the traditional mainstream travel guides held much interest or value for African American travelers, who knew these books could not be trusted to help black motorists negotiate travel in a segregated society. Even the summer haunts of the black elite—towns such as Oak Bluffs on Martha's Vineyard and Sag Harbor on New York's Long Island—were not deemed worthy of inclusion in either the AAA guides or other travel guides. Middle-class black motorists learned about hotels and resorts by word of mouth, through advertisements in black newspapers, or in articles that appeared in such periodicals as *The Crisis*, *Opportunity*, or *Ebony*. That is, until the creation of the first black travel guides.

"The White traveler for years has had no difficulty in getting accommodations, but with the Negro it has been different," proclaimed the first edition of *The Negro Motorist Green Book*. "He, before the advent of a Negro travel guide, had to depend on word of mouth, and many times accommodations were not available. Now things are different. The Negro traveler can depend on the 'GREEN BOOK' for all the information he wants, and has a wide selection to choose from."[25] The author of the guide was Victor Green, a New York publisher who wanted to help blacks identify welcoming establishments, resorts, and places of entertainment, as well as black businesses—barbershops, beauty parlors, hospitals, pharmacists, and stores anywhere in the country.[26] Especially when it was paired with a road map, an African American travel guide provided the perfect combination for a safe and pleasant trip. "In planning your trip or tour, secure a road map from your local service station for the trip that you expect to take," advised *The Green Book*. "Plan your trip from this map, noting the route and cities that you are to pass through, then you can make note of the accommodations in the cities that you are to pass through in case you might want to stop over."[27]

The Green Book was only the most famous entry in a new genre of publications. In the 1930s, individual entrepreneurs as well as some institutions began compiling lists of travel information to meet the very specific needs of black motorists. Black newspapers and magazines had long published articles and advertisements for hotels, restaurants, and resorts welcoming to their readers, but these were not comprehensive guides and the advertisements were not unbiased listings. These new African American travel guides filled a glaring need. In a 1933 article in *Opportunity* magazine, Alfred Edgar Smith wrote about the need for travel guides that identified places welcoming African American guests:

> Obviously, the answer [to the problem of where to stay] lies in an authentic list of hotels, rooming houses, private homes catering to the occasional traveller, tourist camps, and every type of lodging whatsoever, including those run by members of other races and open to Negroes; and the availability of such a list to our growing army of motor-travellers. Such a list would[,] if complete, be invaluable (and I can hear your fervent amens) for I am convinced that within the area of every fifty square miles of the more frequently travelled sections there are lodgings to be found at all times. If we just knew where they were, what a world of new confidence would be ours.[28]

Throughout the twentieth century, as organizations such as the NAACP and the National Urban League sought to integrate public accommodations, they also identified ways for African Americans to live within the existing racial system. They needed to address the present system, even as they sought to change it. The former task meant, among other things, identifying racially specific accommodations for black travelers. Locating black hotels and boardinghouses across the country was a difficult task. "My Dear Madam," wrote W. E. B. Du Bois, editor of *The Crisis* magazine, to Mrs. Sarah Harrison, secretary of the Negro Welfare Council of New London in 1929, "could you tell me if there is a colored boarding house in New London? I expect to be driving through November 14 and would like to spend the night."[29] Such correspondence between African American travelers was very common in the era before the new travel guides were published. Mrs. Harrison and the league were known as a clearinghouse for problems and information.

The Negro Welfare Council, to whom Du Bois' letter was directed, received considerable, similar correspondence each year. It was the first organization to respond to the need for an African American travel guide. In 1930, Sarah Harrison, secretary of the council, and publisher Edwin Hackley established *The Hackley & Harrison Hotel and Apartment Guide for Colored Travelers: Board, Rooms, Garage Accommodations, etc. in 300 Cities in the United States and Canada*. In its second year, 1931, the name of the booklet was shortened to *The Travelers Guide: Hotels, Apartments, Rooms, Meals, Garage Accommodations, Etc. For Colored Travelers*. The guides focused on overnight lodgings for Negro travelers and ran advertisements to help them produce possible future editions.[30] The Hackley and Harrison guides required painstaking research, but the authors admitted the difficulty of trying to account for such a large, diverse, and constantly changing nation, one in which the racial climate was confusing and variable:

> We have not sought and shall not seek to create or solve problems of communities. They are widely diversified and strangely conflicting. We have found directly opposite conditions existing in adjoining cities of the one State regarding racial attitudes and relations. Scattered thru the North and West are some strange anomalies. In many places transformation of sentiment is going on, forward or backward, the causes of which are easily traceable.[31]

Many of the accommodations listed were individual rooms in the private houses of black families, indicating the relatively small number of hotels open to blacks in the 1920s and 1930s. *The Travelers Guide* warned tourists that the quality of lodgings in private houses depended on the individual household and the "restrictions and inadequacies" of their facilities. Although they tried to include only decent accommodations, the authors could not guarantee that inclusion in the guide meant that the establishment would provide just that.

Other guides quickly followed Hackley and Harrison's. Each one, although appealing to the same general audience, also represented particular constituencies, reflecting the great diversity within the black community. For example, some guides were written to help show-business performers and club and association conventioneers in locating buses and accommodations for large groups. All of these publications offered similar information on towns and attractions that would be welcoming and cordial for the black business or family traveler.

The Travelers Guide clearly described its purposes in its opening pages in a way that defines all of these publications, noting that its development was specifically related to the rise in automobile use by African Americans. The guide claimed four reasons for its publication. First, it hoped to help readers learn more about the country. Second, the book aimed to help fraternal, college, and club groups stay in contact with one another by providing information that would facilitate participation in national conventions. Third, *The Travelers Guide* supported African American leisure and vacation travel. And fourth, the guide enabled African American travelers to avoid discrimination and harassment. In the end, keeping African Americans from being killed on the road constituted the overarching, if unstated, goal of all these travel guidebooks.

Most African American travel books included lists of lodging and profiles of tennis clubs, municipal golf courses, vacation resorts, and romantic getaway spots that helped middle-class African Americans find middle-class vacation options similar to those for white Americans. Black travelers could find all of the values and trappings of middle-class life reflected in these travel guides.[32] But black travelers also included those who could be considered by the white community as "working class." Porters and chauffeurs, many of whom were underemployed, were a significant market for black hotels and boardinghouses, because their work involved travel. Many business establishments catered specifically to these groups, in addition to vacationing tourists. Advertisements in some black tourist guides welcomed "colored tourists and chauffeurs."

Nonetheless, African American travel guides generally focused on travel as a leisure or business activity and presented themselves for a more educated audience. "This class of travel," noted *The Travelers Guide,* "in general is efficient, genteel and courteous in bearing and deserving of welcome in any hostelry or home."[33] Writing a justification for *The Negro Motorist Green Book* in 1949, Standard Oil representative Wendel P. Alston identified the variety of audiences who desperately needed a special African American guidebook. His list seems like a partial account of the *talented tenth*, the term used by W. E. B. Du Bois to describe the leaders of the black community. Alston mentioned musicians in "top ranking orchestras and numerous minor ones, concert singers and various musical organizations," as well as black members of the major "Negro" organizations and businessmen and entrepreneurs. His list also included "touring clubs, students and teachers and many others in the field of education, numerous religious, sorority and fraternity groups."[34]

The guides consciously avoided addressing the political challenges African Americans faced. The author of *Smith's Tourist Guide*, for instance, wanted to "establish a closer relationship with all people in order to secure the cause of peace and justice."[35] *Travelguide* offered readers "vacation and recreation without humiliation."[36] Indeed, the guides offered a mix of consumerism and uplift. Some ran advertisements for sophisticated fashions, black beauty

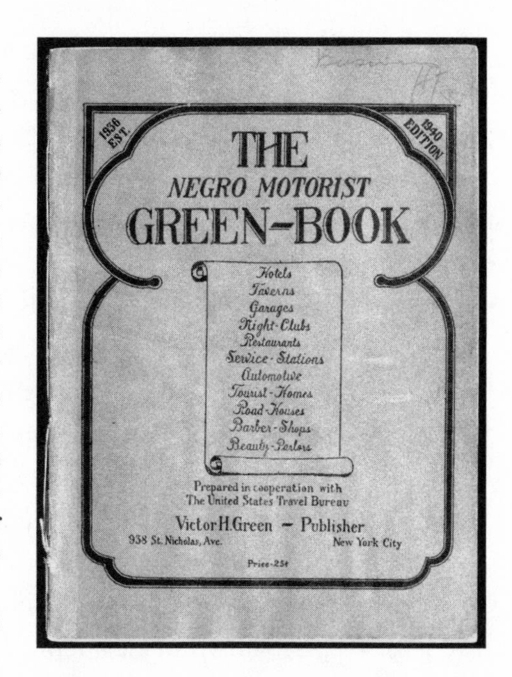

The cover of the 1940 edition of *The Negro Motorist Green Book* indicates that within its pages the reader would find recommendations for hotels, car-repair shops, nightclubs, black barbershops and beauty parlors, and restaurants, among other places. The cover also mentions collaboration with the United States Travel Bureau. (*Reproduced by permission of the Schomburg Center for Research in Black Culture, New York Public Library.*)

pageants, vacation gear, boats, and other middle-class pastimes and consumer goods. Automobile manufacturers purchased ads, hoping to convince readers to buy their brands of automobile for the family vacation. Others provided lists of historically black colleges or profiles of black Americans of achievement.

Even amid a glut of new guides for African Americans, Victor Green's stood out. The most successful and longest-lasting travel companion was produced in his 135th Street office in Harlem. *The Negro Motorist Green Book,* which later became *The Negro Travelers' Green Book,* was first published in 1937.[37] Although born in New York City, Green grew up in Bergen County, New Jersey, where his father worked as a porter for the United States Post Office Department. A striver and entrepreneur, Green secured a position as a mail carrier in northern New Jersey, and later he tried his hand at several business ideas. A nephew remembered an earlier business selling carvings of elephants and crocodiles and other decorative African items, which adorned his publishing office before he turned to the travel-guide business. He advertised some for sale in various issues of *The Green Book,* offering readers a chance to decorate their homes with Nigerian ebony letter openers and brightly colored North African hassocks.[38]

Other individuals and organizations responded to Green's success by launching guides of their own. In 1939, a little-known African American automobile association called Smith's Touring Club established an auto guide in Media, Pennsylvania. Smith himself (we do not know his first name) compiled his booklet in collaboration with Standard Oil, an arrangement later mastered by Victor Green and *The Negro Motorist Green Book,* when he joined forces with the company to distribute his travel guide nationwide. Smith praised Standard Oil for its willingness to sell gasoline dealerships to black owners as well as for its treatment of African Americans at its Esso service stations. Smith also worked with the African Methodist Episcopal Church, hoping to capture that market by printing in the back of the volume a listing of all of the denomination's conventions nationwide. Smith's guide did not last long, and we only know of its contents from advertisements. Other guides—*The Bronze American* and *Grayson's Travel and Business Guide*—also are known today only through their ads in black newspapers and magazines.[39]

As black fraternal groups and clubs attempted to locate venues for their annual conventions, additional special travel guides appeared. For the black traveler, finding a hotel room was difficult enough. Reserving sufficient rooms for an African American fraternity or church convention could be almost impossible in certain regions of the country.

The quality of hotel accommodations—so often a matter of concern for black travelers—inspired the founders of *The Go Guide to Pleasant Motoring* to focus on high-end facilities. Published from 1952 to 1959, the guide promoted hotels and motel complexes that could provide lodging for groups needing anywhere from ten to as many as five hundred rooms or more. To make convention planning easier for fraternal and church groups, many hotels and motels in the *Go Guide* listed the number of rooms available for reservation. The *Go Guide* was the official directory of the Nationwide Hotel Association, Inc. (NHA), a membership organization of black hotel and motel professionals founded to provide superior service and quality to their customers. Members paid no dues to join the NHA, but membership was granted by invitation only. Before receiving the NHA's seal of approval, a hotel would have to pass an inspection. Members displayed the NHA emblem in their windows, as a sort of private accreditation. The emblem ensured that the premises met the standards of refinement and cleanliness sought by black middle-class customers.

The NHA's "Pledge of Service" required hotels to guarantee heat and running water, impeccable cleanliness, daily fresh bed linens, air conditioning, and other comforts. Members were to assure their guests of a genteel atmosphere that included quiet in public hallways; the elimination of "rowdyism and vulgarity"; and the provision of comfortable mattresses, extra towels, and "kind and considerate hospitality" as the very minimum of service. Most important, all members guaranteed truth in advertising to potential patrons. The board of the Nationwide Hotel Association urged any dissatisfied customer to file a complaint directly with its national headquarters in Washington, DC, so that punitive action could be taken, if and when necessary.[40]

William Brown, the manager of Harlem's Hotel Theresa (a building now on the National Register of Historic Places), established the NHA group with Washington, DC, public relations attorney Andrew F. Jackson. The NHA guide pressured some states to consider recognizing black Americans as a desirable market. Hosting conventions could be lucrative, after all. The NHA itself solicited and received letters from several mayors and governors, inviting black tourists to visit their cities or states. The *Go Guide* reproduced copies of these letters to reassure tourists about locales where they would find a warm welcome. But the warm invitations were not always totally reliable. For instance, even though the Atlantic City (New Jersey) Board of Trade enticed tourists with promises of round-the-clock entertainment and "moonlight strolls on the boardwalk," most of the lodgings listed in the guide were black-owned hotels in the black neighborhood, far from the boardwalk and the segregated beach. A few states proclaimed in the *Go Guides* that their Hiltons, Radissons, and Sheraton–Biltmore hotels would be open to black visitors, and the steady opening of these hotels to African American patronage in the 1950s and 1960s was an indication of the gradual—albeit still agonizingly slow—pace of integration of public accommodations.[41]

In addition to providing listings of high-quality lodgings, the Nationwide Hotel Association offered an impressive array of services to its members. The organization promoted black business enterprises in the *Go Guide* and even assisted its members with financial and investment advice. The members gathered annually for a national convention, published a monthly newsletter, sponsored speakers, and established a scholarship fund for black students interested in business careers. The NHA even put on an annual beauty pageant, billing the evening as the vacation event "of a lifetime." The 1959 pageant, held in the Grand Ballroom of the Concourse Plaza Hotel in New York City, included all of the features of the Miss America pageant: bathing suits, evening gowns, talent competitions, and a fashion show of chinchilla and mink coats from Milton Herman, Furriers. The woman crowned as queen represented the NHA for the following year as official hotel hostess.[42]

The concerns expressed by touring musicians and performers about their inability to find housing while on the road served as the initial inspiration for another African American travel guide. Musician William "Billy" Butler spent years on the road arranging and conducting for the Fletcher Henderson Orchestra, Fats Waller, and the Ed Sullivan Orchestra. Finding it difficult to locate decent hotels that would welcome blacks, Butler published *Travelguide,* beginning in 1946, to help other performers find lodgings. As a board member of the Negro Actors' Guild, the National Urban League, and the NAACP, Butler knew that such a guide would find a ready audience.

It quickly became a successful business venture. "*Travelguide* affords a universal, economical and permanent publicity guide direct to the consumer," noted a 1948 article in *Color* magazine, "and gains a part of the $500,000,000 spent annually by Negroes alone 'just getting around.'"[43] *Travelguide* billed itself as offering "authentic guidance for ALL peoples." Butler hoped to support the goals of integration and the civil rights movement; his guide was one of the few with overtly political goals. In the tenth year of operation, an article in *The Crisis* magazine commemorating the milestone described *Travelguide* as "the only business ever started with the express idea that every effort would be made to eliminate those conditions which made it necessary."[44] If *Travelguide* succeeded at promoting integrated accommodations, theorized Butler, there would no longer be a need for it, as the United States would be a fully integrated society.

Between the 1930s and the 1960s, a wide variety of African American travel guides sprang up to address the needs of different black audiences. (*Collection of the author.*)

Interspersed throughout the booklet's commentary on hotel and overnight accommodations were listings for businesses that a traveling performer might need, including drugstores, lawyers, music schools, dry cleaners, and even dentists (for emergency dental work). Unfortunately, while the agents for *Travelguide* located some "mainstream" or "white" hotels, motels, and restaurants that did not discriminate against people of color, most of the listings were for the same African American boardinghouses and hotels found in other travel guides. Even though Butler imagined his publication of *Travelguide* as a form of gentle civil rights activism, the country was not yet ready for his enlightened approach.

Travelguide used an unusual method in its attempt to achieve these broader social goals. At Butler's direction, black couples visited various resorts with the intention of demonstrating, through their supposedly sophisticated middle-class demeanor, their worthiness to be granted full access to the accommodations. Thus, rather than file lawsuits or create scandals in the local newspapers, Butler charged his emissaries with cajoling and convincing hotelkeepers to accept black travelers through gentle persuasion.[45] Then, as the civil rights movement progressed, an additional impetus for change emerged to support Butler's mission. An increasing number of white liberals intentionally chose to stay only at hotels that did not discriminate.[46] White vacationers adding their leisure dollars to those of black travelers only aided *Travelguide*'s campaign to open doors to public accommodations.

Seeking to broaden their mission, the editors of *Travelguide* began to include profiles of prominent and inspiring black Americans. The 1947 edition featured, among others, baseball player Jackie Robinson, described as a modest and clean-cut former US Army lieutenant, and Philippa Duke Schuyler, the child musical prodigy. The biracial Schuyler represented the ultimate triumph of integration—her parents were African American journalist George Schuyler and Josephine Cogdell Schuyler, the daughter of a white Texas rancher. Philosophically, Schuyler's biracial pedigree fit well into *Travelguide*'s integrationist and even internationalist worldview. A brilliant pianist who was hailed as the American Mozart, Philippa was seen by many as a superior human being, in that she combined the best qualities of both African Americans and white Americans. She provided the ideal counterargument to the popular notion that racial mixing would result in inferior humans and a diluted white race. Despite the well-meaning intentions of the Schuylers and those who agreed with them, however, this argument smacked of eugenics, even to integrationists, and sounded as racist as the attitudes of the southern bigots.[47]

Headquartered at New York's United Nations Plaza, *Travelguide* sought not only to help establish equality for African Americans but also to bring together people from all over the world. The guide, whose symbol was, in fact, a globe, promoted international travel both to and from the United States, informed readers about publications by the United Nations, and listed consulates, visa offices, United Nations missions, and embassies in New York and Washington, DC. As with the publishers of *The Negro Motorist Green Book*, the authors of the *Travelguide* hoped that bringing together people of different backgrounds through travel would result in greater understanding and reduced racism.

A host of organizations agreed with this approach, lending their names to *Travelguide* and offering their membership lists in an effort to sustain its international, integrationist passion. In fact, *Travelguide* enjoyed perhaps the most popular support of any of the African American guidebooks. The participation of these organizations demonstrated white liberal support for integration, at least in the abstract. The American Civil Liberties Union, the National Conference of Christians and Jews, the National Council of Churches, and the Catholic Interracial Council participated in *Travelguide* and circulated it to their members.

Notably, the African Methodist Episcopal Church (AME) also joined forces with *Travelguide*. The authors printed a history of the AME church and a list of current leaders in the first pages of the booklet, tying the denomination to the publication. The churches encouraged their members to buy Butler's *Travelguide* and to patronize the businesses listed in it that pledged themselves to its political goals, which paralleled the AME mission to "induce free religious thought and action, to enlighten and uplift humanity and to awaken racial consciousness by stimulating a desire for independence, self-reliance and achievement in the minds of an oppressed minority." The AME mission also complemented *Travelguide*'s internationalist approach.

THE TRAVELERS *Guide, The Go Guide to Pleasant Motoring, Travelguide, The Negro Motorist Green Book*, and other guides like them reflected not only African American needs but also middle-class values. Black Americans wanted to fit into American society and to take full advantage of their ability to travel, just as white Americans could. Black corporate executives knew that they deserved access to hotels and restaurants with the same amenities that white executives expected. "I believe the *Green Book* was created in response to a growing auto tourist business that would support it," Esso executive and corporate traveler James A. Jackson told *The Green Book*'s editor. "The traveler needs a 'home away from home' to the profit of those who make such homes available."[48]

But the most successful travel guides were beholden for their success to powerful interests—oil companies, corporations, and even large hotel chains that wanted black convention business—and they could not reflect just an African American perspective. These were collaborations of enlightened self-interest. Corporations hoped to capture the black tourist market, and black middle-class businessmen and vacation travelers sought the right to rent hotel rooms beside those rented by white Americans. Middle-class white allies found the travel-guide approach to integration particularly appealing, because it involved good manners rather than direct confrontation. These demands did not include permission for black people to move into white neighborhoods, to integrate white schools, or to gain access to a genuinely participatory democracy; they were among the least-threatening demands for civil rights.

With the rise of the automobile, dozens of travel publications—brochures, books, journals, guides, magazine and newspaper inserts, and travel maps—helped both black and white vacationers negotiate the country's roads and learn about the natural and manmade attractions they might visit. Some of these travel publications were literary, others commercial. Commercial messages embedded in travel brochures met the advertising needs of corporations spawned by the tourism industry. For-profit enterprises—bus companies, oil companies, hotels, and resorts—created and circulated a huge array of tourist information and maps as promotional tools to attract consumers to a particular brand of gasoline, or to encourage booking a room at a specific resort hotel.

With the end of the Depression, travel became a commodity to be consumed not only for the good of the individual but also for the good of the nation. The wide variety of travel books, guides, and maps helped to make travel something that every American wanted to access. Families spending vacation dollars on hotels, motels, restaurants, and tourist attractions helped revive the economy and define American prosperity.

Unfortunately, while vacations allowed American citizens to see the beauty in their country, not everyone was welcome to share the public accommodations or even the public spaces around the country.[49] Thus, a new category of travel guide that specifically designated safe spaces for people of color provided freedom of movement, safety, and security. These guidebooks represented both an entrepreneurial spirit and the mores of the black middle class—a consumer's approach but also an approach based on the search for a gradual end to segregation through travel. The creators of these guides all firmly believed the mantra that Victor Green adopted from Mark Twain: "Travel is fatal to prejudice."

Chapter 7

VICTOR AND ALMA GREEN'S *THE NEGRO MOTORIST GREEN BOOK*

> . . . the most important book needed for Negroes who traveled anywhere in the United States.
>
> —Earl Hutchinson Sr., ca. 1950, *A Colored Man's Journey Through 20th Century Segregated America*

When I was a child in the late 1950s, my entire family often made the same trip to my grandmother's house on Cumberland Street in Fayetteville, North Carolina, that my parents had made the evening of my grandfather's death. We rose at four or five in the morning and reached the New Jersey Turnpike before dawn, my brother Gary and I riding in the "wayback" of the black Ford station wagon, playing games or dozing on the pillows and blankets brought from our beds. The trip from Newark to Fayetteville took more than ten hours.

We stopped only to picnic. My mother packed a green metal Coleman cooler with fried chicken, potato salad, brownies, and soda—the same menu every time. It was the only time of year she made chicken this way—fried in a heavy iron skillet and drained on a brown paper bag—and it was the only time of year we were allowed to eat it. My parents worried over the stereotypes about black people and fried chicken. We could never order it in a restaurant or eat it in public. To this day, it still gives me pause when I buy a package of chicken or a watermelon, so conditioned am I to avoiding eating such foods when others might see me. Occasionally we took the train from Newark to Fayetteville, and my father always purchased a compartment for us. I know that he wanted to keep his wife and two kids from having to ride all night in coach, but I also think he felt better knowing that we would not be eating our chicken sandwiches in public. There was no need for him to worry, though: As I recall, everyone getting on the train—nicknamed the "Chicken Bone Express"—was black, and every family brought along a similar picnic.

Gary and I just assumed that families always drove through the

Gary and Gretchen Sullivan behind the Sullivan family station wagon, ca. 1957. The car—its trunk and backseat packed with fried chicken, brownies, coloring books, and pillows for sleeping—made the trip from New Jersey back to Fayetteville, North Carolina, each summer. (*Collection of the author.*)

dark hours of early morning when heading out on summer vacations. I attributed these marathons to my father's enthusiasm for the road, and, on the way home, to his loathing of Fayetteville, but I now realize he had other concerns. I knew that many families, black and white, departed for vacation in the predawn hours, so why did these trips make my father so anxious? For my brother and me, the ride to Fayetteville was an adventure. For my parents, it was a journey filled with potential danger.

The trip "back home" to the South, usually in the summer, was a common annual event for thousands of families who had moved north during the Great Migration. The Seaboard Coast Line train that ran from New York City all the way to Florida was one option, but, by the 1950s, a lot of families drove down. Indispensable for so many families making the trip was The Negro Motorist Green Book.

"**WE OBTAINED** the most important book needed for Negroes who traveled anywhere in the United States," wrote Earl Hutchinson Sr. in his memoir of growing up "colored" in the first half of the twentieth century. "It was called the *Green Book.*" In the summer of 1955, Hutchinson and his wife decided to drive from Chicago to Berkeley, California, to visit friends. In preparation for the trip, they joined the Chicago Auto Club, which had just opened its membership to African Americans, and they bought a copy of *The Green Book* to help them find accommodations along the way. According to Hutchinson, "The '*Green Book*' was the bible of every Negro highway traveler in the 1950s and early 1960s. You literally didn't dare leave home without it."[1]

The *New York Amsterdam News* called *The Green Book* "the beacon light for the traveler and vacationer in the United States—the main instrument in making the Negro's travels more pleasant."[2] The Hutchinsons and other middle-class African American travelers depended on *The Green Book*, which gave black travelers confidence that they would not be stranded in hostile territory. From it they learned where they would be received hospitably, where they would not be, and where they would have to take a chance in an uncharted area. In 1939, a grateful admirer explained the importance of *The Green Book* in a letter to the publisher: "*The Negro Motorist Green Book* will mean as much if not more to us than the A.A.A. means to the white race."[3]

With the book in hand, Hutchinson was even willing to face rejection by testing hotels and motels that weren't listed in its pages. "If it was in the afternoon and I spotted a vacancy sign at a motel not listed in *The Green Book*, and there were few cars in the motel lot, I would try to get a room. In most cases the clerk had an arsenal of excuses ready." Desk clerks suddenly discovered their facilities were full when an African American traveler happened to stop and ask for a room. "We've just rented the last room and haven't taken the sign down yet," was a popular excuse. "We're expecting a large group shortly," was another.[4]

Hazel and Clayton Sinclair never advertised Rock Rest—their guesthouse in Kittery Point, Maine—in African American magazines, newspapers, or travel guides, although some of the other black guesthouses and hotels in the state paid for listings in *The Negro Motorist Green Book* or in *Travelguide*.[5] But when the Sinclairs went on vacation themselves, they always carried *The Green Book* with them. Specialized tourist guides such as *The Negro Motorist Green Book*, *Travelguide*, and the *Go Guide* served as tool kits for middle-class travelers, supplementing word-of-mouth recommendations and warnings. *The Green Book* helped travelers navigate unfamiliar territory and enabled them to preserve their dignity and sense of propriety. It also helped members of the black middle class maintain their class identity while traveling, by recommending suitable lodgings as well as black-friendly beaches, municipal golf courses, black country clubs, and other activities. Hazel Sinclair always had high expectations for hotels and restaurants. When an awful fish dinner greeted the couple in Youngstown,

Ohio, Hazel angrily criticized the African American establishment that served it. "Our colored is a dog," she complained. "I am ready to go home now."[6]

Naturally, *The Green Book* had more listings for cities and communities with larger black populations. As African Americans traveled westward, they found themselves with fewer and fewer options, and almost no accommodations could be found once they reached the mountain states.[7] The Sinclairs, for instance, heading to California, had to search hard every night for a hotel or motel that would rent a room to black tourists. *Green Book* correspondents traveled to the western states to look for places willing to accommodate black visitors, but the results of their missions were mixed. Generally the correspondents came away unsure of the response that travelers would receive in the West. In Dickinson, North Dakota, the consensus statement on the hotel operators was that, "while they themselves had no color prejudice, some of their

Victor H. Green, founder and publisher of *The Negro Motorist Green Book*. (*Reproduced by permission of the Schomburg Center for Research in Black Culture, New York Public Library.*)

regular customers did have." However, "[U]pon occasion, Negroes have been accommodated in Dickinson," which could not have inspired confidence. Businesses in Shelby, Montana, refused to be included in *The Green Book* because they feared that their hotels might be overcrowded with "touring Negroes . . . to the exclusion of old customers," although they believed that Negro patrons had "a right to fair consideration."[8]

THE NEGRO *Motorist Green Book* was the brainchild of Victor Hugo Green, a Harlem entrepreneur. "Let's get together and make Motoring better," he wrote, in explaining the goal of his travel guide. He hoped to make travel as easy and stress-free as possible for black motorists. An astute businessman, he also wanted to reach as many travelers as possible.

An avowed integrationist, Green anticipated that his guide might appeal to white supporters of integration as well as to black travelers. He imagined a time when travelers of all races would be able to sleep in the same hotels. Green courted the black middle class with *The Green Book*'s covers and stationery, as well as articles pitched at black corporate executives, but he advertised his guide as appealing not just to all races but to all classes of people. In pursuit of a large, heterogeneous readership, he included a range of accommodations—from hotels and motels to guesthouses and rooms in YMCAs—at a variety of prices.

The Green Book informed its readers that advance planning would make all the difference between a successful trip and a difficult one. Making and confirming reservations before getting on the road, and prepaying for at least one night's lodging, would make it more difficult for a hotel to deny a black family a room. "DON'T BE DISAPPOINTED—Make reservations in advance," Green exhorted his readers. Indeed, most travel guides made this recommendation because of the difficulty in securing a hotel room if you showed up at the front desk with a black face. With a reservation and a first night paid, the hotel was less likely to deny you a room, although there were no guarantees. "Housing conditions make this necessary," *The Green Book* noted.[9] The consequence of not making advance plans might be a night curled up in the backseat, or even a dangerous encounter with the locals.

Though we know relatively little about Green's life overall, we do know that this purveyor of travel tips rose from a working-class background to build a very successful national business. Born about 1892, he spent his first years in Harlem, then a mixed-race, working-class neighborhood of German immigrants and black migrants from the South. Early in the new century, his parents, both Virginia natives, moved to the growing city of Hackensack, New Jersey, which then was bustling with Italians, Germans, Poles, Greeks, and Russians, as well as with African Americans fleeing southern segregation. Although Hackensack was in the North, it was strictly segregated and Victor and his brother William Jr. and sister Helen attended a colored school. Silk mills, brickyards, shoe factories, government work, and the railroad provided opportunities for the black and white working classes, including William Green, Victor's father, who became a federal employee, working as a porter with the Post Office Department. For his part, Victor Green served honorably in World War I and then married Alma Duke, who not only became his wife but also would emerge as a driving force in his publishing business.[10]

Victor Green founded *The Negro Motorist Green Book* in 1936, and, with his partner George L. Smith, published the first issue the following year. Smith died shortly thereafter, and William Green, Victor's brother, soon joined the company, remaining a partner until 1945. Victor's own retirement "from active participation" came in 1952, probably because of a serious illness or disability. At that point, Alma stepped in and assumed the role of publisher of *The Green Book*, and Victor assumed the role of adviser. With

Alma Green took over management of *The Green Book* when Victor retired in 1952. (*Reproduced by permission of the Schomburg Center for Research in Black Culture, New York Public Library.*)

Alma at the head of the company, an all-female staff managed, wrote, marketed, and distributed *The Green Book* out of the Lennox Avenue offices in Harlem. Most women-run businesses during the 1950s focused on services like childcare, dressmaking, hair care, and laundry work. A female publisher was a rarity, and Alma was a trailblazer.[11]

A strong and creative businesswoman, Alma Green kept the publication humming along when other African American travel guides failed after only an issue or two. Alma's staff stayed with the team well into the 1960s. Evelyn Woolfolk, who worked as a secretary when *The Green Book* began, returned from a hiatus in Cleveland to take on the crucial role of selling advertising. Much of *The Green Book*'s success came as a result of her efforts. Novera Dashiell wrote most of the "articles and commentary," and Dorothy Asch, "the only non-Negro member of the staff," managed public relations.[12]

Alma Green's all-female staff pictured in the 1961 edition of *The Negro Travelers' Green Book*. Green gets credit for the publication, but these women ran the company. (*Reproduced by permission of the Schomburg Center for Research in Black Culture, New York Public Library.*)

Victor Green credited guides written for Jewish travelers as the original inspiration for his venture. "The Jewish press has long published information about places that are restricted," he wrote. During the late nineteenth century and the first half of the twentieth, Jewish Americans experienced discrimination in public accommodations similar to that faced by black Americans, although they generally did not fear physical violence. An advertisement might make a hotel or restaurant sound welcoming, but when the concierge heard a name that "sounded Jewish," no room or table would be available. Several well-publicized cases of discrimination appeared prominently not only in the Jewish press but also in mainstream newspapers.

For instance, early in the twentieth century, the charismatic Jewish leader Rabbi Stephen Wise created a stir when he rose to present a sermon at Carnegie Hall titled, "Peace, Peace When There Is No Peace." Wise announced his refusal to attend the annual Mohonk

Peace Conference because Albert Smiley, owner of the Mohonk Mountain House resort in New Paltz, New York, and the creator of the conference, would not permit Jewish patrons to stay at his hotel during the popular summer season. It was, he argued, a "business necessity" that he deplored, but he nonetheless carried it out. The progressive Mohonk Peace Conference, founded in 1865, had grown to include hundreds of eminent leaders each year, several of them Jews who attended the conference in spite of the policy. "The American Jew has, for years made the foolish and impractical mistake of suffering the humiliating injustice of hotel-ostracism in silence," commented an author in 1911 in the *American Israelite*, agreeing with Rabbi Wise's criticism.[13] Although he supported the concept of the conference, the rabbi felt that Jews needed to stop politely acquiescing to their exclusion from hotels and restaurants and to stand up publicly against the practice. He soundly criticized his brethren who refused to condemn such segregation. "[N]o self respecting Jew," he wrote to them, "ought to be willing to accept such hospitality even for an hour."

In hotel and resort brochures and newspaper ads, code words such as *restricted* and *selected clientele* meant "No Jews allowed." Adirondack Mountain resorts, known at the time for their anti-Semitism, openly stated, "Hebrews as a rule also being objectionable," when describing their prohibitions on dogs and people with active tuberculosis.[14] Others advertised that they accepted Gentile patronage only, stating, "No Hebrews desired."[15] New York State passed antidiscrimination legislation in 1943 outlawing *selected* and *restricted* accommodations. But as late as the 1950s, letters to the *New York Times* complained that the use of a new euphemism, *churches nearby*, in an advertisement communicated the message that Jews should stay away.[16]

In response to these restrictions, Jewish travel guides emerged, serving multiple purposes: They listed hotels that welcomed Jewish travelers or had a largely Jewish clientele, and they also included the names and addresses of hotels and restaurants offering kosher meals. The guides aimed to assist their readers in traveling "Jewishly," which meant helping them find Jewish neighborhoods and community centers, historic sites, synagogues, grocery stores stocking kosher goods, and more.[17]

From 1935 to 1952, the Organized Kashruth Laboratories in New York City published the quarterly *Kosher Food Guide*, a booklet that served "as a guide to the Observant Jewish Woman desiring to uphold the traditional dietary laws." Amid articles about the proper observance of the Jewish holidays and lists of approved packaged foods (for example, Breakstone's cottage cheese and Hershey's chocolate were kosher), the *Kosher Food Guide* also included lists of recommended hotels, summer resorts, camps, and caterers.[18] *The Jewish Chronicle,* founded in 1841 and based in London, developed a Jewish travel guide, perhaps as early as the 1930s, that assisted Jewish travelers around the globe and was widely distributed in the United States. Other Jewish newspapers and periodicals, such as the *Philadelphia Jewish Exponent*, the *American Hebrew*, and the *Baltimore Jewish Times*, included advertisements for hotels, restaurants, and vacation resorts that catered specifically to Jewish travelers and provided for their dietary and religious needs.

WHILE JEWISH travel guides and advertisements provided the initial inspiration for Victor Green to produce a Negro travel guide, his creation was nevertheless distinctive—not only because of its mission to help black people but also because of its longevity and the comprehensive nature of its listings. While other African American guides struggled to survive, *The Green Book*, except for a hiatus of four years during World War II, experienced an otherwise-uninterrupted run from 1937 to 1966. Although no records for the business are known to exist, we can find clues to Green's success in the black press, in the pages of *The Green Book*, and even in mainstream newspapers. A savvy promoter, Victor

Green proudly informed his readers, shortly after he began publication, that the United States Travel Bureau had officially adopted his travel guide.[19] The Travel Bureau gave Green national visibility as well as access to a national network, helping to ensure broad distribution of *The Negro Motorist Green Book*.

Green and his staff also knew how to recruit allies and promote the guidebook broadly and effectively. Crucially, *The Green Book* also abided by the traditional African American aphorism, "Got one mind for white folk to see / Nother I know that is me."[20] Green and his staff kept the language of *The Green Book* polite and inoffensive, rarely mentioning the very reason that the guide was necessary in the first place. It was sometimes vague, but always subtle, calm, and well reasoned. The writers avoided inflammatory political topics. But, even though each edition of *The Green Book* appeared to include little or no politics, it was nonetheless intensely political, very carefully worded, and illustrated to serve the specific needs of black readers, while also taking into consideration the sensibilities of white readers and financial supporters. This was both a tactical concession to potential white readers and a reflection of Green's desire to approach travel with middle-class restraint.

African American readers understood the moderate voice of *The Green Book* as necessary for any publication that required white support or that came under white scrutiny. "It has been our idea to give the Negro traveler information that will keep him from running into difficulties [and] embarrassments, and to make his trips more enjoyable," wrote one of the *Green Book* writers.[21] But Victor Green's black readers, of all social classes, regarded *The Green Book* and other similar black travel guides as activist publications. The 1961 edition, for instance, made it clear that action was required if African Americans were to make progress in ending segregation: "History shows the rewards gained when a race made its own struggle against the ebb and flow of local and national passions. No one esteems freedom given or sought without it being earned."[22] The language of *The Green Book* made readers responsible for interpreting the carefully chosen words according to their own needs, and it helped make Green's business successful.

African American journalist George Schuyler penned instructions to black writers about the kind of writing he deemed appropriate for publication in the Negro press: "Nothing will be permitted that is likely to engender ill feelings between blacks and whites. The color problem is bad enough without adding any fuel to the fire."[23] African Americans were well aware that people in the white mainstream noticed their writings and speeches.

The Green Book authors approached their audiences with the thoughtfulness urged by Schuyler and the well-mannered style of the black middle class. Green's writers also had an innate understanding of the way American business worked. They knew that black people needed white allies if they were to succeed in a national consumer society, so they chose not to offend their white allies because they wanted continued support.

Most white Americans were completely unaware of *The Green Book*, but they would have found its rhetoric inoffensive. Indeed, the guide could even be viewed as maintaining segregation by keeping African Americans contained within black neighborhoods when they traveled. They would not have to stop and ask for accommodations, challenging segregation at white hotels, if they knew how to find black hotels. From the point of view of those anxious to avoid racial confrontation, *The Green Book*, despite its intention to promote African American freedom, could be viewed as supporting separation, and it certainly demonstrated the type of moderate behavior that made white Americans feel comfortable.

Relatively early on, *The Green Book* found a very small white audience. A 1941 article in the New York newspaper *PM Daily* introduced progressive white Americans to the guide in order to boost sales of the book. "Year after year [the new book] grew until 1941 [when] '*PM*' one of New York's great white newspapers found out about it, wrote an article about the guide and praised it highly."

This cover from the 1948 *Negro Motorist Green Book*—showing a stylish couple with matched luggage departing from their suburban neighborhood—demonstrates the Greens' interest in catering to the black middle class. Such images also appealed to white supporters of the Green guides. (*Reproduced by permission of the Schomburg Center for Research in Black Culture, New York Public Library.*)

Titled "Even Off Subways, Negroes Follow the Green Line," the article was a milestone, in Victor Green's view—a sign that his multiracial approach and goals could work.

He had practical reasons for the tone of *The Green Book* that went beyond appealing to white readers. His business relied on the largesse of mainstream—which is to say, white—corporations and government agencies to disseminate his product widely to black readers. These corporate and government interests balanced concern for their African American audience with their need to please their constituents in the segregationist white South. Green understood that his success as a businessman was tied up in these matters.

The affiliation with the Standard Oil Company, and its Esso gasoline stations, became the most advantageous business relationship for *The Green Book*. Standard Oil brought marketing support and a network of nationwide gasoline stations to distribute the travel guide. Needless to say, the relationship was mutually beneficial. Standard Oil enjoyed new cachet among black Americans for the support of *The Green Guide* and for their willingness to permit black patrons to use their gas-station bathrooms. To its credit, the oil company recognized and actively solicited the black community as an important group of potential customers long before other companies did the same.

Although African American newspapers created reports to convince American corporations to market to black communities, it took a long time for many companies to serve black people as Standard Oil had done. Beginning in the 1940s, a few American corporations started to recognize the black middle class as a potential market. Advertising in black newspapers and on radio programs that played "race" music were the most typical approaches used by American corporations to attract this new demographic. African American market researcher David J. Sullivan published a variety of articles aimed at encouraging white businesses, including automobile and oil companies, to reach out to black consumers. The most prominent African American marketing professional during this period, Sullivan proposed a variety of ways to appeal to black customers sensitively and successfully. His recommendations indicate the depth of American and corporate obliviousness about the American black community and the need to review the language they used. Racism was so much a part of everyday life and custom that Sullivan had to inform his white readers not to use such insulting words as *pickaninny, coon, shine*, and *darky*. A 1943 article entitled "Don't Do This—If You Want to Sell Your Products to Negroes" advised corporate advertisers that they had to avoid "exaggerating Negro features" and should treat black people with respect. "Refrain from referring to every black man as 'George,' " and avoid using the Uncle Mose and Aunt Jemima stereotypes, Sullivan cautioned.[24] The article also recommended that white people forgo the use of blackface makeup and use real "brown-skinned" people in advertisements rather than white people in blackface. Sullivan predicted that by 1944, the aggregate income of the nation's almost thirteen million black Americans would rise to $10.5 billion.[25] If businesses wished to cultivate this new audience for gasoline, tires, automobiles, and other consumer products, they would have to avoid racism in their advertisements. While black companies, like Green Publishing, had to be extremely careful not to offend white sensitivity about race, white companies regularly used black stereotypes to promote their products.

As a part of their service to black consumers, Standard Oil and a few other corporations, such as Pepsi-Cola, Marriott, and Seagram's, hired black executives as front men to attract black customers to their companies' products. In 1934, Standard Oil brought on a special "representative to the race," James A. Jackson, and tasked him with conducting research and promoting sales to the black community. His hiring was a coup for the company. The 1939 *Green Book* noted that Standard Oil "created a sensation back in 1934 when it announced that James A. Jackson had been retained." Jackson began his professional career as the first African American bank clerk in Chicago. He then served a stint as editor of the "Negro Department" of the venerable *Billboard Magazine*, a position that made his name familiar in many African American households and resulted in his nickname, "Billboard." Claude Barnett, a black Chicago businessman with considerable influence in the national Republican Party, proposed Jackson to then–Secretary of Commerce Herbert Hoover for a position in the Commerce Department to promote and support black business enterprises.

In 1927, Jackson was appointed the adviser on Negro affairs at the Commerce Department, but Standard Oil lured him away from the federal government to a position in the marketing department of Esso gasoline. In 1945, Standard Oil hired Wendel P. Alston to work with Jackson and possibly succeed him. Together, Alston and Jackson regularly contributed brief articles to *The Green Book*, using their own experiences as corporate travelers to reinforce the need for the book and to sing its praises. As Esso marketing representatives, the two men traveled all over the country promoting "Happy Motoring" with Esso gasoline and motor products. Despite their prominent positions in the corporate world, however, Jackson and Alston found it difficult to locate overnight accommodations. Many African Americans who traveled for the government or for corporations ran into the same problems. Jackson believed that the resulting stress and unpleasantness detracted from his work and peace of mind. He found *The Negro Motorist Green Book* to be an invaluable guide for businessmen and a tool that would have changed his life had it existed when he began working. Travel, he noted, produced considerable strain on the black middle class:

> If there had been such a publication as this when I started traveling way back in the Nineties, I would have missed a lot of anxieties, worries and saved a lot of mental energy which, had it been conserved and used solely to the advancement of the business interests for which I traveled, "my years on the road" might have been concluded long ago, with enough savings to permit my living a life of peace and quiet, now that I am becoming an old codger.[26]

Jackson and Alston—referred to as "[t]he Esso Marketers Public Relations men of the race group"—were so impressed with Victor Green and *The Green Book* that they worked hard to find ways to place it in the hands of more and more black drivers. With its ringing endorsement, Standard Oil widely distributed *The Green Book* through its wholesale outlets—Esso gas stations. Many Esso

Esso marketing executives Wendel P. Alston and James A. Jackson "devised a way to help Victor H. Green Company obtain a more widespread distribution" and to help their own "customer friends to be more certain of finding accommodations . . . wherever they may be going." (The Negro Motorist Green Book, *1948*.)

gas stations sold *The Green Book*, and others gave them away as promotional items. It was good business. "Use Esso Products and Esso Services wherever you find the Esso sign," urged an article in *The Green Book*.[27] In 1946, a newspaper article confirmed the relationship between Victor Green and Standard Oil. In the presence of a black press photographer, James P. Jackson signed a contract with Green to purchase five thousand copies of *The Negro Motorist Green Book*. Presumably, this agreement was the first of many subsequent contracts.[28] At the time of the signing, Green had already established partnerships with several travel clubs, the United States Travel Bureau, and the Idlewild Chamber of Commerce, a large African American resort in Michigan, to help him distribute the travel guide. These distribution agreements extended to travel bureaus, bus and airline companies, the armed forces, bookstores, and automobile clubs, helping to ensure the book's success when so many other guides had failed. As a result of Victor Green's efforts, *The Green Book* boasted a circulation of more than a million in 1954 and more than two million by 1962.[29]

OVER THE years, *The Green Book* expanded its geographical scope. Green's first guidebook for the traveling motorist focused on New York City and Westchester County, just north of the city. A few establishments outside of New York, but east of the Mississippi River and known to the staff, also made it into the volume. The booklet provided readers with a few short articles and lots of advertisements. The guide portion of the booklet listed "Points of Interest in New York City." Recommended places to visit included outdoor or publicly owned sites accessible to all visitors to the city, such as the Triborough Bridge (now the Robert F. Kennedy Bridge), Chinatown, Ellis Island, and Rockefeller Center. Many of the suggested sites, particularly the bridges and tunnels, could be viewed easily on a driving tour without ever leaving the car. The guide proposed a visit to Coney Island as a place offering "bathing and all sorts of open air amusements." A pitch for the 1939 New York World's Fair described this highly anticipated attraction as "the greatest exhibition that has ever been produced by any country in the world." The Hayden Planetarium at the American Museum of Natural History had the distinction of being the only museum to make it into the first edition of *The Green Book*. Its sky show, "The Drama of the Skies," could provide an afternoon or evening's entertainment for twenty-five or thirty-five cents. Whether New York's other museums were unwelcoming to black visitors during the early years of *The Green Book*, or whether their omission was an oversight, we cannot know. In 1962, the guide began including a list of fourteen recommended museums to visit on a trip to New York City.[30]

"Let's Go Places," a feature in the early editions of *The Green Book*, listed regional state parks and public golf courses open to

African Americans. The "ineffectual attempt to put an elusive ball into an obscure hole with implements ill-adapted to the purpose," as President Woodrow Wilson described the game, was becoming more popular at the time. Wilson had played almost every day as a way to improve his health.[31] The African American middle and upper classes took to it as well, but they found it difficult to locate courses where they were permitted to play. Almost all country clubs excluded black players.[32] In the 1920s, a group of African American men purchased the Shady Rest Golf and Country Club in Scotch Plains, New Jersey, to pursue their passion. Reminiscing about the club, a former member commented on the all-black membership, saying, "There was no other place open to us." Shady Rest quickly gained a reputation—not only as the first black golf club in the nation but also as a gathering place for the black upper class. In the summer, famous musicians performed there, and on steamy nights the sounds of Duke Ellington, Count Basie, and Lena Horne wafted through the open windows. White residents of Scotch Plains, seizing the opportunity to hear the music, danced in the parking lot as African American couples danced inside. The club was not mentioned in the American Automobile Association's *Highways Green Book*,[33] but it was included in *The Negro Motorist Green Book*.[34]

In the early editions, Green filled page after page with advertisements for eateries, state parks, and car-care businesses. Writers and advertisers alike encouraged motorists to treat their cars with care to avoid mechanical problems on the road that could leave riders stranded and in a dangerous predicament. In the premiere edition, an article entitled "Preparedness" discussed the necessity of a pretrip tune-up—checking the steering, brakes, and lubrication, and packing extra headlamp bulbs and fuses, just in case of a mishap. While these recommendations could apply to any traveler, they took on special meaning for African American motorists, for whom the automobile was not only a means of travel but also a first line of defense.[35]

Most editions of *The Green Book* included articles, but they tended to be short, and while they offered helpful travel tips, they were but brief interludes between the advertisements and hotel listings. Some editions included no articles at all, instead focusing on lists—from suggestions for protecting your house during vacations to ideas for packing your suitcase properly. A few issues did include substantial commentaries, however. For example, the 1947 guide provided an extensive discussion of all of the new automobile models manufactured in 1946 by General Motors and Ford, delving into the attributes of each in great detail. This postwar issue celebrated the resumption of automobile manufacture after five years of metal and rubber rationing. The writer praised GM for its contributions to wartime production and viewed the inclusion of the Cadillac engine in military tanks, and its ability to meet the "grueling tests of the battlefields," as a recommendation for the car buyer who wanted a car "toughened and hardened to new standards of efficiency and durability."[36]

As the years went by, *The Green Book* ran more extensive, original articles. For instance, it profiled cities with large and welcoming black neighborhoods, like Chicago and Louisville, that catered to tourists. The profiles included a history of each city specifically for African American readers. The article on Louisville encouraged visitors to participate in the excitement of the Kentucky Derby and enjoy the gracious living of southern hospitality—after briefly outlining the city's history of slavery. Hospitality, of course, was a matter of perspective. To the readers of *The Green Book*, southern hospitality meant a bountiful table and cold mint juleps, not the buxom mammy or cotton-picking slaves that signaled cordiality in many white travel guides.[37]

The Green Book's 1949 feature on "What to See in Chicago" focused less on history and more on the excitement travelers would find when visiting the city's museums, ballparks, and sites. A photograph of Comiskey Park, obviously taken from the segregated black section of the bleachers, reminded readers that Jackie Robinson, Roy

Campanella, Satchel Paige, Larry Doby, "Mule" Suttles, and Buck Leonard had played there. Other photographs, instead of highlighting the Chicago Historical Society or the Art Institute—buildings found in most Chicago travel guides—depicted places of interest to black readers: the building that was home to the city's largest African American insurance company, a large black-owned funeral parlor, and the block that housed the Regal Theater and the Savoy Ballroom. These buildings provided visual evidence of the success of black businesses. While not the traditional tourist sites, the architectural monuments of the black community in Chicago were a source of pride for the city's black citizens and were easily accessible for visitors. The issue highlighting Chicago also recommended sites for African Americans to visit in the city's "Ghetto"—by which the writer meant not a black neighborhood but the city's Russian Jewish neighborhood (as the term was originally used in Europe).[38]

The Green Book's 1949 New York City issue likewise reveals an African American perspective on tourism. While the issue offered a very traditional travelogue with photographs of the George Washington Bridge, Times Square, and the Statue of Liberty, it also praised Harlem: "Harlem—The greatest Negro metropolis in the world where over 300,000 colored people live, between 110th and 155th Sts. . . . Here you will find a city in itself: fine restaurants, taverns, nightclubs and department stores." The accompanying photograph reinforced the idea of an active, successful, and vibrant urban community that welcomed black tourists. At the busy intersection of Seventh Avenue and 125th Street, the sidewalks bustled with well-dressed pedestrians walking past cars and taxis, busy shops, and the Alhambra Theater. Following the article, dozens of listings for restaurants, taverns, and nighttime entertainment made the neighborhood sound even more appealing.[39]

In addition to its lists and articles, *The Green Book* also ran advertisements for travel products. All of the guide's ads provided national advertising space for local black businesses of all sizes—a significant service for the African American business community.

Most of the companies that advertised in the guide did not usually have access to the type of broad exposure that *The Green Book* provided, with its national distribution networks. The ads echoed the needs and values of the eras in which they appeared. In the earliest editions, they reflected the novelty of automobiles and the concerns about keeping these modern contraptions from breaking down. Dozens of listings for black-owned businesses in the New York metropolitan area appeared in the first *Green Book*, encouraging readers to patronize "automobile blacksmiths," car and radio repairmen, electric and acetylene welders, and tire salesmen who would be friendly to black people. Clanrod Jones, an "Automobile Technician" who noted that he had been in business since 1913, could be found on East 136th Street teaching driving, repairing cars, and selling generators—a rather unusual collection of businesses. Restaurants, dance halls, beauty salons, and pharmacies catering to black Americans found a ready audience in readers of *The Green Book*. North of Manhattan, "Westchester's Sepia Rendezvous," the Harris Tea Room and family restaurant, publicized good home cooking. Donhaven, in Pleasantville, New York, invited readers to enjoy a sojourn in the country with dinner and dancing for couples and club groups. Many notices targeted southern migrants living in New York with display ads that promoted home cooking, southern hospitality, and the best southern fried chicken.[40]

The Green Book's growth reflected an increase in the number of black tourist accommodations, but it primarily indicated Victor and Alma Green's effectiveness at tracking down lodgings across the country for black tourists. By the 1960s, *The Green Book* ran fewer but more extensive articles; instead, there were many full-page display advertisements designed to inform readers about local and regional businesses. Listings ranged from a simple address to a full-page display ad with art or photography and additional details about their services. Mme. C. J. Walker's College of Beauty Culture in Chattanooga, Tennessee, for instance, offered potential students promising careers in hairdressing.[41] The Wheel Motel

FORT LAUDERDALE

CATHERINE'S BETTER FOOD CAFE............................515 N.W. 4th Street
The Friendly Place to Find the Best Home Cooking

JA 3-1877 25 miles north of Miami
CHESTER'S PLACE
Fine Food
Courteous Service
1312 N.W. 5th Street Fort Lauderdale, Fla.

JA 4-9750 JA 2-0803
Southern Hospitality
OSBORN'S RESTAURANT
Good Food
1904 N.W. 6th Street Fort Lauderdale, Fla.
25 miles north of Miami

2 Miles East of Turnpike
FIVE POINT SERVICE STATION
Gas - Oil - Auto Maintenance - Courteous Service
2590 N.W. 22nd Road Fort Lauderdale, Fla.
at Sunrise Boulevard and 27th Avenue

21

Sample advertisements from *The Green Book*. Most advertisers stressed courteous service and included pictures of the proprietors to demonstrate that they were black-owned businesses. The drawing at the bottom of the page shows that Victor Green hoped to appeal to train travelers as well as motorists. (*Reproduced by permission of the Schomburg Center for Research in Black Culture, New York Public Library.*)

in Texarkana, Texas, included a photograph of tidy tourist cabins beside a small diner with the slogan, "Your Home Away from Home." The Bay Shore Hotel, a resort right on the Chesapeake Bay in Maryland, provided a picture of a private black beach and publicized year-round comfort in rooms that were air-conditioned in summer and heated in the winter. Even more elegant, the Hampton House Motel and Villas in Miami, Florida, catered to "the Negro vacationer who enjoys luxurious surroundings, superb cuisine and an exciting sports and entertainment program designed for all ages," including swimming, boating, fishing, and golf. Calling Hampton House "The Social Center of the South," and using a crown as its corporate logo, the hotel aimed to attract the most affluent black consumers.[42]

The brief *Green Book* listings included basic contact information—names, addresses, and, in later editions, telephone numbers—but the advertisements and their pictures of tourist camps, of room interiors, or of the smiling African American proprietors provided additional detail about vacation locations and the features important to travelers. Most stressed the welcoming, courteous service that patrons could expect, which was key to black Americans so accustomed to discourteous treatment—or worse.[43]

THE GREENS and their staff used a variety of techniques to collect information for the brief lists of lodgings in *The Green Book*. The small staff could not possibly reach every potential site across the country, even though Green, an inveterate traveler, claimed to have visited every state in the union in pursuit of information on hotels. A former mail carrier and a lifelong member of the Cordon Club, an organization of retired mailmen, he may have used this network to keep track of the institutions listed in *The Green Book* and to solicit new advertisers.[44] But much of the information came from readers, although a caveat in each volume explained that the listings were printed as presented and that *The Green Book* accepted no responsibility for errors.

In addition to customers' testimonials, Green's hotel and restaurant listings came through agents. He cleverly enlisted the help of sales and travel agents and also invited his readers to consider selling subscriptions and advertising for the guide on a part-time basis. "*The Green Book* gets much of its information from travel agents," commented an article in *Newsweek* in 1963.[45] Actually, *Newsweek* was incorrect. *The Green Book* "agents" were not all travel agents, but rather field representatives in different parts of the country who had special knowledge and practical experience finding places where African Americans could spend the night.

The 1949 edition of *The Green Book* listed agents living in Mississippi, New Jersey, and West Virginia, but they had nationwide experience. Mrs. Leroy P. (Nellie) Bass of the Piney Woods School—a boarding school for African American children—was an expert at booking travel accommodations for black student travelers and served as the guide's representative from Mississippi. Her job at the school gave her knowledge about lodgings all over the United States.

Nellie Jones Hardy Bass was the sister of Dr. Laurence C. Jones, the well-known and charismatic founder and president of the Piney Woods School. Dr. Jones established his school in 1909 and traveled throughout the country publicizing it and raising money to support it. Often, his fundraising methods, which proved to be very effective, involved performances by the school's talented singing groups. His sister became expert at locating hotels, restaurants, and other African American businesses to serve these young musicians as they traveled.

Between 1922 and 1975, Nellie Bass booked singing engagements for Piney Woods. At various times, she also made housing and travel arrangements for the International Sweethearts of Rhythm, the Cotton Blossom Singers, and the Swinging Rays of

Nellie Bass, who booked housing all over the country for singing groups from the Piney Woods School in Mississippi, played a significant role in identifying lodgings for *The Negro Motorist Green Book*. (*The Piney Woods School*.)

Rhythm, who toured about six months of the year as ambassadors and fundraisers for the school. After 1929, when Piney Woods merged with the Mississippi School of the Blind for Negroes, the Five Blind Boys of Mississippi singing group became one of the school's popular touring attractions. Bass also reserved rooms and helped schedule the Piney Woods baseball team as they traveled the Negro Leagues circuit. Over the decades, her work proved invaluable to Victor and Alma Green as they sought the best accommodations for African Americans across more and more states.

It was never easy to book housing for black students. Sometimes Mrs. Bass had to use her contacts to identify rooms in private homes, because no hotels would welcome them. This task required networking in black communities, and it may even have required her to work with a local minister or funeral director. So difficult

Singing groups from the Piney Woods School traveled all over the country together. Their experiences informed the information that was provided by Nellie Bass to *The Negro Motorist Green Book* staff. (*The Piney Woods School.*)

was the job of finding housing in some parts of the country that Albert Alexander Hyde, a friend of Dr. Jones and a Piney Woods donor, designed a custom vehicle for the Cotton Blossom Singers that included a kitchen and sleeping quarters. This early version of an RV, which could be parked in a church parking lot or campground, was a direct outgrowth of racial segregation.[46]

Although overall he used relatively few sales agents, Green's recruitment of individuals like Nellie Bass, with broad national experience, was a smart business strategy. Without sending staff to visit all of the sites, Green was able to pinpoint the best hotels, tourist homes, and guesthouses outside of the New York metropolitan area. Armed with recommendations from readers, the contacts from his agents, and the lists from the previous year, Green also sent out annual letters and postcards urging business owners to purchase display ads in *The*

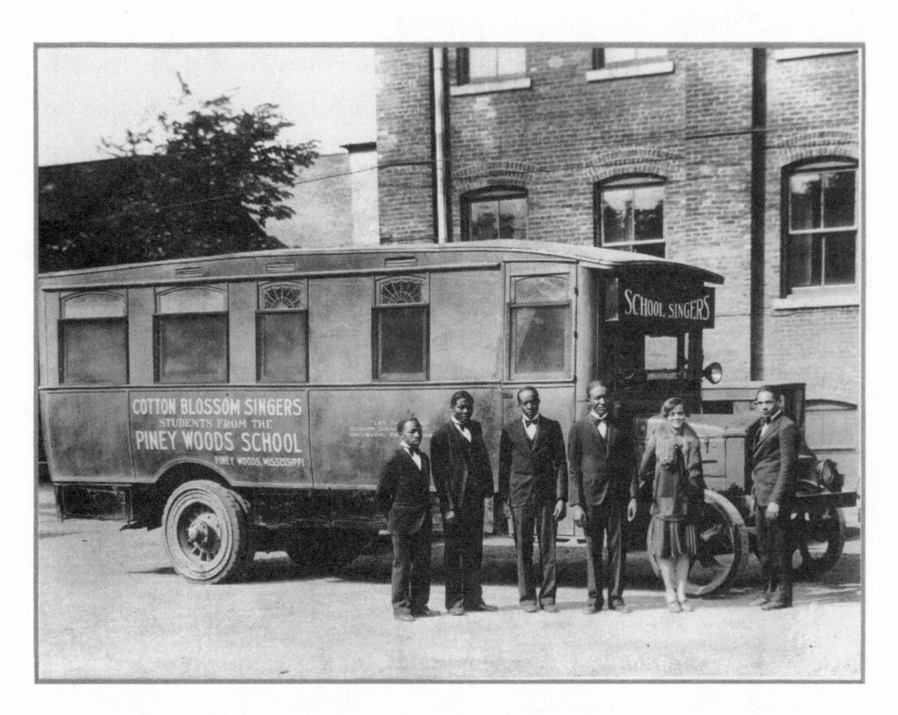

This early version of an RV provided lodging for the Piney Woods School singers when they could not find hotel rooms. (*Piney Woods School.*)

Green Book or to buy copies of the guide to distribute. The annual letter described *The Green Book's* success and reminded potential advertisers of the humiliation that "Negroes have suffered." The purchase of an ad, Green argued, "would help correct this."

In addition to outside advertisers, Green included advertisements for other services offered by his business, Victor H. Green & Company. Acting as a travel agent, Victor (and later Alma) organized bus and boat trips around Manhattan and planned vacation cruises to Africa, South America, Europe, Canada, and the West Indies. The Greens also started a companion business—a reservation service assisting travelers in contacting the hotels, tourist homes, and resorts that appeared in the guide.[47]

Beginning as a sixteen-page pamphlet, *The Green Book* ended its thirty-year run as a paperback containing more than 128 pages. Even two years after the initial publication, the 1939 guide was already considerably larger than previous editions. By the mid-1960s, the book included listings for travel and roadside services all over the United States—and later Canada, Mexico, and the Caribbean. In addition to lodgings and restaurants, it ran listings of black community services and businesses, such as doctors' offices, pharmacies, taverns, grocery stores, barbershops, and beauty parlors. *The Green Book* could never be comprehensive, but it gave black motorists enough information, in most cases, to make prudent and successful travel decisions.

The listings were clustered around major cities in the East, including New York, Cincinnati, Washington, DC, and Baltimore. In California, many of the accommodations listings for black travelers could be found in Los Angeles and San Francisco. *The Green Book* identified relatively few accommodations in South Dakota and Wyoming, which had tiny black populations. There were only six lodging suggestions in the entire state of Idaho. Nevada had only three entries—two in Reno and one in Las Vegas. A respondent from North Dakota, who wrote that the state had no "Negro families," assumed that any black visitors would be treated "as well as anyone else."[48] Thus, the traveler was free to take a chance to visit—or not. On the other hand,

PHONE WADSWORTH 6-5828 TRAVEL BUREAU TOURS AND TRIPS

VICTOR H. GREEN & CO., Publishers

The Negro Traveler's Green Book — A Guide to Travel and Vacation

200 WEST 135TH STREET • ROOM 215-A • NEW YORK 30, N. Y.

Dear Proprietor:

Our 1960 Edition of the "Green Book" will mark the 24th year of publication. This is a long time for one publication coming out year after year to help make traveling conditions better for the Negro and to bring added business to the businessman. If it were not for your cooperation, we could not have done so. We offer our sincere thanks to you!

If you are looking for a sure fire medium to reach the traveler, the "Green Book" is your answer. This guide has been tested by hundreds of advertisers over the years and has been conceded to be the leading medium for Negro travel. An estimated 1,500,000 travelers the year round are looking for places to go, accommodations, service, etc. I am sure that you would be doing our readers a great service, as well as yourself, if you would advertise your place in the 1960 Edition. Negroes have suffered, unfortunately, some social embarrassments in travel; your ad would help correct this.

Enclosed you will find rates on our contract, which, I am sure, you will find economical for twelve months advertising compared with other advertising. We can offer you a deferred payment plan if you wish to take the 1/3-1/2-2/3 or full page space. You may pay 1/3 down with our contract and the balance to be paid in 60 and 90 days. If not, a deposit of 1/2 the cost of your ad space is required along with your filled out and signed contract. We shall bill you for the balance. Listings must be paid for in full. If cash is sent with your contract in full, 2% discount is allowed. All contracts and ad material for our 1960 Edition must be in by November, 1959. Don't overlook the fact that we give you a number of copies in which your ad space appears FREE with your contract. Your guests will be glad to receive a copy.

May we have the pleasure of serving you?

Yours very truly,

VICTOR H. GREEN & CO., Publishers

Victor Green sent this letter to Miss Sing's Tourist Home in Baton Rouge, Louisiana, asking her to renew her advertisement in *The Green Book*. Miss Sing operated a guesthouse for musicians and other black travelers from the 1940s into the 1960s. This letter from 1959/1960, the twenty-fourth year of *The Green Book*, was discovered tucked inside the hotel's guestbook, which Miss Sing gave to Kevan Cullin in exchange for electrical work. (*Kevan Cullin, Baton Rouge, Louisiana.*)

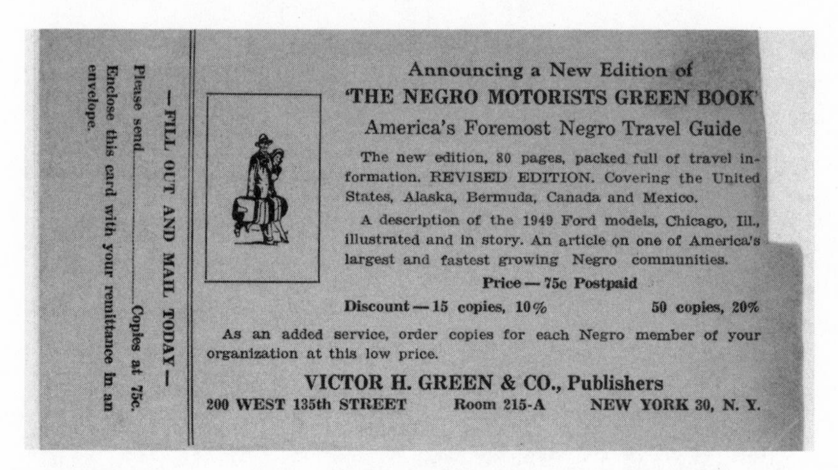

Victor Green sent these postcards to libraries, businesses, and organizations he thought might buy *The Negro Motorist Green Book*. This card was sent to the Durham Public Library in Durham, Connecticut, in 1949. (*Charles Clark III photograph, collection of the author.*)

the list for Harlem, the home of *The Green Book* office and the capital of black America, named 244 places that welcomed African American guests—more than twice as many as several states combined.

Lodgings listed in *The Green Book* ranged from tourist camps and motels in small towns to multistory hotels in urban centers. In many cities, black YMCAs and YWCAs provided the only places for black travelers, although not all black Ys had dormitory rooms. Ys constituted a significant proportion of the listings in *The Green Book,* particularly in the early editions.[49]

Indeed, black YMCAs represented the largest national network of lodgings for Negro travelers during the first half of the twentieth century. Often boasting gyms, cafeterias, and dormitory rooms, black YMCAs offered ideal safe havens. Founded in the 1850s as the Confederation of North American YMCAs, the all-white organization dedicated itself to Christian ideals and building character in men. Canadian YMCAs, troubled by America's slave past and concerned about living up to the organization's Christian mission, pressured the American organization to consider including black men, and separate YMCAs for African Americans were introduced in the late 1870s. From the organization's founding, they gave special attention to historically black colleges to promote the development of black YMCAs throughout the country and to support the growth of black leadership. Black YMCAs offered places for young men to spend the night in clean and commodious lodgings, to meet one another, to conduct business, to share a meal, to exercise, and to participate in educational programs—all in a completely segregated but welcoming environment. Although hardly luxurious, black YMCAs remained popular with ambitious students and some business travelers well into the 1960s.[50] In 1967, the National Council finally passed a resolution certifying that eligibility for membership or participation in programs would no longer be based on race, color, religion, or national origin.

EACH ISSUE of *The Green Book* focused on a specific form of travel or region, keeping the traveling public up to date on trends in the tourism industry, running articles on train travel and air travel, for instance, and helping black travelers feel more confident about how they might be received in particular communities. As the civil rights movement progressed in the 1950s and 1960s, *The Green Book* encouraged readers to experiment with new destinations, especially ones beyond the United States.

While the automobile gave African Americans the freedom to travel from coast to coast, the airplane made travel abroad easier for all Americans. Although black Americans earned less, on average, than white Americans, lower airline fares in the 1950s placed international travel well within the reach of middle-class black families. "Thrifty, medium income Americans who had never previously thought a trans-Atlantic trip possible will soon be arriving in Europe in large numbers, thus bringing into sharp focus the social impact of the 30 percent reduction in fares . . . ," noted one *Green Book* article.[51] And *The Green Book*'s writers urged black

Americans to travel outside of the United States to find welcome respite from the discrimination in their home country.

The 1953 "Airline Edition" of *The Negro Motorist Green Book* included notices from Victor Green proposing international group tours, trips aboard cruise ships, and flights to Europe, Canada, and Africa. Another article in that issue, titled "Air Transportation," gave readers details about the history of Pan American World Airways, American Airlines, and Trans World Airlines, but it made little mention of race or concerns about the possible segregation of airplane seats. The article described the wide variety of destinations available to air travelers and the growing accessibility of flying to middle-income people. Enthusiastically, it also encouraged African Americans to vacation by air. As Green suggested, it was the mode of transportation that, in his opinion, would involve the least amount of prejudice. He continuously pushed against the limits of white tolerance for Negroes on public carriers.

The federal government controlled air travel, and the Fourteenth Amendment, ensuring equal protection under the law to all citizens, protected black travelers from the types of discrimination they experienced on trains and buses. Yet an employee of American Airlines revealed that at least one airline did not follow federal law and found a clandestine way to segregate airplane passengers. In 1951, the district attorney from Queens (New York) opened an investigation into the use of a secret code—E111—by American Airlines for the airline reservations of African American passengers. During staff training courses in New York, employees learned to affix the code to the tickets and the plane's manifest to "warn" the stewardesses that black passengers would be boarding and to enable them to seat these passengers separately from white travelers. When this tactic was discovered, American Airlines announced that the policy would be abandoned immediately and that the training to identify and segregate black passengers had been inadvertent.[52]

Airports were another story, though. Local ownership of airports meant that the same state and municipal laws governing other buildings applied to the bathrooms, waiting rooms, and restaurants in air terminals. Policies differed at every airport terminal, so travelers never knew what to expect. At the New Orleans airport, black passengers had to eat in the kitchen, at the food-preparation table, if they wanted a meal. In some terminals, there were segregated restrooms marked *Ladies* and *Gentlemen* for white passengers and *Men* and *Women* for black passengers. The Houston airport had no bathrooms at all for black travelers. For black passengers, negotiating airports proved to be almost as difficult as other modes of travel unless travelers left the United States.

By the 1951 edition, *The Green Book* was listing lodgings in other Western Hemisphere countries—Canada and Mexico, the Caribbean, Costa Rica, Bermuda, and the Virgin Islands. Chief writer Novera Dashiell admitted that she was the only member of *The Green Book* staff still "earthbound," but she highly recommended that her readers try air travel for a faraway vacation or for a distant business appointment. Dashiell also supported the popular belief that France welcomed black Americans. "We know a number of our race who have a long standing love affair with the tempestuous city of Paris," she wrote. "Their hearts have lingered there long after they have returned home."[53] By the 1960s, *Green Book* readers could find extensive listings for both Europe and Africa. Travel outside of the United States increased in popularity in the 1960s and provided a respite from American racism for middle-class black people. In many countries outside of the United States, black travelers found a tourist industry receptive to their visits. They could often travel without fear.

Ernest Dunbar, a black writer and senior editor for *Look* magazine and frequent international traveler, suggested that going abroad enabled middle-class black Americans to relieve the relentless psychological pressure that racism caused. "When I walk down the street of some small European town and a white policeman smiles and says *bonjour* or *buon giorno*, it renews my faith in the possible humanity of the police officer," he wrote. "When I fall into a conversation with a Dane over *schnapps* or with a Yugoslav awash with *slivovitz* they don't ask me what Stokely Carmichael means by his latest statement." European travel was, for Dunbar and many others, a survival skill. "Away from the pressures and inanities of the racial struggle in this country," he observed, "we pull together our shredded psychic garments and gird ourselves for another round or two."[54] Travel outside of the United States braced black Americans for the struggles they faced when they returned home.

Travel to Africa, in particular, enabled many African Americans to engage with their heritage. Travelers could redefine themselves simultaneously as middle-class travelers, African Americans, and proud descendants of the African continent. In addition to providing an opportunity for self-discovery, travel to Africa spurred a bit of self-education.

Highlighting both the fun of travel abroad and the potential to learn about other cultures, *The Green Book* for 1965 was titled *The Travelers' Green Book: International Edition* and focused on the New York World's Fair of 1964–65. The cover illustration featured a well-dressed African American child in a dress and matching jacket, with a camera hanging around her neck, ready to capture events at the fair or on a trip abroad. In her white-gloved hands, the girl holds a clutch purse and a makeup case. Beside her, two boys—one white and one black—carry a suitcase together. The image reflects the way that members of the black middle class saw themselves—stylish and respectable. The picture also symbolized the hope for integration, which was certainly shared by Victor and Alma Green.

Inside the guide, a tantalizing photo of African American dancers in 1960s dashikis, caftans, and other West African clothing introduced readers to an American interpretation of African culture. The unidentified photograph demonstrated African American curiosity about Africa, but the varied clothing indicated a lack of specific and detailed knowledge about the differences among countries and cultures in West Africa from which many black people in the United States originated.[55] The legacy of slavery left most black

Americans with a yearning to know their backgrounds, but no way of knowing their families' actual places of origin.

Another part of the issue provided details on everything a tourist to the New York World's Fair needed to know. Recommendations of hotels in all five boroughs that would welcome black guests included daily rates for single and double rooms—information offered, perhaps, to make sure that black tourists would not be charged more than others for their accommodations. The list included Howard Johnson's, the Statler Hilton, and the Marriott, among other mainstream hotels. By the 1960s, New York generally did not segregate hotels, although no hotel chain had established a national policy banning the practice. African American guests who were received cordially in some New York hotels might be turned away from other hotels in the same chain elsewhere.

The 1965 edition of *The Green Book* included maps showing the locations of the fair's exhibitions in relation to the major highways that brought motorists to the fairgrounds. An article about inexpensive places to eat while visiting the fair, reprinted from *Look* magazine, recommended international cuisines and, like other articles original to this edition of *The Green Book,* encouraged readers to experience the cultures of faraway people and places.

In general, *The Green Books* of the 1960s reflected the expanded opportunities available to blacks for international travel. The guides also explicitly backed the civil rights movement, even though the publication's run ended in 1966, just two years after the passage of major federal civil rights legislation made segregation illegal in public accommodations. In a feature entitled "Your Rights, Briefly Speaking," drawn from a list compiled by the Anti-Defamation League of B'nai B'rith, *Green Book* writers listed the states that passed laws against any form of discrimination. Arguing in support of the "militancy" of the civil rights organizations—whose sit-ins, freedom rides, and court battles had "widened the areas of public accommodations accessible to all"—this segment sought to inspire readers to challenge the laws by reporting violations experienced during travel to the appropriate human rights commission. Contact information was included for each of the twenty states with such commissions. The descriptions of the violations encouraged readers to file lawsuits, to seek monetary damages against wrongful actions, and to demonstrate peacefully. In Nebraska, for example, violators of antidiscrimination laws faced criminal prosecution through court proceedings. In California, fighting against bias in recreational facilities required plaintiffs to sue in civil court for damages plus $250.[56] A photograph of five black United States congressmen accompanied *The Green Book* article and reminded readers of the progress made toward equal rights up to that point. The author of the text accompanying the photograph commented that the Negro was "only demanding what everyone else wants . . . what is guaranteed all citizens by the Constitution of the United States." Unlike earlier *Green Book* articles that spoke of travel as a fairly passive method of moving civil rights forward, this author proposed direct action. No longer taking refuge in euphemisms that vaguely alluded to the "humiliation" and "aggravation" experienced by black travelers, the rhetoric in the 1960s *Green Books* addressed the legal bases for equal rights and made the case for vigorous political action. The 1960 edition included an indicator of the era's more direct and aggressive attitude toward civil rights. A full-page photograph of C. E. Ware, the African American proprietor of Ware's Super Market in Memphis, Tennessee, shows Ware proudly shaking hands with Dr. Martin Luther King Jr. and Dr. Ralph Abernathy. The store's owner consciously tied himself and his business to King, despite the repercussions that such associations with civil rights leaders tended to have on black businesses in the South.

From its founding in 1936, *The Negro Motorist Green Book* advocated civil rights by implication, in supporting the Negro traveler and finding ways for black Americans to "vacation without aggravation" in the segregated United States. But decades later, in an article titled "Janus" (after the Roman god of open doors), writer Novera Dashiell openly praised 1960 as a year of great

Congratulating the Proprietor, Mr. Ware. Left to right, Dr. Martin Luther King, Dr. Ralph Abernathy of Montgomery, Ala. and Mr. Ware.

WARE'S SUPER MARKET

Fast Free Delivery WH 8-7943

Meats - Vegetables · Dairy Products

Phone Orders - Free Parking
The Best For Less

C. E. Ware, Prop.

226 W. Brooks Road Memphis

95

As the civil rights movement heated up in the 1960s, *The Green Book* supported the black freedom struggle in a more open and forthright manner with advertisements like this one, which included prominent leaders of the movement. Siding openly with the civil rights movement could jeopardize relationships between black business owners and whites in their communities. (*Reproduced by permission of the Schomburg Center for Research in Black Culture, New York Public Library.*)

accomplishment for black people worldwide as a result of direct political action and the drive for independence on the continent of Africa. "Our young people with their successful sit-in demonstrations have prodded the older generation to greater effort in the struggle for civic dignity," she wrote.[57] Members of *The Green Book* staff perceived themselves as civil rights advocates and tied their work for the black motoring public to the efforts of such institutions as the Urban League, the NAACP, the Congress of Racial Equality (CORE), and the Student Nonviolent Coordinating Committee (SNCC). By facilitating free movement throughout the country, the staff believed they were "fighting for minority rights."[58] But, while the words of *The Green Book* grew increasingly forceful, the type of radicalism that they now celebrated in the pages of the travel guide—direct action—was necessary for ending segregation. It could not be ended by words or by travel alone.

Chapter 8

"WHERE WILL YOU STAY TONIGHT?"

See America First, If You Can.

—Ernest Dunbar, *Look* senior editor, 1968

Every year, after school let out, my parents took my brother and me on vacation. Often that meant going south to visit my grandmother, but they thought other destinations could be enriching, too. Besides Niagara Falls (on the Canadian side), there were trips to Toronto, Gettysburg, Philadelphia, and Washington, DC. In 1967, my father decided that we needed to experience air travel, so he booked a trip on Air Canada to Expo 67 in Montreal, and we flew for the first time. During the relatively short flight, which departed from Newark, we were even served a hot meal. My father, a dedicated amateur photographer, took home movies as we rode the Expo monorail. My parents liked Canada. They felt comfortable there.

A few times, our summer vacation consisted of a camping trip. We loaded our Ford station wagon with coolers, sleeping bags, and a camp stove and drove to one of the New Jersey state forests—Jenny Jump Forest was a particular favorite. My parents found comfort in the regular patrols in the state forests, and my father always made friends with the park police. You parked your car right at the campsite and walked a short distance to hike well-traveled trails or go to a swimming hole. Like many African American families, we were not going to walk alone into the wilderness, fearing encounters with dangerous folks. Although some black families chose to visit the national parks, they held little interest for my parents. The idea of hiking without protection of any kind brought to mind white lawlessness and even lynchings. We had no fear of the four-legged animals; it was the two-legged variety that were concerning. Many black families perceived of large wilderness areas like the national parks as white spaces—not necessarily welcoming to everyone. While the parks themselves permitted everyone to enter, the privately operated concessions within the parks often posted Jim Crow signs to keep Negroes out.

Even though we felt safer in New Jersey's parks than we would have in a national park, my father, a licensed gun owner, carried a rifle in a soft case in our station wagon. I recall it coming out of the case only once when we were on vacation—when my father wanted to teach me how to shoot targets. Years later, I wondered about that gun. Why did he really take it for a camping trip in New Jersey?

BY THE 1960s, *The Negro Motorist Green Book* included more than three thousand establishments for black travelers in the United States, Canada, and the Caribbean. But hundreds of additional black establishments were not listed in *The Green Book*—they were known only through advertisements in newspapers or word of mouth. Dozens of resorts, hotels, and camps were scattered throughout New York's Catskill Mountains, for example, but very few of them found their way into *The Green Books*. Catskill vacation spots attracted significant numbers of summer visitors from throughout the Northeast with notices in the black press. Ross Farm in New Paltz, New York, "a haven of rest and recreation," posted the opening of their season in the *New York Amsterdam News*. And Notch Mountain House, which touted the Catskills as a place of "Freedom and Health," advertised in the *Atlanta Daily World*.[1] *The Green Book* itself depended on an informal network of personal recommendations. "The sale of these guide books depends mostly upon the friend-to-friend oral advertising system," noted one edition.[2] While *The Green Book* was the indispensable guide for many black travelers, it could not replace, or exist without, these informal networks of communication.

In the era of Jim Crow, the African American world existed as separate from the white world—often hidden in plain sight, unseen and unknown except by those who lived in it. White residents rarely ventured into black neighborhoods. But black people, many of whom worked service jobs daily, spent a great deal of time toiling within and observing white communities. It was common for whites to refer to black neighborhoods as "niggertown," "darkytown," or "coontown," a grim fact that illustrates this separation. Essayist and writer Dr. Blyden Jackson described the two worlds—one white and one black—with each existing, for the other racial group, "behind the veil." He referred to the white neighborhoods of Louisville, Kentucky, as "the forbidden city," the area where he was not permitted to go. On the other side of the veil, everything and everyone was black: "I knew there were two Louisvilles and in America, two Americas."[3] And within black America, a plethora of barbershops and beauty parlors, lunch counters, clubs, churches, and social organizations constituted networks of informal communication that connected people, sometimes across great distances.

In the 1940s, Fayetteville, North Carolina, had a vibrant black community, a black world totally separate from the world of the white residents. The duplication of businesses and services in the city reveals the extent to which black people and white people lived distinct lives. The city did not have its own black newspaper, but Virginia's *Norfolk Journal and Guide* covered a large swath of the region and provided black Fayetteville with both social and political news. At the same time, *The Fayetteville Observer*, one of the state's oldest newspapers, delivered the news to white readers. Although the *Observer*'s coverage of civil rights demonstrations in the city in the 1960s was quite balanced in comparison with coverage in other southern cities, on the whole the newspaper reflected the values of a segregated city. There were two service stations and two auto mechanics, one of each for blacks and whites. The black neighborhood included wood dealers, a tailor shop, twelve grocery and meat markets of various sizes, a dressmaker, a few restaurants and cafes, shops that sold ice cream and sodas, dry cleaners, eighteen churches, two pool halls, six barbers, eight beauty parlors, and two funeral homes. Parallel businesses existed on the white side of town. Three black dentists, three physicians, two photography studios, two drugstores, St. Joseph's Nursery School, and the public school provided professional services within Fayetteville's black community. A few African American tourist homes offered lodging for travelers and performers.[4] Notably, only six establishments were listed in the Fayetteville section of the 1941 *Green Book*.

On the edge of the city sat Fayetteville State College, then a teachers' college for black students only. Within fifty miles of Fayetteville, white students could choose from more than a dozen higher-education options, all of which refused admission to black students. Taxicabs were segregated, too, and two companies, Bluebird Cab and Eagle Cab, provided black visitors and local black residents with both transportation and information. Fayetteville's black citizens created a variety of social, service, educational, and fraternal organizations, as well as a local chapter of the NAACP.

Despite segregation, some white people found black food and culture too alluring to avoid African American communities completely. Food and music brought black and white people together in some places that ordinarily would have been completely segregated. The spicy fried chicken known regionally as "hot chicken" and served at Prince's restaurant in Nashville, near the Grand Ole Opry, was so popular that it became a local specialty. Prince's served both black and white diners, but it did not adhere to the segregation etiquette practiced at white restaurants. Instead, patrons created a sort of reverse self-segregation. Black diners entered through the front door and white diners used the back door.[5]

Before every American home had a telephone, black travelers seeking overnight accommodations wrote letters to hotels or to individuals recommended by friends or family who lived in the locale they planned to visit, asking where they might find lodgings. During the first half of the twentieth century, the vast majority of these travelers stayed at boardinghouses (private homes with multiple rooms and meals provided for short- or long-term visitors) or private residences with just one or two rooms used occasionally for guests.[6] Desperate travelers who did not write ahead might stop at a local black church, seeking the advice of the minister about where to stay. Remarking on one family's unplanned experience on the road, newspaper columnist Joseph Bibb wrote, "The colored man in his shining car with his dark-brown family says that he drove 500 miles the first day and then was directed to a minister in a small town who found accommodation for him down by the railroad tracks. . . ."[7]

Within the black community, it was traditional for travelers to board with a family. Unmarried individuals, students, and workers saved money by living in a spare bedroom. If the family had another extra space, they might offer it to travelers, who would hear about it from a travel guide or perhaps the local clergyman. Boarding provided income for a family while addressing the dearth of housing for black workers. Popular not only within black communities, boardinghouse life commonly appealed to new immigrants and others unfamiliar with an area or without the means to rent an apartment. From 1900 to 1930, approximately 3 percent of the household population of the United States lived as roomers or boarders.[8] During the Great Depression and the two world wars, when people traveled to find work, including in factories producing war matériel, a great many of them sought these shared accommodations. Boardinghouses afforded both camaraderie and meals for single people and an affordable place to live, but the lack of privacy meant that they certainly were not the preferred lodging arrangement for everyone.

Many a black woman recognized an opportunity to earn extra money for her household by becoming a proprietor of a boardinghouse, sometimes called a rooming house. According to the federal census, widows commonly opened their homes to boarders as a way to make money to pay the rent or the mortgage after their husbands died.[9] Boardinghouse proprietors generally appear in *The Green Book* and other travel-guide listings under women's names—Mrs. Ella Brown, or Mrs. Geo. Robinson, for example. In some communities, people who were not African Americans willingly rented rooms to black travelers. A "w" preceding a very small number of boardinghouse listings indicated a white proprietor—one who was most likely living in or near the black neighborhood. In Seattle, the black neighborhood adjoined Chinatown, where some residents provided lodging for African Americans, including Mar Shue, the owner of the Atlas Hotel.[10]

In resort towns or near beach communities, vacationers rented rooms in guesthouses, tourist homes, or cottages. Tourists might stay for just a few days or for several weeks. The black boardinghouse or tourist home—a precursor to today's bed-and-breakfast—frequently included a home-cooked meal or two.

Relatively few employment opportunities existed for black women outside of service jobs as maids, cooks, hairdressers, and laundresses, so opening their homes to travelers allowed them to manage their own small businesses. Renting rooms gave black women some agency in a racist world, even though the amount of money they made was small. Hazel and Clayton Sinclair's well-documented experience in Maine offers some insight into the operation of these establishments. The Sinclairs welcomed guests to their home from the late 1940s through the 1970s, when a decline in business and their declining health forced them to close shop.

"A SHACK" is what Hazel Sinclair called the small house that her husband convinced her to buy in Kittery Point, Maine. The dilapidated building had no bathroom and no electricity, but at least they could afford to buy it. Hazel refused to live in the house until Clayton spent many months fixing it up. Tucked away in a wooded area on Brave Boat Harbor Road, the house was only a few miles from the beach, so guests could quickly get to the shore in their cars. The property offered privacy for black vacationers in a largely white community. Hazel first visited the Maine coast as a maid traveling from Manhattan with her white employers. The family took her with them on vacation to help out, and she met people in the black community in Portsmouth, New Hampshire, just across the bridge from Kittery. She fell in love with the Maine seashore and decided she wanted to live there. Similarly, Clayton learned

Hazel and Clayton Sinclair's Rock Rest in Kittery Point, Maine, prior to its renovation. Hazel called it a "shack" and refused to move in until Clayton made substantial renovations. (*University of New Hampshire, used with permission.*)

about the region as a chauffeur, when he drove his employer to the state for the summer. He loved to drive and never minded the long trip from New York.

Hazel and Clayton met while attending People's Baptist Church, the heart and anchor of black Portsmouth. Together they explored the coastline, growing more and more fond of one another. In 1939, Clayton and Hazel both worked for a local resident, Mrs. Eleanor Tucker, but by the time they opened Rock Rest—as they called their guesthouse—Clayton had secured a position at the nearby Portsmouth Naval Shipyard, which provided a steady paycheck and money for the guesthouse renovations.[11]

Clayton Sinclair had a vision of what the small "shack" could become. A shrewd businessman, he bought a large tract of land with the house. The renovations included a porch for rocking chairs and for keeping cool on warm summer nights, a living room with a working fireplace, a large dining room, and a kitchen where Hazel cooked her popular meals. Later they added an extra room and bathroom downstairs. Hazel rested in her wide, Mission-style rocking chair in the sitting room off the kitchen after breakfast and before cooking dinner for her guests. The room stayed cool in the summer and served as a quiet sanctuary. She hung pictures of Martin Luther King Jr. and Jack and Bobby Kennedy on its dark-paneled walls.

As a business, Rock Rest grew gradually. The Sinclairs started by renting their own bedroom to guests. Over time, as they saved money, they eventually added five more rooms and two bathrooms to the garage. When all of the rooms were occupied, the main house could sleep about sixteen people. As was typical for most African American guesthouses, Hazel ran the business. She kept the books and did all of the cooking. She hired teenage girls to help her set the tables with her hand-crocheted tablecloths, elegant pink and green Depression glasses, and floral-patterned china. The teenagers also changed the beds every day and washed dishes after meals.

Before guests left for a day at the beach or shopping in nearby York, just eight miles from Kittery, Hazel served them a hearty

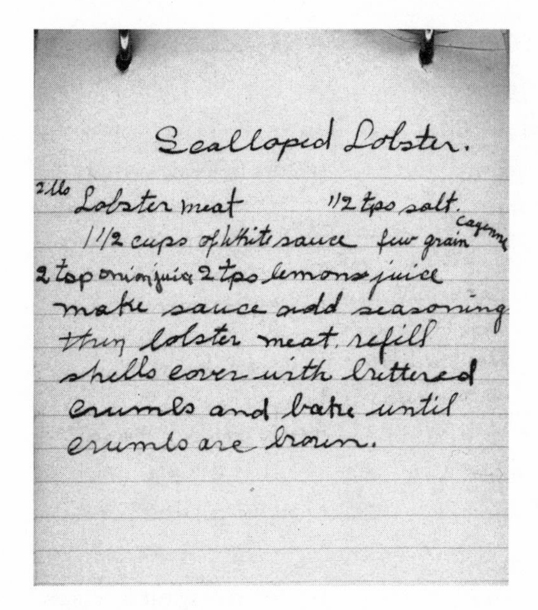

Scalloped Lobster.

2 lb Lobster meat 1/2 tps salt.
1 1/2 cups of white sauce few grain cayenne
2 tsp onion juice 2 tps lemons juice
make sauce add seasoning
then lobster meat. refill
shells cover with buttered
crumbs and bake until
crumbs are brown.

Hazel Sinclair's cooking was well known in Kittery and across the bridge in Portsmouth, New Hampshire. This scalloped lobster recipe, in her handwriting, was one of her specialties. She shared the recipe with Valerie Cunningham, who worked at Rock Rest as a teenager and called her Aunt Hazel. (*University of New Hampshire, used with permission.*)

home-cooked breakfast of eggs and bacon or sausage, with toast, grits, and coffee. On special occasions, one of her signature dishes graced the table. A guest favorite—and a traditional New England recipe inspired by Portuguese culture—was her casserole of codfish balls in cream sauce, topped with slices of hard-boiled eggs. A special treat awaited Sunday diners: Rock Rest's famous stuffed lobster or Hazel's lobster bake served on showy green and red lobster plates.[12] Everyone in the area, black and white, knew about Hazel's delicious food.

Clayton raised vegetables and rhubarb in his garden and gathered fresh eggs for Rock Rest's table each morning. He cared for the grounds and served dinner to the guests each night, wearing a formal white jacket. Guests at Rock Rest spent their days walking along Maine's rocky beaches or visiting local shops. Merchants readily accepted African Americans' money in their shops, but they were not welcome at the local hotels.

Most of the guests stayed for one or two weeks, relaxing and enjoying the company of like-minded folks. But some just were passing through Kittery for a day or two and needed a place that was hospitable to African Americans. Although the Sinclairs owned a copy of *The Negro Motorist Green Book*, they did not advertise in it. Travelers discovered the little guesthouse, in Kittery's woods, via word of mouth and the business cards that Hazel distributed.

The Sinclairs had all the business they could handle, at least in the early years of operation. It came largely through referrals and personal recommendations, as news of their welcoming establishment spread far and wide. "Your place has been highly recommended by Mrs. Gladys (I think the last name is Shirley) to a friend of mine, Mrs. Adelaide Smith, who has left for California," wrote a potential lodger pleading for a room in 1952. "I understand that she stops at your place," she added, "taking and getting her children from school." Guests so enjoyed their time at Rock Rest that they happily passed on the Sinclairs' contact information as a safe and comfortable place to stay.

Even back in the nineteenth century, Bowdoin College in Brunswick, Maine, began accepting African American students and supporting abolition and civil rights. It was one of the first colleges to do so, but black students arriving in the state with their parents in the twentieth century had few available options for overnight lodgings. *The Green Book* listed only two guesthouses in Maine in 1953 and six cottages and guesthouses in 1961. Others surely existed, but, like Rock Rest, they did not advertise in the black travel guides. Bowdoin parents often stayed with the Sinclairs.

Rock Rest's guest register shows that most of the patrons were, as they say in Maine, "from away." Year after year, families returned to vacation with the Sinclairs, enjoying the hospitality and the comfortable accommodations. Most of their guests arrived via car from elsewhere in the Northeast. In the evenings, many visitors shared stories about their experiences with Jim Crow while traveling. Lodgers were primarily African American professionals—teachers, physicians, and clergy. Signers of the register included repeat visitors Dr. and Mrs. Branch, who visited in 1948, 1949, and 1950, and a Mr. and Mrs. Lee, who came every year between 1949

Living close to Maine's rocky shoreline, the Sinclairs named their cottage "Rock Rest." The original sign made by Clayton Sinclair is now in the collection of the National Museum of African American History and Culture at the Smithsonian. (*Photograph by Gretchen Sorin, 2007.*)

A group of well-dressed ladies enjoying one of Hazel Sinclair's delicious meals in the dining room at Rock Rest, sometime in the 1950s. According to the guestbook, regional African American clubs and church groups made reservations to eat at Rock Rest even if they were not overnight guests. Hazel also made extra money by catering for black and white groups both on-site and off. (*University of New Hampshire, used with permission.*)

and 1952. Dozens of other individuals and families discovered Rock Rest as the name was passed around.[13] Many people made long-lasting friendships at the guesthouse. Conversations at dinner could be open and relaxed. Their children could make friends and meet suitable (in the eyes of their parents) middle-class marriage prospects. For the young African American girls from Portsmouth who worked for the Sinclairs, their jobs at Rock Rest gave them access to role models—professionals they may not otherwise have met.

As they became more successful, Clayton and Hazel reinvested in their building and made improvements. They converted the first floor of the garage into an activity center and game room for inclement weather, stocking it with board games, books, and chairs for sitting and talking. They renovated the guest rooms and added gardens. The automobile made possible the success of Rock Rest because the guesthouse was off the beaten path and away from the beach. Some evenings, guests might even drive into nearby York, where there was an African American inn with a jukebox and a dance floor.[14]

NOT ALL boardinghouses offered the comforts of Rock Rest. Many travelers complained about the inconsistent quality. Surely white travelers could also find filthy motels or rooms infested with vermin, but they had far more choices and far more travel guides to rely on. Unless a black traveler received information from a previous boarder, there was no telling what he might find. Did the guesthouse or boardinghouse have a meticulously clean suite of rooms with a private bathroom or simply a dirty room in the back of a house and a bathroom shared with strangers? Was the room infested with bedbugs? One black traveler described the conditions he discovered when he finally located housing in a black neighborhood. "I was lucky to find a Negro hotel at all," lamented Saunders Redding of his trip to Charleston, South Carolina, in the early 1940s:

> This one smelled of damp. . . . The brass was peeling from the bed. A washstand in the corner was fastened upright to the wall with wire. The shattered mirror in the bureau cast a thousand twisting images. At the window a dirty rag of lace, yellow from rain, served for curtain. "Two dollars," the man said and held out his hand. . . . "And for a week?" I asked. "A week?" he

hesitated. "Two dollars a night just the same. . . . We ain't got bellboys neither."[15]

Redding suspended his possessions from a pipe running across the ceiling and covered the thin, filthy, and stained mattress with newspapers. He slept with the light on, believing that would potentially ward off the bedbugs, and noted with disgust the prostitute who came knocking at the door in the middle of the night, "looking for a match."[16]

In the late 1940s, as the first generation of black corporate executives traveled for their jobs, the demand increased for high-quality hotel rooms for African Americans. Denied access to the major hotel chains such as Howard Johnson's and Hilton, where their white colleagues were staying, African American executives, professional athletes, and musicians went to black neighborhoods to search, albeit sometimes futilely, for a boardinghouse or black hotel with the amenities they expected. If they failed to find such lodging, they could end up sleeping in their cars—or, for musicians and baseball players, their tour bus. Trainmen—dining-car waiters and Pullman porters who crisscrossed the country—also found accommodations variable, so recommendations and guidebooks proved critical.

In the 1950s, more and more middle-class black families joined the growing number of black businessmen traveling throughout the United States. Both groups expected and could afford well-appointed business and luxury accommodations, but far fewer hotels and guesthouses that met these standards catered to black patrons. Boardinghouses did not offer much privacy, and communal bathrooms were common. Black business travelers did not have the time or interest to chat over dinner with other guests. And one- and two-room guesthouses did not have the capacity to serve the growing number of travelers.

To be sure, an ever-increasing number of African American hotels offered the basic necessities for overnight accommodations—clean rooms with running water, steam heat, and tiled private bathrooms. The most sumptuous facilities were at the largest luxury hotels—the Hotel Theresa in Harlem, the Majestic Hotel in Cleveland, the Hampton House in Miami, and Detroit's Carlton Plaza, for example. On the West Coast, the Somerville Hotel (later renamed the Dunbar, in honor of poet Paul Laurence Dunbar) provided upscale lodgings for the Los Angeles black community and for travelers. Several of these hotels purchased display advertisements in *The Negro Motorist Green Book* or were highlighted in feature articles. Besides catering to business travelers, all of these hotels provided luxury accommodations for celebrities on the nightclub or concert circuit who performed in the city.

From guesthouses and tourist homes to motels and luxury hotels, a broad range of accommodations greeted black motorists as the twentieth century progressed. But only large-scale hotels could support banquet and convention spaces for group gatherings, and large hotels that served African Americans were scarce—unlike the mainstream chains that could be found just about everywhere in the country. The histories of three of these hotels provide a glimpse into the role that these institutions played in their cities and in the lives of black travelers across the United States.

The Majestic Hotel

A few large hotels existed within black communities prior to the spread of the automobile, and they were well prepared to take advantage of the spike in black travel when the age of the automobile really began. Close to rail lines or city centers, these hotels served black train workers who needed a place to stay during layovers. *Negro Traveler* magazine sang the praises of Cleveland's new Majestic Hotel, noting that, "besides regular transit guests and permanent guests, the Majestic Hotel houses dining car cooks, waiters and porters from the large number of railroads that enter the city."[17] With a commanding presence on East Fifty-Fifth Street in the city's black neighborhood, the Majestic's clientele included

Cleveland's commanding Majestic Hotel, with its nightclub and restaurant, became a popular late-night gathering place for both black and white patrons who wanted to hear great music. (*Courtesy Cleveland Historical Society.*)

athletes, entertainers, and convention-goers as well as business travelers and musical groups.

In 1932, representatives of all the major black baseball teams from across the nation gathered at the Majestic for a two-day summit to hash out a new East–West Colored League. (Cumberland "Cum" Posey, the primary owner of the Homestead Grays, convened the meeting, which resulted in the new eight-club circuit and reduced players' salaries.) In 1946, the *Cleveland Call and Post* reviewed the Majestic and found it to be elegant and refined, "the top in American transient lodgings." After World War II, new owners renovated all of the guest rooms, focusing on the amenities: tiled private bathrooms, showers, new furniture, draperies, and carpets. Covering an entire city block, the hotel was "a city within a city," large enough to include everything that African American guests in Cleveland might need without ever leaving the building, including "a barber shop, drug store, tailor shop, beauty parlor, cleaners, laundry shop, a bar and one of the finest grills and dining rooms in America."[18]

In the 1930s, a jazz club opened in the Majestic. Called the Furnace Room (and renamed in the 1950s as the Rose Room), it became the best place in Cleveland to hear great jazz. The décor was as striking as the music. A polished oak dance floor invited guests to really swing. Cushioned benches lining the walls were covered in green-and-gray striped fabric. Chartreuse draperies hung from the windows. Tapestry wallpaper and a patterned rose carpet completed the whimsical but elegant interior design.[19] Beginning about 1952, Gay Crosse and His Good Humor Six started a Monday morning jam session that became a citywide sensation. Musicians jammed at the Majestic from 5 a.m. to about 10 a.m. on Monday mornings. While this might seem like an unlikely time to attract an audience to a jazz club, hundreds of Clevelanders lined up for the privilege. The Monday morning sessions became the most popular event of the week. The house performers—Duke Jenkins and his five-piece band: Duke at the piano, his brother Fred playing alto sax, baritone sax, and clarinet, Roy Clark playing trumpet, Junior Ragland on bass, and Johnny Brown on "skins"—packed the Rose Room six nights a week, as well as for the Monday jam sessions. "Every Monday morning from five a.m. until ten o'clock, we had a 'Blue Monday' party," Jenkins recalled in an interview. "You couldn't get near the place. People lined up to get in." Male and female vocalists, dancers, quartets, whoever happened to be playing at a club or concert hall in Cleveland showed up at the Majestic. Jenkins remembered the Ink Spots and Nancy Wilson being a part of the Rose Room's Blue Monday parties.[20] White Americans traditionally accepted African Americans as performers, and an integrated audience watched these black musicians at the Majestic.

The Hampton House

Miami's Hampton House was unusual as one of only a small number of white-owned hotels that catered exclusively to black patrons. The brightly colored yellow-and-turquoise building featured an

Hampton House in Miami, Florida, boasted fifty rooms and a magnificent tropical courtyard. Elegant resort hotels enabled members of the black middle class to enjoy the same kinds of luxurious accommodations that attracted white vacationers. (*Historic* Hampton House.)

Olympic pool and courtyard amid an environment of lush tropical trees and plants. Guests in formal attire listened to jazz as they sipped cocktails at the circular bar. A story about Hampton House in the 1962 issue of *The Green Book* touted its "luxurious surroundings, superb cuisine" and exciting sports and entertainment program—all just ten minutes from Miami's airport.[21] In one of the nation's premiere getaway spots, this large, well-known black hotel catered to celebrities as well as well-heeled vacationers. The Hampton House figured prominently in the famous heavyweight fight between Cassius Clay and Sonny Liston on February 25, 1964.

After the brash young Clay defeated Liston, the heavyweight champion of the world, in one of the most iconic moments in the history of the sport, he and his retinue (which included Malcolm X) needed a place to celebrate. Ordinarily a beachside party at the Fountainebleau, the city's most luxurious hotel, would have been

Malcolm X snaps a photograph of Cassius Clay (later known as Muhammad Ali) at the snack bar in the elegant Hampton House Motel in Miami. Dozens of prominent African Americans stayed here because they were not welcome in Miami Beach. (*Photo by Bob Gomel/LIFE Images Collection/Getty Images.*)

chosen. But until the early 1960s Negroes as guests or revelers were not welcomed on Miami Beach, and they felt most comfortable at local black hotels.[22] No victory party had been planned in advance, because Clay had not expected to win. So Clay and his fans headed triumphantly to the Hampton House and celebrated with his favorite treat, a large bowl of vanilla ice cream.

The Hampton House had an unusual history. About 1961, Harry Markowitz, a prominent builder and entrepreneur, and his wife, Florence, rehabilitated the old Booker Terrace Motel as a resort for black people, who could not stay anywhere in exclusive Miami Beach, and renamed it. Florence inherited the property from her father, and it came to the couple as the result of a foreclosure. "My parents were not political," their son Jerry Markowitz remembered, "but people in the Jewish community in south Florida in the 1950s and 1960s were open minded and liberal." Although they did not consider themselves part of the civil rights movement in any way, the Markowitz family's values dovetailed with the goals of the movement. They engaged in daily support for the local black community and black travelers and worked to impede local segregationists. The Markowitzes hired both black and white employees in professional and wage capacities; they did not discriminate. Jerry Markowitz worked at the hotel during the summer and "did everything from answering telephones to being a bellman, carrying bags to the rooms." He was the white Jewish kid carrying the black folks' suitcases in segregated Florida in the 1960s. "I remember serving coffee to Malcolm X," he said. Life at the hotel, he added, certainly did not mirror the segregated world in other parts of Florida, or even Miami Beach: "There was never any separation, not in the bathrooms, not anywhere. And, it never dawned on me that there could have been or should have been."[23]

As with other African American luxury hotels, Hampton House became a destination for people in show business. Lena Horne, Duke Ellington and his band, Sam Cooke—anyone who headlined in Miami Beach spent the night at Hampton House or at the nearby Sir John Hotel. As a teenager, Jerry Markowitz found life at the Hampton House very exciting. Although he was too young to spend his evenings in the lounge, he saw the performers come and go. "There was no end of celebrities. Late at night—after midnight—many of the musicians playing at the clubs on Miami Beach came here and jammed together in the lounge with whomever happened to be there. I remember Sammy Davis and Tony Bennett. Flip Wilson saw a female impersonator here and I think that inspired his character Geraldine."[24]

Martin Luther King Jr. relied on the Hampton House as a place to refresh and recharge. Miami became a retreat for him, a place to think and to write, and he loved the freedom that a swim in the pool provided. King stayed there before giving his famous "I Have a Dream" speech on the Mall in Washington in 1963, and, according to local lore, he wrote the speech and practiced his delivery at the Hampton House.

Although the vast majority of the guests at the hotel were black, the restaurant and lounge, like other jazz clubs, attracted a variety of Floridians, tourists, and performers—those who could see past skin color and simply wanted to enjoy a good meal or to listen to great music. "Lots of white folks came to the lounge and to the restaurant," Jerry Markowitz remembered. "The owners enticed a chef away from the Carillon Hotel in Miami Beach and the food was excellent." This oasis in the middle of Miami's Brownsville offered a comfortable, integrated environment in the segregated South, for those who could afford it.

The police strictly enforced curfews in nearby Miami Beach, a sundown town. Local ordinance 457, passed in 1936, required the compulsory registration of all "casual visitors" with the local police department. "Casual" included all seasonal employees of the hotels as well as domestic servants and chauffeurs of individual families. The police fingerprinted and photographed every worker on Miami Beach. The requirement to obtain identity cards was based on the pretext that such precautions protected the wealthy residents. Anyone not carrying the appropriate papers could be arrested or expelled from the jurisdiction. Since African Americans were easily identified as "casual visitors," law enforcement officers profiled them within Miami Beach, where their every movement was controlled. "The police during that day were very suspicious of any black person walking around on Miami Beach," remembered Enid Pinkney. "They wanted to know where you were going and what you were going to do."[25] With the exception of performers, black people working in Miami Beach had to be out of the area after 6 p.m. or they were subject to arrest. Performers left immediately after their last set of the night. Embracing tactics reminiscent of the era of slave passes, the Miami Beach Police actively and enthusiastically enforced Jim Crow.[26]

The Hotel Theresa, Seventh Avenue (Adam Clayton Powell Boulevard) at 125th Street, Harlem's flagship hotel.

The Hotel Theresa

The Theresa, one of the most famous African American hotels and a popular stop for vacationers in New York City, originated as a segregated building. Built by George and Edward Blum in 1912–13, the elegant thirteen-story edifice, located in the heart of Harlem, with its white terra-cotta ornamentation, still stands as one of New York City's most distinctive structures, although it is no longer a hotel. During the mid-twentieth century, a vibrant community surrounded the Theresa. The Harlem section of *The Negro Motorist Green Book* listed more than 240 establishments, more than in any other US city. The directory included dozens of locations nearby for dining, having hair done, or buying aspirin, but the most distinctive listings promoted Harlem's nightlife—a place where "celebrities rendezvous."

The Theresa was Harlem's flagship, yet the hotel did not accept black patrons until 1940, when the management decided to permit

African Americans to stay in their guest rooms. Soon, well-known figures such as boxer Joe Louis, singer Dinah Washington, and activist and labor leader A. Philip Randolph, among many others, booked rooms there. National attention fixed on the Theresa in 1960, when Fidel Castro and his huge entourage took over dozens of rooms during the opening session of the United Nations and used Harlem and the hotel "for their own political purposes"—a charge leveled against the Cuban leader by Harlem's congressman, Adam Clayton Powell.[27]

Usually, only the black press documented the events in Harlem, but the mainstream news covered Castro's attempt to embarrass the United States in front of the United Nations and the world. The problems began, however, even before the Cuban delegation to the UN arrived in New York. Cuba–US relations were already at a low point, following Castro's successful overthrow of the Fulgencio Batista government in 1959. When Castro proceeded to nationalize all businesses on the island, the United States broke off diplomatic relations.

Prior to the session at the United Nations, the Cuban government contacted multiple hotels but failed to find rooms in Manhattan for their ten-day stay. No hotel wanted to rent to the controversial foreign leader and the large entourage traveling with him—even though the heads of many African countries and the Soviet bloc had had no trouble finding accommodations. Pressured by the State Department and the United Nations, the Shelburne Hotel on Lexington Avenue relented and provided rooms for the delegation.

The Cubans, however, quickly ran afoul of the manager of the Shelburne. Furious, Castro dramatically strode out of the hotel, traveled uptown to Harlem, and checked in to the Hotel Theresa, where he had visits from the likes of Nikita Khrushchev, Malcolm X, and Langston Hughes. It seems that the Shelburne Hotel manager's concerns had merit. The group left their rooms in disarray—littered with empty milk cartons and chicken feathers (since they decided to pluck and cook fresh chicken in the rooms). Ashes and cigar butts had been ground into the rugs.[28] The Cuban leader's move to Harlem meant that the black capital, not midtown, became the site of demonstrations for and against Fidel Castro.

Not everyone agreed with Adam Clayton Powell's belief that Castro's choice of Harlem was nothing more than cynical propaganda merely designed to draw a favorable contrast between Cuba and the United States. Many African Americans understood Castro's selection of the Hotel Theresa, and his subsequent emphasis on segregation in the United States, as the Cuban leader's way to stick "a knife . . . into the heart of America's racism." Castro went so far as to declare himself an African American because of the solidarity he said he felt with black people in the United States.[29] A segregated hotel—confirmation of the way the United States restricted its black citizens' movement—provided the Cuban leader with the ideal symbol of American hypocrisy concerning race.

African Americans were happy to have someone, anyone, call attention to their struggles. One newspaper commentator courageously described the reasons for black support of the communist leader:

> Read me loud and clear. I said the people of Harlem got a big lift out of Castro's and Khrushchev's visit uptown. But I did NOT say that as a result of this, all or any Harlem Negroes are now going to join the Communist party and start spending their summer vacations in Cuba instead of at Sag Harbor or Oak Bluffs. . . . The Negro understands his role much more clearly than the white. That is why he will stand up and cheer Khrushchev in Harlem on Tuesday—drop everything and go off to fight against Khrushchev on Wednesday if America should call him.[30]

The black community's response to Castro's visit reflected their social predicament and their frustration with American indifference to racism. Many black Americans viewed shaming the nation for its bigotry as a useful weapon. As one writer put it, "[T]he moral issue is the Negro's greatest ally."[31]

In October 1960, national politics again brought the Hotel Theresa into the public eye when presidential candidate John F. Kennedy used the hotel as a backdrop for his appeal for African American votes. Campaigning with Eleanor Roosevelt, the popular former first lady who was widely admired in the black community, he hoped to demonstrate that the Democratic Party had not forgotten the Negro.

The Theresa, however, was much more than a symbolic site for international and national politicians. It was more frequently a community meeting place for African American groups representing many different points of view—from Malcolm X's Organization of Afro-American Unity (OAAU) to A. Philip Randolph's March on Washington Movement, which also had offices in the building in the early 1940s.[32]

Despite their popularity with black travelers, the Majestic, the Hampton House, the Theresa, and other large African American hotels faced serious challenges. As more and more Americans trav-

In addition to large city hotels, small segregated motor courts and tourist cottages like McKenzie Court in Hot Springs, Arkansas, were listed in *The Negro Motorist Green Book*. Motels were new and convenient and had parking adjacent to guestroom doors. (*Curt Teich Archives, Newberry Library, Chicago.*)

eled by automobile, these hotels, whose central locations within cities made them hard to access and made parking difficult, found their businesses dwindling. They could not attract white customers to their guest rooms, and the new modern motor hotels enticed many African American travelers. Segregated motels, often situated right off of highway exits, offered accessibility, convenient parking, and competitive nightly rates.

The Majestic Hotel was razed in 1967 to make way for the Goodwill Industries Rehabilitation Center. Hampton House closed in the 1970s and was scheduled for demolition, but a dedicated group of community members saved the building, and it reopened in 2015 as an event venue with much of its former glory restored. The Hotel Theresa closed in 1967, by then badly in need of updating. The new owners reimagined the interior as Theresa Towers, an office building.

THE NETWORK of black hotels and restaurants across the country served as places of refuge not only for vacationers, businessmen, and entertainers, but also for demonstrators and black leaders. It would have been difficult, if not impossible, to plan and mount protest marches without the support of these business owners. Private individuals and churches provided lodging and food for those who marched for civil rights, but hotels and motels also played significant roles.

The argument that *The Green Book* and other black-oriented travel guides offered safety in an unsafe world is largely true. But as proprietors openly demonstrated their support for the civil rights movement and the commitment to end segregation in the United States, they placed their own lives and their businesses in peril. Behind the scenes, the movement needed considerable funds, meeting spaces, lodging, and food—which successful hotel and restaurant owners were uniquely able to supply. Their participation in civil rights work, however, brought these otherwise invisible or at

Martin Luther King Jr., Fred Shuttlesworth, and Ralph Abernathy held a press conference in May 1963 in the courtyard of the Gaston Motel in Birmingham. They announced an agreement with the city's business leaders that would get jailed protesters out on bail and gradually result in the desegregation of Birmingham's lunch counters, restrooms, and drinking fountains. The agreement angered hard-line segregationists. (*Bettmann, Getty Images.*)

least ignored black spaces into the crosshairs of an angry white community. Gaston Motel, the Birmingham headquarters for Martin Luther King Jr. and for out-of-town protesters, is an example of a black business's active participation in the movement.

Self-professed conservative and Booker T. Washington supporter Arthur George Gaston, known as A. G., believed in gradual desegregation and self-reliance. A millionaire many times over, he hoped that African Americans could make social gains through economic success, and he started at least ten businesses during his lifetime—among them funeral parlors, a bank, a motel, and an insurance company—to prove it. Gaston's autobiography, *Green Power*, promoted his philosophy of gradualism through self-help, education, and black-owned business success, certainly an outdated philosophy by the 1960s. But throughout his life he worked quietly, behind the scenes, to use his influence to push civil rights forward. He paid the bail of arrested civil rights workers, urged his customers to register to vote, and engaged in conversations with white business owners about ending segregation. Gaston put pressure on the local Birmingham bank, threatening to move his account if they did not take down their Jim Crow signs. They came down. All this he did without public knowledge or recognition.

In 1963, after seeing children rolled down the street by the high-pressure water of fire hoses as they peacefully participated in a demonstration, he decided that he could no longer be a quiet, behind-the-scenes protester. "My people are out there fighting for their lives and my freedom. I have to go help them," he told Birmingham attorney David Vann, who was on the phone with him as he watched, in horror, from his window. Children participating in the march were being knocked to the ground by torrents of water. Once he decided to support the movement openly, Gaston did so very publicly—a dangerous move in the city Martin Luther King Jr. called "the most thoroughly segregated city in the United States."

Gaston had connections to some of the movement's leaders. He had worked actively with the Birmingham NAACP when, in 1956, the state sued the organization and sought to obtain the names and addresses of its members. The state claimed that the NAACP harmed the people of Alabama as well as the state's reputation through its involvement in the 1955–56 Montgomery bus boycott and other civil rights actions. State Attorney General John Patterson hoped to hobble the civil rights movement. But in 1958, in *NAACP v. Alabama*, the United States Supreme Court recognized the NAACP's right of freedom of association and the right to privacy in one's associations. It would be another five years before the NAACP's operations in Alabama were declared legal once again, but activists in the state were not idle in the interim. A group of local residents, including Gaston, formed the Christian Movement for Human Rights and elected Reverend Fred Shuttlesworth as their leader. Working with the Southern

Christian Leadership Conference, founded in 1957 by a group of sixty people in the wake of the Montgomery bus boycott, the Central Committee, an amalgamation of the two groups, met regularly in Room 30 or in the lounge of the Gaston Motel. A. G. Gaston served as a member of the committee.

In 1963, the Central Committee launched Project C (for "confrontation"), a series of direct-action, nonviolent demonstrations and boycotts designed to end segregation in Birmingham. They began with sit-ins at lunch counters in the stores downtown. Marches and a boycott of local businesses followed, with increasing numbers of protesters joining in.

Law enforcement and the White Citizens' Council met the protesters with some of the ugliest and most violent weapons seen during the civil rights movement, including fire hoses, vicious police dogs, and even bombs. The scope of the boycotts and sit-ins and the intensity of the response required that the committee meet every few days to keep track of new developments. Civil rights leaders went in and out of Room 30 at the Gaston Motel on a regular basis. In April, they met eight times, even getting together on Easter Sunday to discuss funding and what to do about those who had been arrested. Early in May, children joined the marches, some as young as six. As the police jailed black children, hundreds of others waited in the wings.[33]

It was in Room 30 of the Gaston Motel that Martin Luther King decided to submit himself for incarceration in the Birmingham jail, the site where he wrote his famous response to criticism from the city's white ministers. King's "Letter from the Birmingham Jail" helped to define the civil rights movement and gave voice to the suffering of black Americans under segregation. "Freedom is never voluntarily given by the oppressor," he wrote. "It must be demanded by the oppressed. . . . [W]hen you take a cross-country drive and find it necessary to sleep night after night in the uncomfortable corners of your automobile because no motel will accept you; when you are humiliated day in and day out by nagging signs reading 'white' and 'colored'; when your first name becomes 'nig-

Jazz musician Al Hibbler, a member of Duke Ellington's orchestra whose runaway hit *Unchained Melody* made him a popular singer, became a civil rights activist in the 1950s and '60s. In this photograph, he leads a march in Birmingham, Alabama. Police arrested several hundred peaceful protesters, including Hibbler. Blind since birth, he was driven to the Gaston Motel after the demonstration. *The Negro Motorist Green Book* recommended the Gaston as a place for black travelers to stay, but the owner's strong support of the civil rights movement eventually made the motel a target of segregationists. (*Associated Press.*)

ger' and your middle name becomes 'boy.' " The letter offered these poignant examples of the pain of the discrimination faced daily by black Americans, including the perils of traveling or driving while black. Fortunately, black hotels and motels still seemed to be safe havens. In addition to sheltering King and Ralph Abernathy, the

Gaston Motel's modern, comfortable, and air-conditioned rooms provided a sanctuary for many other civil rights workers.

Unfortunately, A. G. Gaston paid a heavy price for his courageous stand in favor of civil rights. Sometime before Saturday, May 11, 1963, King and Abernathy left Room 30 and returned to Georgia. Both men were scheduled to preach in Atlanta on Sunday. After their departure, a bomb was hurled directly at Room 30, reducing it to rubble. The Klan had made an attempt on the lives of the civil rights workers. If anyone had been in the room, the bomb would have killed its occupants. Almost simultaneously, a second bomb exploded on the front porch of the Birmingham house owned by A. D. King, Martin's brother. No one was killed, but the blast at the Gaston Motel injured three people. Black residents rushed into the street to see what had happened. Alabama state troopers arrived with guns leveled at the African Americans on the scene. More police arrived with dogs, apparently suspecting that the black citizens fleeing the area needed to be contained. An armored riot car then roared up the street with a loudspeaker blaring at the crowd to disperse. The vehicle, originally designed for use by the US Army during World War II, and completely shielded by metal plating, sprayed tear gas at bystanders. A uniformed officer manned the machine gun atop the vehicle as the driver navigated through the crowds. The presence of the military-style vehicle, along with the dogs, served only to heighten the anger that such tactics would be used with civilians. Meanwhile, Klansmen staged a rally nearby. Furious about a recent agreement to desegregate the downtown stores, they burned two twenty-foot-high crosses. Despite the menacing nature of the Klan rally, it was completely undisturbed by law enforcement.[34]

The bombing did not bring an end to the terrorizing of guests at Gaston's. James Williams, a correspondent for the *Baltimore Afro-American* newspaper who was staying at the Gaston, noted, "Five minutes after I checked into the Gaston Motel an unidentified woman rang the switchboard to warn a bomb had been planted and would go off in ten minutes. It was just a frightening prank, no dynamite was found—at least, not yet—but I'll sleep uneasy. . . ."[35] Gaston's home was bombed several months later, but no one was injured. In 2017, President Obama recognized the importance of the Gaston Motel, designating it as part of the Birmingham Civil Rights National Monument. Another motel also listed in *The Green Book* would become the site of violence in 1968, when James Earl Ray murdered Martin Luther King Jr. on the balcony at the Lorraine Motel in Memphis.

IN ADDITION to the hotels and motels that supported the movement, kitchens known only within the black community served travelers and also funneled much-needed revenue to civil rights causes. Many black women in the South made their living as cooks and housekeepers for white families. They also baked and cooked for their own families and their communities—coconut cakes, cookies, smothered chicken, and brownies, among other favorites, graced the tables at church suppers and socials, bake sales and catered events. Their livelihoods depended on keeping secret their association with the mass demonstrations disrupting the status quo in the South, yet these women used their skills as cooks both to raise money and to feed the members of the movement.

Georgia Gilmore, a domestic, midwife, and cook-turned-activist ran such a kitchen in Montgomery, Alabama, using her well-known recipes to raise money by selling food in and around her community.[36] This was not a woman to be trifled with. Gilmore was tough and determined. As Reverend Al Dixon, a DJ and radio-personality-turned-minister, described her, "Everyone will tell you Georgia Gilmore didn't take no junk." She lost her job at the National Lunch Company when her employers discovered her efforts on behalf of the Montgomery Improvement Association, an organization founded to support direct action and end segregation on the city's buses. Martin Luther King Jr. suggested that she start a restaurant in her home, and he helped her do so by providing start-up money for her business. Word of mouth brought travelers to her dining room, and she had all the diners she could handle.

Civil rights workers who traveled to the South to demonstrate needed places to eat, and Gilmore's dining-room restaurant took care of them. She cooked up her southern classics—fried chicken, baked macaroni-and-cheese, collard greens, stuffed pork chops, black-eyed peas, stuffed peppers, chitterlings with coleslaw. King shared many delicious meals here, and Gilmore's home provided the space for secret meetings and strategy sessions—reason to keep the existence of her restaurant from public knowledge. At Georgia Gilmore's home, too, King could trust that the food was safe to eat.[37] She also fed Robert Kennedy, Morris Dees (who headed the Southern Poverty Law Center), Lyndon Johnson, and dozens of other well-known figures who were sympathetic to civil rights and who passed through Montgomery in the 1950s.

Gilmore was part of a group of women from Montgomery who sold baked goods and entire meals to raise money to support the bus boycott in 1955 and 1956. The hard work of these women helped to keep the movement humming along. The money they earned (sometimes as much as six hundred dollars a week) purchased station wagons (and gasoline) that transported people to work in lieu of riding the buses—they literally fueled the boycott. The women called their enterprise "The Club from Nowhere," so that if anyone asked where the money went, they could honestly say that it went "nowhere." The name protected the anonymity of both the cooks and the donors so they would not be punished by association with the protest. The cryptic name of the group also meant that the women could quietly collect money from white people familiar with the good food they prepared, many of them unsuspecting contributors to civil rights. Gilmore found that there were many more people of goodwill than she imagined. "After the boycott . . . we found that we had so many white friends, then they could let it be known that they were really and truly interested in you as a human being, not of your color, but as a human being."[38]

Martin Luther King Jr. and other civil rights workers enjoyed meals in the homes of women whose clandestine support for the movement was significant and rarely acknowledged. (*Michael Ochs Archives, courtesy Getty Images.*)

In other communities, professional restaurateurs opened their doors to civil rights workers in support of the movement. Paschal's in Atlanta, established by brothers Robert and James Paschal in 1947, started as a thirty-seat luncheonette and sandwich shop and evolved into a large, luxurious restaurant and grill that gave "Negro Atlantans the very finest atmosphere for enjoying a wonderful meal."[39] The brothers added La Carrousel, a jazz club with two hundred seats, making the site Atlanta's hottest music venue, and in 1960 they built a motel.

Paschal's served as the city's seat of black power as a gathering place, source of pride, and driving force for local activism. Elected officials, civil rights leaders, demonstrators, and anyone in Atlanta with political aspirations showed up at Paschal's and met with Robert and James. The two reserved Room 110 in the motel as a headquarters for meetings and put their considerable resources to good use to end segregation. Martin Luther King and other civil rights leaders frequently held meetings over dinner at Paschal's. When the Freedom Riders came through Atlanta, they dined here. Often the restaurant provided meals for civil rights workers free of charge or at discounted rates.[40]

If protesters needed to post bail, the Paschal brothers put up the funds, and they supported those who were jailed. After each march or sit-in, they kept the restaurant open late to provide a place where families could be reunited. James Paschal described the process in a recent oral history:

> [T]he students used to meet at Paschal's before they would go to the downtown to do the sit-ins for the purpose of being arrested. So hundreds of students at a time would be arrested and by the time they were fingerprinted and got released from jail it would be late into the night sometimes. The parents would come to Paschal's and wait. . . . And of course, my brother and I would always provide a hot meal for them after they had been released from jail.[41]

The Paschals welcomed all comers. Black people and white people could meet and eat together here even though it violated Atlanta's segregation laws. The food was so good, especially the chicken, that it was worth the risk.[42]

Dooky Chase's restaurant played a similar role in New Orleans. It started with small investments and expanded into a full-service restaurant specializing in American southern and creole cuisine—red beans and rice, gumbo, and po'boy sandwiches. Owners Edgar Dooky and Leah Chase cultivated a friendly relationship with the local police, frequently handing out sandwiches and drinks. In exchange, the police looked the other way when someone entered the doors at Dooky Chase's. Local law enforcement never bothered them. "[T]his was a safe haven for all of us," noted Leah Chase, who died in June 2019. "See, they knew they could come and sit down here. Nobody would worry them. Even when the civil rights people came, the policemen didn't worry us. So they felt safe coming here, all the civil-rights movement, the Freedom Riders who left from here met here. Because once they were inside this building, nobody was gonna worry them."[43]

ACROSS THE United States, this black world unseen by most white people provided a network of places and institutions that supported black communities and black travelers. Women played a key role in providing lodgings—particularly in the early years of the automobile, when there were relatively few places that accepted black travelers—by opening their homes and their kitchens to overnight guests. The increasing number of black hotels, motels, and restaurants did similar work. Within the hidden world of black travelers, people felt comfortable and safe. It was an environment that gave them the support to face the humiliation that they might encounter every day and to use any means, whether subtle or overt, to defeat segregation.

In many cases, the wealthiest members of the black community, particularly black business owners in the South, stepped up to provide shelter, food, and meeting space for activists in the civil rights movement—at their peril. Their support took great courage, as it could lead to a loss of revenue or even to violence. In addition to providing overnight accommodations, meeting spaces, and meals, black businesses also funneled money into the movement, paying bail bonds for jailed protesters or simply making cash donations. Black hotels, no longer safe havens, became targets. Businesses were threatened and in some cases vandalized—or worse, as A. G. Gaston discovered. But this work was crucial, in the end, in that it helped lay the foundation for the movement's many achievements. Though the world of black travel—the guides, the motels, the boardinghouses—was gradualist in its politics, if it was political at all, by the 1960s it had become an important part of the push for civil rights.

Chapter 9

"VACATION WITHOUT AGGRAVATION"

It will be a great day for us to suspend this publication for then we can go wherever we please, and without embarrassment.

—*The Negro Motorist Green Book*, 1948

My maternal grandmother died when I was twenty-one. Born in 1892, Nana was a devout Southern Baptist. She grew up in a world far different from the Newark, New Jersey, neighborhood of my own childhood. Both of her parents had been born slaves. Her mother was three years old when emancipation came. My grandparents and my parents had to work incredibly hard to reach the middle class. They lived through the worst of the Jim Crow South.

When my brother and I were young, Nana would leave her house in Fayetteville each fall and live with my immediate family for much of the school year. She enjoyed shopping and going to the park with us, but she would never go to our church, insisting that on Sundays my father drive her to downtown Newark for the charismatic services at Hopewell Baptist. She never could abide the staid Episcopal liturgy that was part of my father's family tradition. My brother and I were very close to Nana, because she looked after us while our parents were at work. Every day, we walked home around noon and Nana made us a delicious hot lunch—chicken and rice, soup, macaroni-and-cheese, her famous apple pie, and the fried potatoes she cooked in a cast-iron pan.

When we went to Fayetteville for her funeral, I had not been to the town since my childhood, but the memories flooded back immediately. I remembered running through the streets with cousins and friends, stopping at Uncle Julius' small store—Wooten's Handout—in the middle of the black neighborhood. It was little more than a fancy shack, but all the kids loved it. My favorite thing at the Handout was the Coca-Cola cooler filled with freezing-cold bottles. You thrust your hand down into the frigid water and pulled up your favorite—grape or orange or Coke. On the counter was a gallon jar of pink, briny pickled pigs' feet. Once I carried one around like a popsicle and sucked on it for hours—an unpleasant idea to me now, but not so as a little kid trying to fit in with my southern cousins. "Why do you talk proper?" my young cousin Francine asked me then, confused by my northern accent.

I brought a simple black dress to wear to the funeral. As a grown woman, it seemed an appropriate way to honor my grandmother. But my mother's older sister, Aunt Nell, instructed me that all of the "children" would be wearing white. I told her that I would be wearing black, but my mother asked me to do as Nell said. As the oldest cousin and the only one who could drive, I was told to "go downtown and get white shoes for yourself and your cousin Francine." I drove Aunt Nell's enormous Cadillac to downtown Fayetteville. In the shoe store, we waited and waited for someone to serve us. White people came in and went out with their packages. They were waited on. After a while, I understood. The salespeople would wait on every white person before they waited on us. In a huff, I refused to buy anything in the store and dragged my protesting cousin home. This was in the 1970s, when such discrimination was illegal. To my shock and horror, Aunt Nell ordered me to go back to the store and wait my turn. Aunt Nell lived in town—she had a business in Fayetteville—and she did not want her northern niece to make a fuss. I did as I was told, to please my mother. But I learned an indelible lesson. Even though Jim Crow segregation had legally ended in 1964 with passage of the Civil Rights Act, white southerners still found ways to discriminate. And, like Aunt Nell, African Americans often just made do. They knew that racism runs deep and doesn't disappear overnight.

FROM ITS first edition in 1937, *The Negro Motorist Green Book* advocated for civil rights. Although this effort was implicit at first, by the late 1950s and 1960s, the travel guide actively championed direct action. *Green Book* writer Novera Dashiell praised 1960 as a year of great accomplishment for black people worldwide as a result of protests and the national independence movements in Africa. "Our young people with their successful sit-in demonstrations have prodded the older generation to greater effort in the struggle for civic dignity," she wrote.[1] *The Green Book* staff considered themselves civil rights advocates and tied their work to that of the Urban League, the NAACP, the Congress of Racial Equality (CORE), and the Student Nonviolent Coordinating Committee (SNCC), among other institutions and organizations. By facilitating free movement through the country, *The Green Book* was actively "fighting for minority rights."[2] Full of idealism and hope, Alma and Victor Green believed that equal rights in the United States were truly achievable and that travel would ultimately help defeat prejudice.

Victor Green would not live to see racial discrimination legally banned. He died in 1960 at the age of sixty-seven. Just two years later, Harlem businessman Langley Waller and *New York Amsterdam News* cartoonist Melvin Tapley purchased *The Green Book* from Alma. Although the guide continued to bear the names of Victor and Alma Green, the new publishers put their own stamp on it. One of the most striking changes was the addition of line drawings and cartoons by Tapley, one of the black press's leading cartoonists. He drew for the *New York Amsterdam News* from the 1940s until he retired in the late 1990s.[3] The Waller–Tapley *Green*

Books included not only more line drawings but also a didactic feature called "Green-Book's History-Makers," highlighting little-known black American heroes. "One of the founders of Denver, Colorado," black hunter and trapper Jim Beckwourth, appeared wearing a fringed shirt. Beckwourth—who lived with the Crow Indians for many years, trapped in the Rocky Mountains, and mined gold in California—was presented as embodying the American spirit of adventure.[4] Another of Tapley's "history-makers," William Leidesdorff, a seaman from St. Croix, earned a profile for launching the first steamboat in San Francisco and building the city's first hotel. Born in 1810 to a Jewish sugar planter of Danish origin and a "mulatto" woman from St. Croix, Leidesdorff also helped to found the first schools in San Francisco and was known as the nation's first black millionaire.[5] Beckwourth and Leidesdorff were exemplars of *The Green Book*'s new ambition to highlight black heroes and places related to black history—to encourage readers to take risks, as they had, and travel the country. Although ownership of the company had changed, the writers remained the same.

As the places that accepted African American patronage slowly increased (reflecting the changing nature of the travel and tourism market), Waller and Tapley changed the name of their guide from *The Negro Travelers' Green Book* to, simply, *The Travelers' Green Book* in 1961. The following year, they had a change of heart and renamed it again, this time as *The Green Book Guide for Travel and Vacations*. The new owners hoped to attract a white audience in addition to the black one, but the changes failed to help broaden the guide's readership. On the contrary, there already were plenty of guides for white readers, and many longtime loyal devotees of *The Green Book* still expected a publication created specifically for them. The broader approach could not have inspired confidence among black readers that the guide would address the racism that continued to exist in public accommodations.

Victor Green had predicted the end of *The Green Book*. Indeed, he had hoped that someday it would no longer be needed. By the late 1950s, more and more white hotels were opening their doors to black travelers. As Green had said, the black travel guides would achieve their ultimate goals when they were no longer needed. "There will be a day sometime in the near future when this guide will not have to be published," he wrote. "That is when we as a race will have equal opportunities and privileges in the United States. It will be a great day for us to suspend this publication for then we can go wherever we please, and without embarrassment."[6] His vision of full equality was too optimistic, but mainstream travel guides, including the *Mobil Travel Guide,* held new appeal for African American readers in the 1960s and thereafter.[7] *The Negro Motorist Green Book* and *Travelguide*, which had a run of about twenty years, ceased publication in the 1960s.

Victor Green was correct that things had improved, but he gave too much credit to travel as the reason for gains in civil rights. The will to maintain segregation, in much of the country, was too strong for that. Ending segregation required the concerted effort of generations of black people and their allies; direct action in the streets and legal action in the courts; and the aggressive tactics of organizations like SNCC and CORE. But Green's contribution cannot be ignored. As we've seen, many in the African American tourist trade—hotel and motel operators and restaurateurs, both formal and informal—fed and housed the civil rights workers when they gathered to participate in demonstrations. And travel itself did change minds.

In the late 1950s and early 1960s, some white hotel and motel owners realized that African Americans would constitute a new and substantial market: There was money to be made from black vacationers and businessmen. For purely economic reasons, many started to form new opinions about black travelers. In Miami Beach, for example, the exclusive Copa City Club "melted away the icy grip of jim crow" in 1951 by integrating the audience at a Josephine Baker concert, the first mixed-race performance on the

Beach. Baker refused to sign a contract to perform unless the hotel abandoned its segregation policies during her stay. The popular actress and singer insisted that the previously segregated hotel provide her with a suite, and she danced with her husband (they were a mixed-race couple) in the ballroom among the white guests. The hotel may have been most comfortable meeting Baker's demands because she was a French citizen and therefore a foreign national, not an American black woman, but the effect was significant: Baker's one-week engagement helped to pull down the invisible wall that kept black travelers out of the hotels in Miami Beach.[8] In the activist political climate of the late 1950s and the 1960s, performers found that they had gained the power to push hotels and theaters in some parts of the country to agree to similar contracts.

In the middle of the latter decade, President Lyndon Johnson oversaw and signed one of the crowning achievements of the civil rights movement, the Civil Rights Act of 1964, which prohibited discrimination on the basis of race, religion, national origin, or gender in all public accommodations. Passage of the bill was not easy. Congressmen from the southern and border states staged a filibuster that lasted for seventy-five days. When it became law, Martin Luther King referred to the act as "a second emancipation." In his first State of the Union address in 1964, Johnson spoke with pride about this accomplishment, saying, "Let this session of Congress be known as the session which did more for civil rights than the last hundred sessions combined." Of course, without the years of hard work and constant agitation of generations of African Americans, and those white Americans who collaborated in the black freedom struggle, the legislation would not have been possible. Many Americans—black and white—suffered and died for the cause. "Gone are the nightmares of yesterday's travel for Negroes," read an article in the *New York Amsterdam News* in 1966. "[The] civil rights act with its emphasis on public accommodations has caused facilities across the country to mend their ways. . . ."[9]

As hotels and motels opened their rooms to black travelers, the black businesses that had supported the African American traveling public went into a period of decline. In Maine, Hazel Sinclair tracked Rock Rest's summer guests carefully, recording who visited and when they stayed. Rooms rented for forty dollars a week per person in 1957 and increased gradually to ninety-five dollars per week by 1974.[10] Her account book also recorded how much she spent on meat and groceries, vegetables and fruit, lobsters for her famed Sunday dinners, milk, bread, ice cream, eggs, laundry, and electricity. She listed occasional expenditures for dishes, glasses, and linens and carefully calculated her profit for each season.

The guesthouse served between thirty-three and forty-two guests each summer from 1957, when the account book begins, to 1964, when the number of guests started to decline—just when the federal civil rights legislation outlawed segregation in public accommodations. Most guests stayed for one week. During some seasons, the profits from the guesthouse were extremely small—only $286 for twenty-two guests in 1965. The number of summer visitors dipped perilously low later in that decade, with only thirteen visiting in 1969. The business never recovered or even came close to matching its success in the 1950s.

By the 1960s, the black middle class was using its increasing clout to boycott chain hotels that discriminated. A chain hotel company's bookings for large black national church or club conventions would evaporate if any one franchise kept black customers out. With the support of business travelers and vacationers, fraternities and sororities, and religious groups, the NAACP put increasing boycott and legal pressure on two corporations with a record of discrimination—Hilton Hotels and Howard Johnson's.[11] Other civil rights organizations, such as the Southern Christian Leadership Conference (SCLC) and the Congress of Racial Equality (CORE), also targeted segregation in public accommodations. Some mainstream associations, such as the National Association of Social Workers, refused to book their annual conferences in hotels that discriminated. But one unintended and ironic effect of this work, and of the Civil Rights Act of 1964, was to hasten the decline of black businesses related to travel. Russell Toppin recalled his father operating a cab company in Cleveland when the city was strictly segregated and mainstream cab companies would never pick up a black person. He found his fares at the Majestic Hotel. "My grandfather filled that void until the Yellow Cab found out that black folks paid and ran him out of the business," he remembered.[12]

One historian has argued that prosperous African Americans began to consider black-owned hotels as second-rate and wanted to stay in higher-quality, white-owned lodgings.[13] But the situation was much more complex and nuanced than that. African Americans were torn. Segregated lodgings by their very nature were second class, but not always second rate. And white-owned lodgings were certainly not always first rate. Many black resorts and tourist houses welcomed returning black families summer after summer—not only because these vacationers could not stay in major hotel chains but also because the businesses provided clean, comfortable, welcoming lodgings in surroundings where their guests would not be humiliated. Melvina Jackson's regular column in the *Baltimore Afro-American*, "Vacationland Notes," sang the praises of the summer season's accommodations in the *Afro Travel Guide*. The column urged readers to purchase the guide and highlighted plush accommodations such as those found at the new Park Plaza in Atlantic City, which had made "a quarter of a million-dollar investment in luxury accommodations."[14]

Early in the 1970s, *Ebony* magazine admonished its readers not to forget about black businesses that for years had supported black travelers in segregated America. *Ebony* confidently informed readers that black resorts were competitive and could retain their clientele. But, on the whole, black travelers flocked to the national hotels and restaurant chains to which they had pushed so hard to gain access. In addition to offering broad coverage across the country (most African American hotels were single-location businesses), chain hotels were reliable, if bland. Black corporate executives could now stay at the same hotels as their white counterparts, and most executives usually found it more convenient to rely on a chain as they traveled to different cities rather than stay at unfamiliar hotels. It wasn't just a matter of convenience, though. For many black travelers, integrating public accommodations constituted an act of protest and defiance. Even if the law had changed, after all, the minds of many segregationists had not. Once the color line was broken, black travelers stayed at these hotels because they could.

In 1971, Jesse Jackson's Operation PUSH sponsored a Black Expo in Chicago to showcase black culture and business and to support black entrepreneurship. Much like the marketing surveys of the 1940s and 1950s, the black business community hoped to persuade participants at the Expo to support black-owned enter-

The NAACP sponsored numerous protests to end hotel segregation, often facing angry groups of white supremacists and Klansmen, such as in this July 1962 protest in downtown Atlanta. African Americans worked so hard to open public accommodations to everyone that when they could stay in these chain hotels, they did. (*Bill Young photograph,* Atlanta Journal-Constitution, *Associated Press.*)

prises, to deposit money in black-owned banks, and to demonstrate the value of black consumer dollars to the United States economy. Four hundred firms exhibited their products and services to about 250,000 potential customers. During the Expo, John H. Johnson, the owner of *Ebony* magazine, gave a speech in which he dismantled what he described as the five myths about black business. Johnson argued strenuously that black people will support their own businesses and had been doing so for a long time. Indeed, churches, funeral homes, cosmetic companies, and publishers thrived in black communities. "The problem of black business," he said, "is not the absence of black support, but the absence of white support."[15] When some African Americans chose to patronize the large chain hotels, the guesthouses and tourist hotels that they had supported for years, and that had supported them, lost business. The problem was that these black enterprises did not gain any white customers. While segregation had been ended legally, encouraging white Americans to fully integrate their buying habits would take much longer.

DE FACTO segregation itself did not end overnight. Indeed, resistance to the 1964 Civil Rights Act was widespread. Atlanta lawyer and owner of the Heart of Atlanta Motel Moreton Rolleston Jr., a staunch and unapologetic racist and segregationist, sued, arguing that the legislation was unconstitutional because it violated his right to exclude Negroes from his motel, particularly since he operated his business only within the borders of Georgia. His case was based on claims that the legislation violated the Fifth Amendment, protecting him from self-incrimination, and the Thirteenth Amendment, protecting him from involuntary servitude. Of course, the Thirteenth Amendment, passed after the Civil War, was designed to end slavery for African Americans, not to protect the right of segregationists to discriminate. In a unanimous decision in *Heart of Atlanta Motel v. United States* (1964), the Supreme

Court found that at any given time a substantial proportion of the motel's patrons came from many other states, and therefore it could be regulated under the Constitution's interstate commerce clause. The motel was ordered to accept business from people of all races and ethnicities.

Meanwhile, in Shreveport, Louisiana, the Justice Department filed suit against the mayor and the superintendent of parks, who arrested African Americans attempting to use the city swimming pool. Some trains running to the South continued to include Jim Crow cars. When confronted, the railroad companies claimed that they felt the ruling did not apply to them. In other places, segregationists tried to use the letter of the law to maintain discrimination. Because the law applied only to establishments in which food was consumed on the premises, one restaurant tried to flout the law because "50 percent of the food was consumed off-premises," a contingency not specifically addressed at the time. Many African Americans continued to take the rear seats in buses, conditioned from years of segregation and fearful of what might happen otherwise.[16]

At the same time, businesses often found subtler ways to discriminate. Particularly in rural areas, small hotels and independent restaurants resisted admitting black travelers. Montgomery, Alabama, removed all of the seats from the local airport's waiting room to ensure that black and white passengers would not be sitting together. And the city's attorney announced that the public bathrooms would be locked and water fountains plugged—to resist integration.[17] Better for no one to drink water than for white people and black people to drink from the same fountains. Driving while black still entailed uncertainty and risk. An article entitled "Negro Traveler—Still Weary in '67," in Norfolk's *New Journal and Guide*, reported: "[T]he Negro traveler here and there is still standing in the doorways wearing their 'never' buttons—trying to hold back the dawn." In a line that could have been written decades earlier, the guide explained that African Americans responded to the unpredictable nature of travel by confining their travel to "places where they have friends or relatives or to foreign shores—such as the Caribbean."[18]

The NAACP and other groups continued to file lawsuits that addressed discriminatory practices. "The Negro traveler can expect a crazy quilt pattern of desegregation mixed with traditional Jim Crow in the South—depending on the route that is taken," noted one article about travel conditions in the wake of the 1964 Civil Rights Act. Among the first places to open their doors in compliance with the law were the large chains, such as Holiday Inn and Hilton. But, in some small towns, "colored people still watched the movies from segregated balconies." Fortunately, but perhaps not surprisingly, twenty-two of Alabama's most influential businesses took out a full-page advertisement in the state's twenty-two daily newspapers and *The Wall Street Journal* that advocated abiding by the new law of the land. As businessmen, it was in their interests to exploit their new market. "In light of recent developments in Alabama," they wrote, "we feel that the business community has an obligation to speak out for what it believes to be right." While the group's members disagreed with the Civil Rights Act, they felt that they had an obligation to follow it.[19]

FROM THE time that Victor Green began writing his travel guide in 1936, he dreamed of the day when it would no longer be needed. African Americans traveling by automobile throughout the country, he believed, would calm racial fears, end segregation, and reintroduce white Americans to their black countrymen as equal fellow citizens who shared their values and believed in a truly democratic republic. While Green's dream was certainly overly optimistic, he witnessed tremendous change in the nation during his lifetime—much of it the result of the automobile.

World War II had energized black soldiers, who returned home ready to take on racism in this country as they had fought it in

Europe. At the same time, many black workers and women who had entered the labor market gained expertise and confidence and used their new skills, and the new opportunities open to them, to enter the middle class. After the war, one of the most important purchases for these upwardly mobile citizens—particularly those who lived outside of city centers and away from public transportation—would be an automobile.

By the time *The Negro Motorist Green Book* ceased publication in 1966, the United States had become a nation of cars and highways. The automobile spurred the complete alteration of the physical landscape to meet the demands of a new culture built around gasoline, speed, and traffic. Owning a nice car had become synonymous with attaining the American dream. For African Americans, the automobile held a particularly special meaning and provided a level of freedom that many had never known. Cars enabled the escape from peonage and racial hatred in the South and allowed black travelers to avoid Jim Crow buses and trains. Crucially, the automobile facilitated the civil rights movement by providing transportation for bus boycotts, rental cars to get to and from airports, and general transportation for people and supplies.

At the same time, however, the black-owned businesses that grew up around the automobile—guesthouses, tourist homes, hotels, and motels that had supported black travel for decades—quickly went out of business as civil rights legislation opened public accommodations to African Americans. There is much to celebrate in the story of black travel in the twentieth century, but also much to mourn: not only the loss of so many black businesses, but also the failure of these businesses to attract a white audience. In other words: our failure to become one nation, a failure that continues to this day. Nowadays, the phrase *driving while black* refers, needless to say, to the ongoing mutual mistrust between African Americans and law enforcement in so many communities across the country.

"[The Negro] has seen the promised land," commented a

reporter for United Press International in 1965, "but it still lies in the distance."[20] Although *The Negro Motorist Green Book* stopped publishing in 1966, it resonates today for Americans, both black and white. Across the decades, the book celebrated the intrinsic joy of driving. But, more importantly, it reminds us of the fragility of our freedom and the ingenuity of a people to prod the country continuously toward true equality.

EPILOGUE

When our son, Gregory, reached the age of sixteen, he anxiously awaited the moment when he would get his driver's permit. Because we live in a rural area, my husband, Martin, and I took him out to drive on backcountry roads and made him practice driving in snow. He even learned what to do if a deer ran in front of the car. Most important, I cautioned him to be extremely careful if a policeman stopped him. "Keep your hands on the wheel," I said. "Don't reach for anything, your cell phone or your wallet. Be extremely polite. Don't give him any reason to get angry, or to get nervous." My son (and, later, Rob, my son-in-law) chided me for these warnings. "I know, Mom." "Don't worry so much, Mom." I couldn't imagine anyone assuming that either of these kind, sweet men could be dangerous. But I do worry.

Recently, when the "Driving While Black team" gathered a group of senior American historians together to discuss the themes of this book and the accompanying documentary film, my son heard similar warnings from the African American members of the group. "If you are stopped by the police, your job," my colleague Faith Ruffins, senior curator at the National Museum of American History at the Smithsonian, said, "is to live long enough so that we can get to you." We have to assume that a policeman stopping a black driver will be adversarial, not respectful—suspicious and afraid of you, just because of the color of your skin.

I am afraid of the police. I admit it. This doesn't mean that I am anti-police or that I believe all policemen and policewomen are anti-black. It means that as an African American woman and a his-

torian familiar with the history of the relationship between African Americans and law enforcement, I don't want to encounter that policeman who will be terrified of me or one of my family members or who may be a racist bent on killing black people because they know they will get away with it. Sadly, police misconduct seems all too often to result in the death sentence being handed down to an unarmed driver. I am also aware that many individuals and groups have pushed our society in the direction of greater equality for all Americans. We have come a long way since my father's drives through the night on the way down to Fayetteville, when he feared what might happen if he stopped at any moment. Yet I still must warn my son that "driving while black" can get one killed.

TODAY, AFRICAN AMERICANS generally do not worry about being lynched by white mobs or being turned away from hotels simply because of skin color. For the most part, driving into "unknown" communities is less dangerous today than it was fifty years ago. Nevertheless, dangers still exist for black Americans. In 2017, author Jan Miles created *The Post-Racial Negro Green Book*, her modern-day take on *The Negro Motorist Green Book*. The guide is a state-by-state compendium of carefully documented acts of police brutality, racial profiling, and everyday racist behavior by businesses and private citizens. Also in 2017, the NAACP, for the first time in its history, issued a statewide travel advisory in Missouri. As a result of numerous racial incidents—and a report by the Missouri attorney general that black drivers were 75 percent more likely to be stopped by police in the state than white drivers—the nation's oldest civil rights organization took the unprecedented action of warning African Americans against traveling in the state. The legacy of the (mostly recent) history recounted in this book can be seen in these events and in everyday traffic stops.

Of course, the unjust treatment of African Americans by the authorities, and the resulting fear of the police, goes back much further than Jim Crow; it began with slave patrols.[1] Scholars have identified a pattern of intentionally arresting African Americans for minor or arbitrary offenses and using the arrested individuals as a source of free labor—effectively, the reinstitution of slavery in the guise of criminal justice.[2] More broadly, Jim Crow intimidation was supported by police power. Perhaps the most egregious example was Bull Connor, who gained national attention in the 1960s as a vocal segregationist. He became the nation's best-known "law-enforcement" officer in 1961, when he ordered police dogs and men with fire hoses to attack lawful civil rights demonstrators and enabled the Ku Klux Klan to commit murder with impunity in Birmingham, Alabama.

Nor was this just a southern phenomenon. African Americans and the police clashed during the social upheavals of the 1960s in northern cities: New York, Newark, Detroit, Los Angeles, Chicago, and Baltimore. I remember riding in the car with my mother on our way home to Colonia, a New Jersey suburb, one dark night during the unrest in Newark. We were, she thought, quite far from downtown, the focal point of the disturbance, and she had her headlights on. As we approached a checkpoint, a National Guardsman, his rifle leveled at us, started screaming at her to turn off the headlights. My mother had no idea that she was supposed to be driving in the dark without headlights. From the guardsman's perspective, this woman was trying to blind him and perhaps hurt him. Clearly, there was misunderstanding on both sides.

THIS BOOK has shown how a local ordinance in Miami Beach in the 1960s empowered that city's police department to profile and monitor African American mobility by keeping black people under constant surveillance and requiring identity cards for everyone entering the jurisdiction. More recent research indicates that a pattern of profiling by the police, based on racial criteria, can be documented statistically. A 1970 study of the police department in

"Midwest City," a real but anonymous city of more than half a million residents, provided the first critical examination of the disproportionate targeting of black drivers. Midwest City's police force, typical of other urban police departments in the 1970s, included only one African American officer and no women officers. Some officers "routinely used racial slurs" to describe the black residents of the city. The research, a random sample conducted by trained observers who accompanied police cars on patrol, found that African Americans were stopped more frequently than white people, although they were not more likely to commit traffic violations or be involved in traffic accidents than other drivers.[3]

Many police departments and the officers themselves, by contrast, regard racial profiling in traffic stops as a "media invention" that demeans hardworking and conscientious policemen simply trying to protect law-abiding citizens. They interpret police practices as legal and warranted and feel themselves unfairly targeted by activists. The dangerous nature of police work, and the fact that policemen and policewomen put their lives in jeopardy every day, justifies their actions. They themselves are just trying to stay alive.

Many policemen and policewomen also believe that because African Americans are more likely to be the victims of crime, and to call upon the police to protect their communities, the police are often unfairly maligned for doing the job black people often ask them to do.[4] For a variety of reasons, many policemen view black men as more likely to be involved in drugs, therefore more likely to be engaged in criminal activity—an assumption not borne out by studies. Nonetheless, these beliefs have resulted in more black drivers being stopped.[5]

Ironically, some of the behaviors that police departments have used to profile drivers include some longstanding customs that enabled black travelers to navigate a country where hotels and restaurants discriminated against them. Some of the "red flags" that police used to identify "suspicious drivers" were ones that black travelers used to protect themselves along the road. For example, carrying a stash of pillows and blankets to allow for sleeping in the car if necessary might be seen by the police as a sign of drug dealers who did not want to stop for the night. Driving a large or nice car for safety, or because you could afford it, might cause the police to stereotype the car's occupants as involved in some criminal enterprise.[6] A dilapidated car—presumably the only kind the driver could afford—might be interpreted by the police as a vehicle whose occupants were up to no good because they should not have been driving through a neighborhood where the residents owned expensive houses or cars.

Even some police training videos included not-so-subtle messages that African Americans driving expensive or rental cars were likely to be criminals—a contemporary version of the old idea that black people should not be driving nice automobiles. In some states, police training materials primarily depicted minority individuals as the examples of perpetrators, reinforcing the idea that most criminals are black men.[7]

This training as well as these fears have real-world effects. A significant body of research documents racial profiling of black and brown drivers since the 1990s. Temple University Professor John Lamberth studied traffic stops in both New Jersey and Maryland. In response to arrests made on the New Jersey Turnpike, black defendants contended that police stopped their cars and searched them disproportionately more than they stopped white drivers. In 1996, the Supreme Court of New Jersey agreed, finding a long-standing pattern of discrimination and the violation of African Americans' civil rights under both the United States Constitution and the Constitution of New Jersey.

Research on Maryland's profiling record began with a lawsuit brought in 1993 by Robert Wilkins, whose family had rented a car to travel to Chicago for a funeral.[8] On their return from the Midwest, a Maryland state trooper stopped the car, allegedly for speeding, but he inexplicably decided to hunt through their vehicle for drugs. Without probable cause, the trooper forced the family to stand at the roadside in the rain, at night, while they waited for police with drug-sniffing dogs to arrive and search the car. The dogs found nothing and the trooper released the family, but Wilkins happened to be a Harvard-educated lawyer who knew that the intrusion was illegal. He filed a lawsuit against the Maryland State Police, which led to a settlement in his favor that required the State of Maryland to provide researchers with additional data on police traffic stops for analysis to determine the extent of the problem.[9]

Professor Lamberth's studies also showed that while African Americans comprised 15 percent of the speeders on the New Jersey Turnpike, they comprised 35 percent of those stopped. In Maryland, 17.5 percent of the speeders were black, but 28.8 percent of the drivers pulled over by the police and 71.3 percent of the cars searched belonged to black drivers. And in the current century, a 2015 United States Justice Department investigation following the killing of Michael Brown in Ferguson, Missouri, found a clear pattern of racial bias, violation of the United States Constitution, intimidation, and practices "shaped by revenue rather than by public safety needs." The local police department issued tickets and stopped vehicles not to protect the citizens but to generate as much revenue as possible for largely white suburban communities. More than 50 percent of the revenue of several Missouri communities near St. Louis came from traffic tickets and court fines imposed for traffic violations that typically were minor. Inability or failure to pay the fines led to increased fees, fines, and even stints in jail—even for parking violations. Black drivers were ten times more likely to be pulled over for these predatory stops than white drivers. Police officers in Ferguson routinely violated the First and Fourth Amendment rights of citizens by stopping motorists without reasonable suspicion and making arrests without probable cause.

One man, sitting in his car to cool down after playing basketball with friends, was arrested at gunpoint for being a pedophile because children were playing in the nearby park. A charge of not wearing a seatbelt was added, even though the car was parked.

He was also charged with making a false statement for giving his name as "Mike" instead of "Michael." These charges, despite being invalid, led to the loss of his job as a federal-government contractor.

Dozens of such stories revealed a culture in which officers were "inclined to interpret the exercise of free-speech rights as unlawful disobedience, innocent movements as physical threats, indications of mental or physical illness as belligerence." Overall, the investigation found evidence of a deeply flawed police department and court system in which discriminatory intent contributed to disparities in the treatment of black people and white people.[10]

The most comprehensive study of police traffic stops, The Stanford Open Policing Project, begun in 2015, gathered and continues to collect information from multiple states. The dataset, which includes information from twenty-one state police agencies

Stuart Carlson, former editorial cartoonist for the *Milwaukee Journal Sentinel*, took on the concerns of black Americans who worried about being stopped by the police. (*CARLSON © 2015,* Milwaukee Journal Sentinel. *Reprinted with permission of Andrews McMeel SYNDICATION. All rights reserved.*)

and twenty-nine police departments, covers more than a hundred million traffic stops. Analysis of the data found significant racial disparities: African American drivers are about 20 percent more likely to be pulled over than white drivers.[11] This research is not an indictment of all police, but it does help explain why African Americans feel frightened, anxious, distrustful, and even angry during and when hearing about police encounters.

Still, there is some reason for optimism. In 2014, President Barack Obama, concerned about the growing erosion of trust between law enforcement and the public, convened a task force in the wake of the fatal shooting of Michael Brown and the subsequent decision not to pursue charges against the officer who shot him. The charge to the task force was to identify best practices in law enforcement and to offer "recommendations on how policing practices can promote effective crime reduction while building public trust." The eleven members met with dozens of stakeholders and produced a final report that proposed a way forward for the federal government, American police departments, and communities.[12] "Ferguson has changed the landscape in this country," noted Laurie Robinson, cochair of the president's task force. "It is difficult to advance the ball, but it has been striking how many chiefs are aware of this task force and are using it. They are using it and checking all the boxes. The basis for our report is building bridges between police and communities."[13]

One recommendation that Robinson found important for improving relations between African American communities and law enforcement is the need for understanding the history between the two groups and for encouraging them to engage in dialogue about it. If nothing else, my hope is that this book contributes to that understanding, and that dialogue.

APPENDIX

POLICE RESEARCHERS, POLICE DEPARTMENTS, COMMUNITY advisory groups, and activists throughout the United States have weighed in on the problems of racial profiling, implicit bias, and law enforcement–community relations. By no means comprehensive, some stakeholders with creative ideas to share on this subject have offered their ideas:

DENNIS PARKER, DIRECTOR OF THE AMERICAN CIVIL LIBERTIES UNION (ACLU) RACIAL JUSTICE PROGRAM, has personal experience of driving while black. He urges states and the nation to collect data that will provide a basis for understanding the scope of the problem and perhaps lead to a more informed discussion.

One of the problems is that there's frequently an absence of data that reflects the extent of the problem. So that is one thing that I think is important—making sure that records are kept but also that they're reviewed and that action is taken accordingly. I think one of the big dangers is that you allow settlement agreements or court orders saying that a police department or law enforcement agency has to keep records and then nothing happens to them. There are no consequences to them. Instead, there should be people who are looking at records and looking at things like the racial breakdown of people who were stopped and looking at whether there are patterns of individual officers or precincts where there is a disproportionate number of stops. It is frequently important to take a look at what the outcomes of the stops were. I think one thing that we have seen and other groups have seen consistently is that both in automobile stops and in street stops for people who are walking, there tend to be what is called a lower hit rate. In other words, that people of color are less likely to have contraband or to have engaged in illegal activity, which suggests that they are being overtargeted. So that is one statistical thing that has emerged. The other is that there is frequently a greater use of force when people of color are involved, and those cell-phone videos have provided horrifying examples of inappropriate use of force. The Guardian *conducted a study of police shootings and was shocked to find out that there was no source of data on the number of police shootings, that there was data on the number of police who were shot, but that other data wasn't required. And so, in order to even find out the extent of these police shootings, the newspapers had to basically go through local papers and look for stories about shootings. You measure things that are important to you, and the failure to measure things raises questions about how much you care about that issue.*

Parker also emphasized the importance and success of training for police officers:

One of the implicit bias studies suggests that in some ways there's at least the potential for the police to be better at dealing with implicit bias than others. There was a test that was done, where they would show people and tell them either they have a harmless item or they have a gun, and you have to decide which, as quickly as possible, because if it's a gun, you want to basically shoot them before they shoot you.[1] *When they give the test, people tend to overestimate the number of times that black people had guns and underestimate the times that white people had them, and tended to shoot more quickly when people believed that black people had weapons. So they made mistakes more and they shot more quickly. The exception was that police tended to do better than most people in these tests, and part of it was because of training that emphasized the need to look at all the circumstances. One of the things that that argues is that training is an important factor when dealing with these issues. Both training to make clear what implicit bias is and training in how to deal appropriately when you are faced with it. So those are things that police departments can do.*

SYLVAIN BISSONNETTE, POLICE COMMANDER IN THE CITY OF MONTREAL, QUEBEC, CANADA, brings an outsider's perspective to the issue of police stops, as a police officer looking at the United States from nearby Canada. A native French speaker, Bissonnette stressed the importance of continuous training for law enforcement officers, particularly utilizing scenarios and regular coaching so that officers are less likely to make mistakes and shooting is not a course of first action. He also stressed the importance of police work as problem-solving rather than finding reasons to "put on the handcuffs." His most important advice is to de-escalate tense situations rather than use a gun. Police departments should practice their community-engagement skills as frequently as they practice target shooting.

To say that you fear for your life it's one thing, but I use a military term which would be "rules of engagement." A rule of engagement is when you're facing a certain situation, and before getting to the point of taking out your weapon, you analyze the situation and consider what the right moves should be. Did you analyze the situation? Did you place yourself into a vulnerable situation, perhaps by approaching a car too quickly? What was the training that was done for these officers? What were the department's rules of engagement? What were the procedures and the policies of the police service regarding such situations? And, are you making sure that your officers understand what they should do, how they should react? Do you do simulations? I mean, there is a solution. You have to train your people. You have to make sure that they work well, that you have good procedures. But if your people don't react the way they should in training, well tomorrow morning, when they are patrolling, chances are they won't react well at all. If they're not following procedures, they must understand that there are consequences. When you're a police officer, usually when there's a mistake, someone ends up dead. So this is very serious. And from a community point of view, if nothing gets done when it happens, well obviously there's a big problem. It needs courage.

Policework is about problem-solving, not only about law enforcement. You have to assume that your people have the good reflexes to know when to speak instead of handcuffing someone. You have four or five officers, you simply jump on someone, put the handcuffs on, and bring him to the station—that doesn't resolve anything. If you simply take a step back, start talking with the person, usually you should be able to deflate the situation. If you are in a domestic violence situation versus someone that is drunk and on the street, it won't be the same approach. . . . I'm telling you one of the key issues is training. If you recruit and your people are trained regularly with various scenarios on what goes wrong in the street, and you have time to say, well you know in this kind of situation, you do this. If you give people scenarios, what will happen is that they give you a plan. And when you are faced with a situation you didn't expect, well you will fall back on your training. If I gave you some plans during training, chances are that you will take one of the situations and you say, "Okay, in training they said this. I'll try it." So if you look at another example, not police—let's say the military—they train, they train, they train. It's the same reflex. We expect that if some situation happens, they will have the reflex to do this, this, this, and that. And you know, in every situation . . . you could be an airplane steward and something happens inside the airplane. They train so much that they will react the right way, so it's not different for a police service. They should do the same thing. Usually when it's a large police force, training is not really a problem. The problem is when you have a small police force and you don't have the money. You don't have the resources. You don't have the personnel. Chances are that you took someone from the police academy after their training. The first day, he gets his gun and gets his badge, walkie-talkie—here's the key for the car. Let's go, my friend, you have a twelve-hour shift to do. And that's it. Where's the coach? No coach. And, well the situation does happen and then you say, well, this person was simply sent like this on their own and, if nothing happens, fine. If it does, well, we'll face the music. Well, facing the music when someone is dead makes a lot of heat. . . .

We all consider it normal going to the firing range let's say every three months or five months, because we have to make sure that we are good shooters. But we should do the same thing with community relations. We should practice the community side of policing. Our job is not all law enforcement.

Bissonnette, who is also the Montreal police historian, described how historical changes in policing have put additional distance between the police and their communities rather than helping the two groups understand one another better. Just as the automobile provided an enclosed, safe space for African Americans hoping to escape the indignities of the Jim Crow railcar or bus, the police car isolated neighborhood police officers from the communities they served.

Years ago, we had what we call cop. *You know, the origin of* cop *is "constable on patrol." The constable on patrol was someone who would start from the station. He would have a patrol area and he would walk his streets, making sure everything was okay. Then he would go back to the station. So by doing his beat he would simply speak to various people and yes, he would know everybody because he was walking. Then we had a great revolution—cars. With all the problems it gave us. We had a police officer who would quickly respond to a call. So as we did that, we've decided we no longer needed someone to do the patrol by foot—we'll go by car. . . . During summer, it's very warm so you close your window because you need the air-conditioning! So, you don't speak to anybody and the only time you get out of the car is to speak to someone. And when it's very warm, it's like when it's very cold. You don't want to stay there for two hours. You want to resolve the thing as fast as possible because you want to get back in your car. . . . Well, you know what, that's . . . the evolution that changed policing. Let's say a hundred years ago, it was the beginning of cars, but cars were very expensive. It was like having an airplane. So the first problem is, you needed someone to be able to drive the car, so that's why we didn't touch the cars until, let's say, 1910, 1920s. Maybe you had the car but there was only one. Maybe the first cars were more trucks and would be used to carry prisoners and carry many police officers around. Eh, then you have the beginning of motorcycles. Motorcycle? Well, it was only practical for moving from one station to the other.*

So, as you have more transport, people are living in the suburbs, then you realize that you need transport to do the job, so, in the beginning you had small stations, you got to a point that, okay, now it's cheaper to buy cars. They were stuck with horses—you had to feed the horses. So gradually, mostly in the thirties, we could get rid of some of the horses and use cars or trucks to move around. By that time, you have fewer and fewer COPS, constables on patrol. You still had some, but you could simply reduce the force. In Montreal, it was about in the late seventies, beginning of the eighties, that we simply got rid of that system. Because now, we had communication, good transport, good cars. I mean, you could move around. So, in most of the cities, the way of doing policing in the fifties and the sixties simply changed in the eighties, and in the eighties . . . the police had to adapt to a new society . . . which means that you have a different police force.

LAURA ANDERSON, OPERATIONS DIRECTOR AT THE ALABAMA HUMANITIES FOUNDATION, believes that police training is too focused on enforcement. Police regularly practice target shooting and engage in tactical training, but they never receive training focused on building empathy, working with communities, and addressing inherent bias. At the suggestion of her brother, a police officer, she is experimenting with humanities training for police officers. Anderson designed a humanities program to engage Alabama policemen in discussions about the history of policing in the state. The program has garnered a great deal of interest around the country. Rather than beginning with current issues, the program uses the infamous 1931 Scottsboro case as a reference point. Nine African American teenagers, erroneously accused of raping two white women, faced the death penalty and spent as long as twenty years in prison before finally being released after one of the women admitted that she falsely accused them. Anderson's program is largely experimental. She has not yet evaluated its success, but it is a creative attempt to help police officers understand the context in which they are doing their jobs today.

The story of the Scottsboro case and those defendants is so rich, there are stories within the story. . . . It's useful because law enforcement really looked good in much of the story. The defendants would have been lynched very early on, were it not for law enforcement in Jackson County, Alabama. There was a murder later of a sheriff who again did his job, and people for years suspected that it was because he didn't step aside and let the lynch mob take over.

There are stories like that within the story, too, so what the Scottsboro story does for us is not threaten law enforcement so much as implicate all of us—Americans, our culture, especially Alabamians, the government—in what happened. It's about thoughtfulness, giving law enforcement time to be thoughtful.

Time to discuss something. It's not part of the culture for people who don't question, like we do in the humanities world all the time.

[Humanities training for police has] garnered a lot more interest from my colleagues around the country than it has in Alabama, but we didn't promote it a lot. We were trying to play with it, see how it works best, where it works best, what we need to do to improve it. The conversations, the discussions that are built into the eight-hour schedule really end with a lot of discussions about current events.

We wanted to see what happens when people who don't have a good grounding in the humanities and history get a day of it. What does it do for them? How do they respond to it? That's as simple as my idea was. You know, somebody recently said, "Oh, I can't believe you don't have somebody who does diversity training, like race relations workshops." I don't want that. At least not right now. I wanted to deliver the story and see what happens. The story of the Scottsboro case and those defendants is so rich. So since law enforcement looks good, it was a good place to start a conversation.

All I can say is that I started the whole thing with a hunch and with my brother, a chief deputy who spent thirty years in law enforcement, telling me that he thought it would be very worthwhile. All of this professional development that people in law enforcement are offered has to do with how to fire weapons and very tactical-type skills, and they don't get anything humanities-based, and there's a place for it. And so, we have tried it and it seems like something we need to pursue.

LAURIE ROBINSON IS THE CLARENCE J. ROBINSON PROFESSOR OF CRIMINOLOGY, LAW AND SOCIETY AT GEORGE MASON UNIVERSITY. She served as cochair of President Obama's Task Force on 21st Century Policing, and for six years she was cochair of the International Association of Chiefs of Police (IACP).

She stressed the importance of building trust with the community and treating all members of the community with respect.

The basis of our report is about building bridges between police and communities. Police departments need to embrace a guardian mindset rather than a warrior mindset. There are instances where they need a warrior mindset, but they should approach the community as a guardian. And, we must embrace procedural justice. Procedural justice is a principle of respectful treatment of citizens. We must give them an opportunity to state their case. It's the notion of being treated by the government respectfully. I was heading to a meeting with the International Association of Chiefs of Police and I was stopped for speeding in Arlington, Virginia. The officer was extremely polite and explained why they had stopped me and why they had lowered the speed limit there. This was a good approach in terms of how to treat citizens—all citizens. He treated me with dignity. The notion of paying heed to the citizen is important. And we need to inculcate in new officers a strong sense of humanity.

It's also important to develop a culture of transparency and accountability. Everything should go up on the department's website—the demographics of the department, how many shootings there have been. That's how you build a relationship with the community. We envision community policing as a collaboration to find solutions. Listening to citizens is important—about what they see as concerns and what they are going to do about it. We need community buy-in. All of this is about building trust with the community.

ACKNOWLEDGMENTS

I STARTED THINKING ABOUT THIS BOOK IN THE 1990s, when my colleague Myra Young Armstead introduced me to a small pamphlet that she discovered while studying the history of summers in Saratoga Springs, New York. All I knew about it then was that it was published during the 1950s and 1960s, when I was a child. It was popular in the African American community, and I was unaware of it. I was intrigued. I asked my friend David Lewis to make a photocopy at the University of Chicago, which held a collection of the guides. David brought me my first *Green Book.* That little book stayed with me, and Ann Withington—my mentor, colleague, and friend—encouraged me to do something with it. Ann was initially more enthusiastic than I, since the dearth of information seemed a daunting obstacle. I owe my gratitude to Ann and to my other University at Albany colleagues Dan White, Ivan Steen, and Jerry Zahavi, who offered thoughtful critiques of my work. And thanks also to The Ephemera Society of America. The society supported my research travel with the Philip Jones Fellowship for the Study of Ephemera, and Philip Jones and his family offered ongoing enthusiasm for the topic.

Several of my colleagues at the State University College at Oneonta offered suggestions, helpful reviews, and research recommendations along the way, including Christopher Sterba and Cindy Falk. Richard Lee, my colleague and friend in the English department, patiently taught me about semiotics and hermeneutics, information that proved useful in thinking about the language of *The Green Book.* James Mackin shared the lessons he learned as a white administrator at a historically black college. My friend and provost, the late historian Daniel Larkin, spent hours poring over my photographs and teaching me to identify car makes, models, and details about specific automobiles. William Walker, my colleague at the Cooperstown Graduate Program, gave the manuscript a thoughtful reading and offered helpful suggestions, particularly about the black middle class. Kathy Meeker worked tirelessly with me to locate funding and edited grant proposals and prepared project budgets. She is truly one of SUNY Oneonta's most valuable stars.

Many librarians did yeoman work in helping me track down obscure sources, including Kay Benjamin, Sally Goodwin, Mary Lynn Benson, Andrea Gerberg, Terrisa Rowe, and Joe Festa. Joanne Van Vranken, a librarian at the New York State Historical Association Library (NYSHA), located numerous obscure articles and books and persuaded libraries to lend them or to extend already extended interlibrary loans. Wayne Wright, associate director of the NYSHA Library, offered boundless enthusiasm and talked with me endlessly about my topic and how to locate specific rare materials. Their assistance enabled me to take this story far beyond the story of *The Negro Motorist Green Book*.

Many graduate students scanned images and assisted with image research, including Sylvea Hollis, Alan Rowe, Laura Ayers, Amanda Cohen, Audrey Wolf, Georgiana Drain, Matt Wagner, Christian Stegall, Charles Clark III, and Katherine Chaison and her dad, Ken Chaison, who saved me a trip back to Washington, DC.

My friends and colleagues Rosemary Craig and Catherine Raddatz exhibited endless enthusiasm for my topic and offered support that never waned. Rosemary effortlessly transcribed all of my oral histories, making them easily accessible and saving me hours of excruciating work. I also owe my gratitude to Renee Jaussaud, Kay W. Garrett, Charles Granquist, John Armstrong, Debra Gust, and Peggy Pearlstein for their research assistance. Valerie Cunningham and Richard Candee introduced me to Hazel and Clayton Sinclair's tourist home, Rock Rest, in Kittery Point, Maine.

Through a series of oral histories, many people generously shared their personal experiences, which greatly enriched this story, for which I owe them my gratitude: Vernell Allen, Dorothy Arumburo, Patricia Barker, Lonnie Bunch, Avery Clayton, Willie Cooper, Kevan Cullin, Angela Stewart, Valerie Cunningham, James Timothy "Mudcat" Grant, Ramona Green, Bill Gwaltney, Sylvester Hollis, Henry Johnson, Walter Edwards, Doris and Morris Johnson, Jerry Markowitz, Ken Jackson, Danny Earl Clay, and the late Leah Chase. Our adviser team for the book and the documentary graciously shared both their expertise as scholars and their personal experiences: Spencer Crew, Thomas Sugrue, Craig Wilder, Fath Ruffins, Dennis Parker, Sylvain Bissonette, Laura Anderson, Laurie Robinson.

Special thank-yous to my good friends Jonathan Collett, Robin Campbell, Carla Lesh, Carlyn Buckler, Susan Goodier, John and Florence Carnahan, David Schuyler, Susan Turell, and Doreen DeNicola for their support, suggestions, and thought-provoking discussions.

In the African American community, beauty parlors and barbershops are essential local resources for information as well as hair care. I feel very fortunate to know Vernell Allen, owner of Vernell's House of Styles in Albany, New York. Vernell fortuitously introduced me to the Green family. She also shared wonderful stories and photographs and permitted me to conduct many interviews in her beauty parlor. I am very grateful for her friendship and her participation in this project. Special thanks also to my friends and colleagues at Steeplechase Films. They are an amazing, passionate, and creative team. Ric Burns and Bonnie LaFave, Kathryn Clinard, Emily Pfeil, Emir Lewis, and Greg Sorin (our son) brought this story to life in a moving and important film.

I am very thankful that my husband, a prolific reader, spotted the name of the indomitable Alice Martell, my literary agent, in the acknowledgments of another book and tracked her down. She is one of those women whose friendship enriches your life, and I am so grateful to her for her guidance, expertise, and wonderful sense of humor.

I am grateful to Bob Weil at W. W. Norton, who saw the potential in this story and its importance to our understanding of race in the United States. I am grateful for his enthusiastic support and initial suggestions on shaping the narrative. I feel equally fortunate to have had the support and expertise of Dan Gerstle, senior editor at Norton and the editor of this book. I appreciated his good humor and kind manner, his persistent prodding and positive reinforcement, but, most important, his thoughtful understanding of this book and its author. And thank you to Gina Iaquinta, who answered my endless questions with good humor, and Kathleen Brandes for her meticulous reading of the manuscript.

It is truly impossible for me to adequately thank my husband, Martin, the most honorable human being I know, for his support, good humor, thoughtful ideas along the way, thorough reading of drafts, and assistance with numerous illustrations. I am very lucky to have him as a life partner.

And thanks to my daughter and son—both children when I began this research and now grown into kind and responsible adults—Meredith, now a museum director, and Gregory, a writer and documentary film producer. For so many years, they generously shared their mother.

My thanks to Robert, our son-in-law, whose presence in our family enriches us all. And finally to Naomi, Lily, and Maya, who remind us all of the most important things in life. May you always be judged by the content of your character.

NOTES

Introduction

1. Mark Twain, *The Innocents Abroad, vol. 2* (New York: Charles L. Webster and Co., 1889), 444.
2. Pew Research Center on Social and Demographic Trends, "On Views of Race and Inequality, Blacks and Whites Are Worlds Apart," http://www.pewsocialtrends.org/2016/06/27/on-views-of-race-and-inequality-blacks-and-whites-are-worlds-apart/, accessed January 19, 2019.

Chapter 1: THE JOURNEY

1. Olaudah Equiano, *The Interesting Narrative of the Life of Olaudah Equiano* (London: 1793).
2. *Born in Slavery: Slave Narratives from the Federal Writers' Project, 1936–1938*. Oklahoma Narratives, vol. XIII, 134 Ida Henry, age eighty-three.
3. *Born in Slavery: Slave Narratives from the Federal Writers' Project, 1936–1938*. Texas Narratives, vol. XVI, part 4, 55 Patsy Southwell, age eighty-three, Jasper County, Texas.
4. Sally E. Hadden, "Slave Patrols," *New Georgia Encyclopedia*, January 10, 2014, http://www.scencyclopedia.org/sce/entries/slave-patrols/, accessed July 13, 2018.
5. Article IV, Articles of Confederation.
6. William Walter Hening, ed. *The Statutes at Large*, vol. 2, pp. 481–82, June 1680, "An Act for Preventing Negroes Insurrections."
7. United States Constitution, article IV, section 2, clause 3: "No Person held to Service or Labour in one State, under the Laws thereof, escaping into another, shall, in Consequence of any Law or Regulation therein, be discharged from such Service or Labour, but shall be delivered up on Claim of the Party to whom such Service or Labour may be due."
8. The Code of Virginia: With the Declaration of Independence and

Constitution of the United States; and the Declaration of Rights and Constitution of Virginia Pursuant to an Act of the General Assembly of Virginia, Passed on the Fifteenth Day of August 1849. Richmond.

9. Henry Mayer. *All on Fire: William Lloyd Garrison and the Abolition of Slavery* (New York: St. Martin's Press, 1998), 307.
10. Elizabeth Stordeur Pryor, *Colored Travelers: Mobility and the Fight for Citizenship before the Civil War* (Chapel Hill: University of North Carolina Press, 2016), 10–16, 62–63.
11. In *Slave Patrols: Law and Violence in Virginia and the Carolinas* (Cambridge: Harvard University Press, 2001), Sally E. Hadden makes the case that slave patrols in North Carolina, South Carolina, and Virginia who enforced the laws of slavery and helped to ensure limited movement among enslaved African populations also laid the groundwork for the violence and brutality that characterized Jim Crow enforcement in the twentieth century.
12. John Wood Sweet, *Bodies Politic: Negotiating Race in the American North, 1730–1830* (Baltimore: Johns Hopkins University Press, 2003), 91.
13. Aiken Town Council, *Slave Patrol Book*, 1839–1860, South Carolina Historical Society, Charleston.
14. Austin Steward, *Twenty-Two Years a Slave, and Forty Years a Freeman* (Rochester, NY: William Alling, 1857), 28–29.
15. K. B. Turner, David Giacopassi, and Margaret Vandiver. "Ignoring the Past: Coverage of Slavery and Slave Patrols in Criminal Justice Texts," *Journal of Criminal Justice Education*, 17, no. 1 (April 2006): 183–86.
16. Angela Y. Davis, *Blues Legacies and Black Feminism* (New York: Pantheon Books, 1998), 73.
17. *Chuck Berry: The Autobiography* (London: Faber and Faber, 1987), 147, 149. For a wonderful video of "You Can't Catch Me": https://www.youtube.com/watch?v=9jKrHzps0XM, accessed July 17, 2018.
18. A. H. Lawrence, *Duke Ellington and His World* (New York: Routledge, 2001), 44, 265.
19. Victor H. Green, "A Chat with the Editor," *The Negro Motorist Green Book: The Guide to Travel and Vacations* (New York: Victor Green, Inc., 1952), 1.
20. Pauli Murray, "Negroes Are Fed Up," *Common Sense* (August 1943): 274.
21. "The Courier's Double 'V' For a Double Victory Campaign Gets Country-Wide Support," *Pittsburgh Courier*, February 14, 1942.
22. Cora Daniels, "Pioneers: Meet Six Unsung Civil Rights Heroes—Among the First Black Men to Fight Their Way into the Executive Suite," *Fortune*, August 22, 2005.
23. Ibid.

Chapter 2: "HUMILIATION STALKS THEM"

1. Elliott Ferguson, "To Expand Defense School," *Pittsburgh Courier*, January 8, 1941; "365 Register for Defense Classes," *Baltimore Afro-American*, January 25, 1941.
2. C. H. Gattis to Thurgood Marshall, April 24, 1942. Papers of the NAACP, Part 15: Segregation and Discrimination—Complaints and Responses, 1940–1955, Series A, Microfilm 10786: Legal Department Files, Bethesda, MD.
3. Ibid.
4. R. H. Boyd, *The Separate or "Jim Crow" Car Laws or Legislative Enactments of Fourteen Southern States, Together with the Report and Order of the Interstate Commerce Commission to Segregate Negro or "Colored" Passengers on Railroad Trains and in Railroad Stations* (Nashville, TN: National Baptist Publishing Co., 1908), 5.
5. Timetable included in letter from Dr. George Miller to NAACP, December 12, 1943. Papers of the NAACP, Part 15: Segregation and Discrimination—Complaints and Responses, 1940–1955, Series A, Microfilm 10786: Legal Department Files, Bethesda, MD.
6. Manfred Burleigh and Charles M. Adams, eds., *Modern Bus Terminals and Post Houses* (Ypsilanti, MI: University Lithoprinters, 1941).
7. Jerrold Packard, *American Nightmare: The History of Jim Crow* (New York: St. Martin's Griffin, 2002), 244–45.
8. *Atlanta Daily World*, August 17, 1944.
9. *Pittsburgh Courier*, July 10, 1943.
10. *Philadelphia Tribune*, December 13, 1952.
11. Kathryn Schulz, "The Many Lives of Pauli Murray," *The New Yorker*, April 17, 2017, https://www.newyorker.com/magazine/2017/04/17/the-many-lives-of-pauli-murray, accessed November 25, 2018.
12. "Jim-Crow Bus Dispute Leads to Girls Arrest," *Carolina Times*, April 6, 1940; "Appeal from VA. Jim Crow Law Conviction," *New Journal and Guide* (Norfolk, VA), April 6, 1940.
13. "The Supreme Court Decision," *Chicago Defender*, June 15, 1946.
14. Letter, July 26, 1941, C. G. Pennington, General Passenger Agent, to Thurgood Marshall, General Counsel, NAACP. Papers of the NAACP, Part 15: Segregation and Discrimination—Complaints and Responses, 1940–1955, Series A, Microfilm 10786: Legal Department Files, Bethesda, MD.
15. Madge Washington, interview by Gretchen Sorin, February 27, 2016.
16. Vernell Allen, interview by Gretchen Sorin, June 17, 2006.
17. Pauli Murray, ed., *States' Laws on Race and Color* (Athens, GA: Women's Division of Christian Service, 1950).
18. *Chicago Defender*, February 26, 1944.

19. Walter Edwards, interview by Ric Burns, July 2016.
20. "The People Report" was a column that appeared in the *Chicago Defender* during the summer of 1961. See, for example, July 13, 1961, 10; August 19, 1961, 1.
21. *Chicago Daily Defender*, July 19, 1969; ProQuest Historical Newspapers, p. 3.
22. *Cleveland Call and Post*, December 27, 1947.
23. "The People Report on Racial Bias," *Chicago Defender* (National edition), July 8, 1961.
24. Roy Wilkins, "Humiliation Stalks Them": Text of the testimony of Roy Wilkins, NAACP Executive Secretary, July 22, 1963, in supporting the public accommodations section (Title II, S.1731) of the proposed civil rights bill being considered by the Senate Commerce Committee.
25. Ruth Thompson-Miller, Joe R. Feagin, and Leslie H. Picca, *Jim Crow's Legacy: The Lasting Impact of Segregation* (New York: Rowman and Littlefield, 2015), 15–33; "Racism's Psychological Toll, Interview with Jenna Wortham," *New York Times Magazine*, June 24, 2015; Robert T. Carter, "Racism and Psychological and Emotional Injury, Recognizing and Assessing Race-Based Traumatic Stress," *The Counseling Psychologist*, January 1, 2007.
26. Walter Edwards, interview by Ric Burns, July 2016.
27. "When Black Death Goes Viral, It Can Trigger PTSD-like Trauma," *The Nation*, July 22, 2016, https://www.pbs.org/newshour/nation/black-pain-gone-viral-racism-graphic-videos-can-create-ptsd-like-trauma, accessed January 26, 2019.
28. Jonathan Scott Holloway, *Jim Crow Wisdom: Memory & Identity in Black America since 1940* (Chapel Hill: University of North Carolina Press, 2013), 14–15.
29. "Negroes Spend Half a Billion Dollars on Cars a Year," *Our World* (March 1955): 16.

Chapter 3: AFRICAN AMERICANS AND THE AUTOMOBILE

1. For example, NAACP records in the Library of Congress include reported incidents of African Americans being accosted while in their cars. A photograph of Billy Middlebrooks of Clinton, Tennessee, trying to talk a mob out of "hauling a Negro motorist from his car," is included in the collection. Prints and Photographs Division, photograph LC-USZ62-117234. One of the most notorious instances of African Americans being hauled from their cars by a white mob is the Moore's Ford lynching. Two young African American couples, Roger and Dorothy Malcom and George and Mae Murray Dorsey, were

stopped, pulled from their car, repeatedly kicked, beaten, and hanged. No one was ever prosecuted for the crime, although the perpetrators were known. The white community closed ranks and kept the terrible secret. George Dorsey had recently returned home from service in World War II. Clearly the lynchers did not view the couples as human beings. The belly of Dorothy Malcom, seven months pregnant, was slashed open and her unborn baby was ripped from her womb.

2. Emily Post, *Etiquette: The Blue Book of Social Usage* (New York: Funk and Wagnalls, 1955), 582.
3. David Levering Lewis, *W. E. B. Dubois: The Fight for Equality and the American Century, 1919–1963* (New York: Henry Holt, 2000), 296.
4. Herbert Aptheker, comp. and ed., *Writings in Periodicals Edited by W. E. B. Dubois: Selections from the Crisis*, vol. 2, 1926–1934 (Millwood, NY: Kraus-Thomson Organization, 1983), 536.
5. W. E. B. Du Bois in *The Crisis*, "Jim Crow Cars Usually Empty," reprinted in the *Baltimore Afro-American*, February 16, 1929.
6. Charles S. Johnson, *Patterns of Negro Segregation* (New York: Harper and Brothers, 1948), 270.
7. Alfred Edgar Smith (1903–1986) toiled throughout his life for civil rights. A native of Arkansas with an MA in history from Howard University, Smith worked for several federal agencies, including the WPA. He served as a member of President Franklin D. Roosevelt's Federal Council on Negro American Affairs, also known as his "Black Cabinet." A well-known journalist in the African American community, Smith served as a bureau chief and writer for the *Chicago Defender* and also wrote for the *Negro Digest* and *Ebony* magazine.
8. Alfred Edgar Smith, "Through the Windshield," *Opportunity* (May 1933), 142.
9. "Driving Old Betsy," interview with Desiree Cooper, *All Things Considered*, PBS, August 22, 2006.
10. Smith, "Through the Windshield," 142.
11. Spencer Crew, interview by Gretchen Sorin, September 19, 2006.
12. "Negroes Spend Half a Billion Dollars on Cars a Year," *Our World* (March 1955): 16.
13. Booker T. Washington, Louis R. Harlan, and Raymond Smock, eds., *The Booker T. Washington Papers*, vol. 13, 1914–1915 (Urbana: University of Illinois Press, 1972), 124.
14. For the purposes of this study, the black middle class included the professional class—doctors, teachers, clergy, lawyers, artists, writers, corporate executives, and business owners. The black middle class encompasses a broader range of occupations than the white middle class. Automobile workers, postal workers, barbers, and railroad porters, for example, are part of the black middle class. Traditionally shut

out of entire categories of employment, many members of the black middle class were underemployed. Porters fit into this category. Pullman porters were highly esteemed within the black community. They had steady employment and received a great deal of respect because they were so well traveled and knowledgeable about the country. In his memoir of growing up in the era of Jim Crow, Clifton Taulbert remembered that "being a porter on a train was a good job in those days. The porter seemed to represent the best in colored." Other African American workers attended technical schools or found positions as skilled workers. Before, during, and after World War II, for example, the automobile industry employed black workers at rates higher than other industries. Northern motor cities, such as Detroit, Flint, and Pontiac, needed workers to meet increasing demands for new automobiles and for the war effort. Between 1937 and 1941, more than 12 percent of Ford Motor Company employees were African American. Industries such as plate glass, metal foundries, and upholstery leathers and fabrics that supported car manufacture provided skilled and unskilled positions for southern migrants. The automobile industry contributed to the changing status of African Americans in the United States, facilitating the entry of black Americans into the middle class.

15. "Negroes Spend Half a Billion Dollars on Cars," *Our World*.
16. Arthur F. Raper, *Preface to Peasantry: A Tale of Two Black Belt Counties* (Columbia: University of South Carolina Press, 2005), 175.
17. W. E. B. DuBois, "Jim Crow Cars Usually Empty," *Baltimore Afro-American*, February 16, 1929.
18. James H. Bagley Papers, 1936–1956, Alabama Department of Archives and History; Valorie Lawson and John Shryock, "Attic Discovery Tells Different Side of Montgomery Bus Boycott Story," *WSFA News* (Montgomery, AL), February 9, 2018, http://www.wsfa.com/story/37471428/attic-discovery-tells-different-side-of-montgomery-bus-boycott-story/, accessed December 5, 2018.
19. Ross Eldridge, "The Auto and the Civil Rights Movement," *New Pittsburgh Courier*, November 25, 1972.
20. Ibid.
21. C. W. Churchill, "Owner Judged by the Car He Drives," *Harper's Weekly* 62 (March 4, 1916): 235.
22. Robert Russa Moton, *What the Negro Thinks* (Garden City, NY: Doubleday, 1929), 42.
23. Ibid., 41. Robert Russa Moton was a lawyer and educator who became president of the National Negro Business League in 1900. A friend of Booker T. Washington, Moton took over leadership of Tuskegee Institute after Washington's death in 1915. Moton was a prolific writer

on the African American condition and won the NAACP's Spingarn Medal in 1932.

24. Ibid., 37.
25. Juan Williams, *Eyes on the Prize: America's Civil Rights Years, 1954–1965* (New York: Penguin Books, 1988), 209.
26. Marcus Alexis, "Racial Differences in Consumption and Automobile Ownership" (PhD diss., University of Minnesota, 1959), 68.
27. "The U.S. Negro" *Time,* May 11, 1953, http://www.time.com/time/magazine/article/0,9171,935334,00.html, accessed August 30, 2008.
28. *The New Philadelphia Story: A Survey of America's Third Largest Negro Market* (Baltimore: The Afro-American Company of Baltimore, 1946), cover.
29. *America's Fifth Largest Negro Market* (Baltimore: The Afro-American Company of Baltimore, 1946), 22.
30. Almost 305 of those responding to the questions said they would buy a new car after the war when production resumed. Research Company of America, *The Washington Afro-American Report on Characteristics of the Washington Negro Market, Its Product Buying and Brand Preferences in 1945* (Washington, DC: The Washington Afro-American, 1945), 35; *America's Fifth Largest Negro Market.*
31. *America's Fifth Largest Negro Market*, 82.
32. Ibid.
33. "Negroes Spend Half a Billion Dollars on Cars," 15.
34. *America's Fifth Largest Negro Market*, 1.
35. *The Washington Afro-American Report on Characteristics of the Washington Negro Market.*
36. D. Parker Gibson, *The $30 Billion Negro* (London: Macmillan, 1969), 7–8.
37. *Consumer Analysis of the Pittsburgh Negro Market*, p. F-1: 19.4 percent purchased Buicks, 13.7 percent purchased Fords, and 9.7 percent purchased Chevrolets.
38. Edgar A. Steele, *The National Negro Market* (New York: Interstate United Newspapers, 1944), n.p.
39. "4 Out of 5 Negro Families in Cities Now Own Cars," *Chicago Defender*, September 29, 1962.
40. Fred C. Akers, "Negro and White Automobile-Buying Behavior: New Evidence," *Journal of Marketing Research* (August, 1968): 288.
41. J. Trinkle, "Why Negroes Are Buying Foreign Cars," *Sepia* 7 (1959): 9.
42. *The Washington Afro-American Report*, 34.
43. Mamie Garvin Fields and Karen E. Fields, *Lemon Swamp and Other Places: A Carolina Memoir* (New York: The Free Press, 1983), xiii.
44. Dorothy Height, *Open Wide the Freedom Gates* (New York: Public Affairs, 2003), 106.

45. Valerie Cunningham, interview by Gretchen Sorin, August 19, 2006.
46. American RadioWorks, "Remembering Jim Crow," Jerry Hutchinson, Indianapolis, IN, http://americanradioworks.publicradio.org/features/remembering/blacks.html#70, accessed September 23, 2007.
47. James Timothy "Mudcat" Grant, interview by Gretchen Sorin, July 30, 2006.
48. Ibid.
49. Spencer Crew, interview by Gretchen Sorin, September 19, 2006.
50. Lonnie Bunch, interview by Gretchen Sorin, March 2006.
51. Henry Johnson, interview by Gretchen Sorin, March 1, 2006.
52. Bill Gwaltney, interview by Gretchen Sorin, April 3, 2006.
53. Walter Edwards, interview by Ric Burns, July 2016.
54. Mahalia Jackson, *Movin' On Up* (New York: Hawthorne Books, 1966), 97.
55. Johnson, *Patterns of Negro Segregation*, 125.
56. Dick Gregory, *From the Back of the Bus*, ed. Bob Orben (New York: E. P. Dutton, 1962), 36.
57. Trinkle, "Why Negroes Are Buying Foreign Cars," 9.
58. "Why Negroes Buy Cadillacs," *Ebony* 4, no. 11 (1949): 34.
59. Ibid.
60. Horace Sutton, "Negro Vacations, a Billion Dollar Business," *Negro Digest*, July 1950.
61. The U.S. Negro, *Time*, May 11, 1953, http://www.time.com/time/magazine/article/0,9171,935334,00.html, accessed August 30, 2008.
62. "Why Negroes Buy Cadillacs."
63. "Negroes Spend Half a Billion Dollars on Cars," 15–19.
64. *The New Philadelphia Story* (Philadelphia: Harry Hayden Company, 1946).
65. Donald L. Caruth and Thomas E. Barry, "The Black Consumer," *Western Advertising News* (September 2, 1969): 25.
66. Stephen Grant Meyer, *As Long As They Don't Move Next Door: Segregation and Racial Conflict in American Neighborhoods* (New York: Rowman & Littlefield, 2000), 7.
67. For information on African American home ownership and redlining, see sociologist Amy Hillier's website about her doctoral and postdoctoral research on redlining in Philadelphia. This site provides an excellent overview of the history of this practice in one northeastern city: http://cml.upenn.edu/redlining/intro.html, accessed March 2, 2008; Kristen Crossney and David Bartelt's article, "Residential Security, Risk, and Race: The Home Owners' Loan Corporation and Mortgage Access in Two Cities," confirms the link between race and

restrictions on mortgage awards, but it also offers a more complex analysis of the HOLC's policies and history.

68. Black and white consumers spent their leisure dollars in very different ways. While white consumers had access to expensive clubs, sporting events, and restaurants, these avenues were closed to members of the black middle class, who spent more of their disposable income on support of the black church and other social responsibilities. Marcus Alexis, "Patterns of Black Consumption, 1935–1960," *Journal of Black Studies* 1, no. 1 (1970): 55–74; Richard Rothstein, *The Color of Law: A Forgotten History of How Our Government Segregated America* (New York: Liveright, 2017).
69. Raymond A. Bauer, Scott M. Cunningham, and Lawrence H. Wortzel, "The Marketing Dilemma of Negroes," *Journal of Marketing* 29 (1965): 4.
70. Sherwin Badger, "The 15 Billion Dollar Market," *Negro History Bulletin* 18, no. 1 (October 1954): 12.
71. *America's Fifth Largest Negro Market*, 97.
72. "Harlem Women Fight High Prices: Meet at 'YW' Next Week to Push. . . ," *New York Amsterdam News*, October 11, 1947.
73. James Booker and Les Matthews, "Consumers Conference Hears Minority Beefs," *New York Amsterdam News*, December 14, 1963.
74. *America's Fifth Largest Negro Market*, 97.
75. D. Parke Gibson, *The $30 Billion Negro* (London: Macmillan, 1969), 31–53.
76. Fred C. Akers, "A Study of Negro and White Consumption Behavior: Automobiles, Gasoline, Tires, and Batteries" (PhD diss., University of Chicago, 1966), 67–68.
77. Ibid.
78. Morris and Doris Johnson, interview by Gretchen Sorin, September 16, 2006.
79. *The New Philadelphia Story*, 67.
80. "Hotels on the Highway: Tourist Courts Worth Millions Beckon to Negro Vacationers on U.S. Highways," *Ebony* 10, no. 8 (1955): 93.
81. Caruth and Barry, "The Black Consumer," 25.
82. See, for example, Michael L. Berger, *The Devil Wagon in God's Country: The Automobile and Social Change in Rural America, 1893–1929* (Hamden, CT: Shoe String Press, 1979); James Flink, "Three Stages of American Automobile Consciousness," *American Quarterly* 24, no. 4 (October 1972): 451–73; and John Keats, *The Insolent Chariots* (Philadelphia: J. B. Lippincott, 1958).
83. Sarah A. Seo, *Policing the Open Road: How Cars Transformed American Freedom* (Cambridge: Harvard University Press, 2019), 10.

Chapter 4: "THROUGH THE WINDSHIELD"

1. Karl Raitz, "American Roads, Roadside America," *Geographical Review* 88, no. 3 (July 1998): 364.
2. Horace Hutton, "Vacations Across the Color Line," *Saturday Review* 33 (February 25, 1950): 40.
3. James Avery, "African-American Pioneers in the Corporate Sector" (1997), http://www.black-collegian.com/african/avery.shtml, accessed April 26, 2007.
4. For example, in *Red Lines, Black Spaces* (New Haven, CT: Yale University Press, 2001), Bruce Haynes explores the development of residential segregation in the middle-class suburb of Runyon Heights in Yonkers, New York. See also geographer Mark Purcell, "Neighborhood Activism Among Home Owners as a Politics of Space," *Professional Geographer* 53 (2001): 78–194; and *Blacks and American Society* (Washington, DC: National Academy Press, 1989), 58–60.
5. In 1961, the women's division of Christian Service of the Methodist Church commissioned attorney Pauli Murray to research and write a book identifying the segregation laws in each state, to distinguish racial custom and tradition from statute. The book, *States' Laws on Race and Color,* records a dizzying array of more than seven hundred pages of regulations governing illegal conduct between black and white people in each state.
6. Dozens of books trace the history of racial segregation in housing. An excellent recent overview is Stephen Grant Meyer's *As Long as They Don't Live Next Door.* The Institute on Poverty at the University of Wisconsin developed an Index of Racial Segregation for 109 cities in the United States from 1940 to 1970. Most monographs on the history of suburbanization also include discussions of how the growth of the suburbs affected the partitioning of space along racial lines. See, for example, Kenneth Jackson, *Crabgrass Frontier: The Suburbanization of the United States* (New York: Oxford University Press, 1985); and Mary Pattillo-McCoy, *Black Picket Fences: Privilege and Peril among the Black Middle Class* (Chicago: University of Chicago Press, 1999).
7. Rothstein, *The Color of Law*, 94.
8. Colin Flint, ed., *Spaces of Hate: Geographies of Discrimination and Intolerance in the U.S.A.* (New York: Routledge, 2004), 2–3.
9. Robert R. Weyeneth, "The Architecture of Racial Segregation: The Challenges of Preserving the Problematical Past," *Public Historian* 27, no. 4 (Fall 2005): 13.
10. Fisk University sociologist Charles Johnson undertook his study of segregation in urban and rural areas in the North and the South. The

survey, supported by the Carnegie Corporation of New York, was originally undertaken by Gunnar Myrdal. Johnson, *Patterns of Negro Segregation*.

11. Johnson, *Patterns of Negro Segregation*. Schools in twenty-one states either required or permitted black and white children to be educated in separate facilities by law. Weyeneth, "The Architecture of Racial Segregation," 15. In many states, the law even separated the insane and the "feeble-minded" by race. In Texas, it was unlawful for African Americans and white Americans to face one another in the boxing ring. California (like most other states) outlawed miscegenation, fearing the eventual amalgamation of the races and a decline in the purity of the white race. Delaware authorized separate hospitals to care for "colored tubercular" patients, and Tennessee legislated the creation of separate washrooms for the workers in the state's mining industry. South Carolina mandated separate tent entrances for circus-goers, although domestic servants accompanying children to otherwise-segregated facilities were permitted to sit with their charges. Murray, ed., *States' Laws on Race and Color*, 55, 72, 408, 418, 437, 443.
12. Adolph Schalk, "Negroes, Restaurants, and Washington, D.C.," *Catholic World* (January 28, 1952): 280.
13. Murray, ed., *States' Laws on Race and Color*, 419.
14. *The American Israelite*, "No Jewish Race," March 27, 1913: 1.
15. "Allyson Hobbs, The White Student Who Integrated Ole Miss," February 2, 2014, http://www.cnn.com/2014/02/05/living/black-white-ole-miss-integration/, accessed June 27, 2014.
16. Steeplechase Films, on-camera interview with Leah Chase, Fall 2017.
17. Meredith Melnick, "Passing as Black: How Biracial Americans Choose Identity," *Time*, December 16, 2010, http://healthland.time.com/2010/12/16/passing-as-black-how-biracial-americans-choose-identity/, accessed July 11, 2013.
18. Walter White, *A Man Called White: The Autobiography of Walter White* (New York: Viking, 1948), 40–43.
19. Joe Wilder interview with Monk Rowe, October 12, 1998, Hamilton College Jazz Archive.
20. Johnny Otis, "I Pass for Negro," *Our World* (August 1953): 30–33.
21. George Schuyler, "Keeping the Negro in His Place," *American Mercury* 17 (August 1929): 470.
22. M. T. Church, *A Colored Woman in a White World* (Washington, DC: Ransdell, Inc. Publishers, 1940).
23. Joan Quigley, *Just Another Southern Town: Mary Church Terrell and the Struggle for Racial Justice in the Nation's Capital* (New York: Oxford University Press, 2016).
24. Burma-Shave signs consisted of six small signs spaced evenly along

the roadside. Each bore a few words of a poetic jingle that were read consecutively. For example, "Does your husband / Misbehave / Grunt and grumble / Rant and rave / Shoot the brute some / Burma-Shave": John A. Jakle and Keith A. Sculle, *Signs in America's Auto Age: Signatures of Landscape and Place* (Iowa City: University of Iowa Press, 2004), 41.

25. Martha Carver, "Driving the Dixie: The Development of the Dixie Highway Corridor," *SCA Journal* 13, no. 1 (Fall/Winter 1994–95): 11–13.
26. For a discussion of the history of the song "Dixie," see Howard Sacks and Judith Rose Sacks, *Way Up North in Dixie: A Black Family's Claim to the Confederate Anthem* (Washington, DC: Smithsonian Institution Press, 1993).
27. John A. Williams, *This Is My Country Too* (New York: New American Library of World Literature, 1964), 36.
28. University of Dayton School of Law/Race, Racism and the Law, "Speaking Truth to Power," http://academic.udayton.edu/race/03justice/LegalEd/Whitest/HWLS405a.htm, accessed February 13, 2008.
29. Information on the history of Greenville, Texas, can be found in Neil Foley, *The White Scourge: Mexicans, Blacks, and Poor Whites in Texas Cotton Culture* (Berkeley: University of California Press, 1998), 204, and *The Handbook of Texas Online*, http://www.tsha.utexas.edu/handbook/online/articles/GG/heg3.html, accessed June 26, 2007.
30. "P.R.R. Removes Jim Crow Signs Through Action of N.A.A.C.P.," *Pittsburgh Courier*, July 25, 1931; Ralph Matthews, "Jim Crow Sweeps Across America to Take Root in Cheyenne," *Baltimore Afro-American,* March 30, 1946; "Iowans Win Fight Against Jim Crowism," *Chicago Defender*, October 29, 1932.
31. "Tears Down 'Jim Crow' signs: Fired," *Chicago Defender*, July 3, 1926.
32. Sam Slaymaker, "For Whites Only: Harlem Still Faces Color Bar Problem," *New York Amsterdam Star-News*, June 28, 1941.
33. Ibid.
34. "Jim-Crow Signs Up and Down!" *Pittsburgh Courier*, January 21, 1956.
35. Robert Ratcliffe, "Behind the Headlines," *Pittsburgh Courier*, March 10, 1956.
36. James W. Loewen, *Sundown Towns: A Hidden Dimension of American Racism* (New York: The New Press, 2005), 65–66.
37. Ibid.
38. Ibid.
39. Tracey Maclin, "Justice Thurgood Marshall: Taking the Fourth Amendment Seriously," 77 *Cornell Law Review*, 723 (1992).

40. James W. Loewen, *Sundown Towns: A Hidden Dimension of American Racism* (New York: The New Press), 2005.
41. Patsy Sims, *The Klan* (New York: Stein and Day, 1978), 147.
42. Wayne Greenhaw, *Fighting the Devil in Dixie: How Civil Rights Activists Took on the Ku Klux Klan* (Chicago: Lawrence Hill Books, 2011), 69.
43. Sylvester Hollis, interview by Gretchen Sorin, October 19, 2007.
44. Matt Bowling, "The Ku Klux Klan Comes to Palo Alto," *Palo Alto Daily News*, December 9, 2007.
45. Sims, *The Klan*, 29.
46. In the 1940s, when the KKK's association with the German-American Bund exposed its "Americanism" as dangerous to the war effort, membership dwindled and members drifted away. Although New Jersey's governor condemned the rallies and worked to put the Klan out of business, its popular appeal obviously touched a need and a fear among some of the state's white residents, particularly before the war. The *New York Times* closely covered the activities of the Ku Klux Klan and its growth in New Jersey. See "12,000 of Klan Out at Jersey Meeting" (May 3, 1923); "To Keep Names Secret" (May 28, 1923); "Robed Riders Lead Public Klan Parade" (June 23, 1923); "They Need Watching" (August 20, 1940); "Klan Outlawed in New Jersey" (October 11, 1946).
47. Richlyn Faye Goddard, "Three Months to Hurry and Nine Months to Worry" (PhD diss., Howard University, 2001), 67–68.
48. Spencer Crew, interview by Ric Burns, January 4, 2016.
49. Vernell Allen, interview by Gretchen Sorin, June 17, 2006.
50. Patricia Turner, "Ambivalent Patrons: The Role of Rumor and Contemporary Legends in African American Consumer Decisions," *Journal of American Folklore* 105 (Autumn 1992): 424–41.
51. For a history of advertising in the United States, see especially Juliann Sivulka, *Soap, Sex, and Cigarettes: A Cultural History of American Advertising* (Belmont, CA: Wadsworth Publishing, 1998).
52. A variety of articles in the popular media argued that if African Americans were admitted to white establishments or were used in advertising, whites would be discouraged from using the products or services. A questionnaire mailed to resorts across the country noted that responses "very often" included a notation that "I don't mind personally, but if we accepted Negro guests it would have an unfavorable reaction on our business." See, for example, "Vacations Across the Color Line," *Saturday Review* (1950): 40–41.
53. For images of dozens of stereotypes of black children, see the Jim Crow Museum of Racist Memorabilia at Ferris State University, http://www.ferris.edu/htmls/news/jimcrow/picaninny/more/homepage.htm,

accessed February 17, 2008. The mission of the museum, founded in 1996, is "to use objects of intolerance to teach tolerance and promote social justice."

54. Victor Green, *The Negro Motorist Green Book* (New York: Victor Green, Inc., 1953), 2; Victor Green, *The Negro Motorist Green Book* (New York: Victor Green, Inc., 1949), 3–4; Victor Green, *The Negro Motorist Green Book* (New York: Victor Green, Inc., 1947), 10–12.
55. Morris Johnson, interview by Gretchen Sorin, September 16, 2006.
56. Edgar A. Steele, *The National Negro Market* (New York: Interstate United Newspapers, 1947), n.p.
57. David J. Sullivan, "Don't Do This—If You Want to Sell Your Products to Negroes!" *Sales Management* 52, no. 1 (March 1943): 50.
58. A descendant of the restaurant's founder wrote the history of the Coon Chicken Inn for Ferris State University's online Jim Crow Museum of Racist Memorabilia: http://www.ferris.edu/jimcrow/links/chicken/, accessed on June 25, 2007.
59. "There Is No Race Problem for the 'Old Black Mammy' as Long as They Act This Way," *Pittsburgh Courier*, September 19, 1931.
60. Lillie S. Lustig, S. Claire Sondheim, and Sarah Rensel, *The Southern Cook Book of Fine Old Recipes* (Reading, PA: Cuneo Press, 1935), 5.
61. Tony Horwitz, "The Mammy Washington Almost Had," *The Atlantic*, May 21, 2013; "Proposed Mammy Monument Raises Much Commotion," *New Journal and Guide*, March 10, 1923; "A Monument to the Mammies," *The Afro-American*, March 30, 1923.
62. David J. Sullivan, "Don't Do This."

Chapter 5: DRIVING WHILE BLACK

1. This quotation appears in an open letter to President Lyndon Johnson, titled "See America First, If You Dare," that appeared in *Look* magazine in 1968.
2. Speech given by Martin Luther King Jr. on December 18, 1963, on the campus of Western Michigan University, Kalamazoo, Michigan.
3. James Mackin, "The Man on the Bus," unpublished manuscript, 2018, p. 24.
4. Valerie Cunningham, interview by Gretchen Sorin, August 19, 2006.
5. Walter Edwards, interview by Ric Burns, Steeplechase Films, July 2016.
6. Spencer Crew, interview by Gretchen Sorin, September 19, 2006.
7. Mahalia Jackson, *Movin' On Up* (New York: Hawthorne Books, 1966), 97.
8. Esther Balderston Jones, "Where Should a Negro Get Hurt?" Christian Century 49 (July 20, 1932): 907–8.

9. "Auto Tie-up Began 1943 Detroit Riot: Rumors Followed a Fracas and Led to 34 Dead," *New York Times* (1923–current file) (New York), July 25, 1967.
10. Turner Catledge, "Detroit Watchful in 'Mop Up' of Riots: Quiet Continues as the Courts. . . ." Special to *The New York Times*, June 28, 1943.
11. "Detroit Riot Killing Charged to 4 Youths: Three Said to Confess Shooting Negro," Special to *The New York Times*, July 31, 1943.
12. Adam Nossiter, "Murder, Memory and the Klan: Special Report: Widow Inherits a Confession," *New York Times*, September 4, 1993.
13. Thirteen/WNET New York, "The Rise and Fall of Jim Crow," Eyewitness to Jim Crow, Joseph Holloway Remembers, http://www.jimcrowhistory.org/resources/narratives/Joe_Holloway.htm, accessed September 23, 2007.
14. Ernest Dunbar, "Memo to LBJ: See America First . . . If You Can," *Look* (April 16, 1968), 48.
15. Thirteen/WNET New York, "The Rise and Fall of Jim Crow," Willie Wallace interview, http://www.jimcrowhistory.org/resources/narratives/Willie_Wallace.htm, accessed February 17, 2008.
16. James "Mudcat" Grant, interview by Gretchen Sorin, July 30, 2006.
17. Danny Earl Clay, interview by Gretchen Sorin, July 12, 2012.
18. White, *A Man Called White*, 134–38.
19. Ibid.
20. Alfred Maund, *The Meaning of Segregation in Hospitals* (New Orleans: Southern Conference Educational Fund, 1956), n.p.
21. Mitchell F. Rice and Woodrow Jones Jr., *Public Policy and the Black Hospital: From Slavery to Segregation to Integration* (Westport, CT: Greenwood Press, 1994), 31.
22. "Clark Athlete Killed, 6 Hurt in Accident: Mishap Occurs on Highway near Pelham, Tenn.," *Atlanta Daily World*, April 27, 1947; "Barred from Hospitals!: White Institutions Refuse Dying Athlete," *Pittsburgh Courier*, May 3, 1947.
23. Ibid., 27.
24. Paul B. Cornely, "Trends in Racial Integration in Hospitals in the United States," *Journal of the National Medical Association* 49, no. 1 (January 1957): 8–10.
25. Rice and Jones, 95.
26. The Kellogg African American Health Care Project of the University of Michigan Medical School is an online resource that documents black hospitals and black health care in Michigan. The oral histories describe conditions in the hospitals and the discrimination faced by the physicians and the hospital staff. The site also includes photographs, primary documents, and hospital plans: http://www.med

.umich.edu/haahc/aboutpro.htm, accessed January 2, 2009; Booker T. Washington Community Hospital Association, *The Community Hospital: A Brief History* (Newark, NJ: Board of Trustees of the Community Hospital, 1939), 5; "Another Angle to Color Prejudice," *Atlanta Daily World*, June 15, 1949; Russell F. Minton, MD, "The Hospital as a Humanitarian Institution: With Special Reference to the Negro Hospital," *Journal of the National Medical Association* 39, no. 2 (March 1947): 72–73.

27. A controversial piece of legislation slowed the progress of hospital integration. In 1945, to address a general need for more hospitals, and with urging from the American Hospital Association, two senators—progressive Democrat Lister Hill of Alabama and Ohioan Harold Burton—introduced the Hill–Burton Act—or just Hill–Burton, as it came to be known. Designed to investigate, plan, and fund the development of public hospitals all over the United States, and in some cases to provide medical care for the neediest patients, Hill–Burton offered the promise of a revolution in health-care delivery. However, shepherding the bill through Congress could only be accomplished with an odious compromise. The southern states insisted that the Supreme Court's "separate but equal" provision—the provision that in 1896 became the landmark Supreme Court case *Plessy v. Ferguson*—be enforced in the planning and construction of all new public hospitals. This compromise placed the federal government in the position of legally authorizing segregation—the only time in the twentieth century that federal legislation specifically sanctioned the practice. By 1968, Hill–Burton supported the development of 9,200 health-care facilities.
28. Danny Earl Clay, interview by Gretchen Sorin, July 12, 2012; Rice and Jones, 32, 110.
29. *Historical Sketch of the Community Hospital* (Newark, NJ: Board of Trustees of the Community Hospital, June 1939), 5.
30. Jones, "Where Should a Negro Get Hurt?," 907.
31. Herbert Aptheker, comp. and ed., *Writings in Periodicals Edited by W. E. B. DuBois: Selections from The Crisis*, vol. 2, 1926–1934 (Millwood, NY: Kraus-Thomson Organization, 1983); 649–53; W. E. B. Du Bois, "Dalton, Georgia," *The Crisis* (1932), 85–87.
32. "Refused First Aid by Hospital Officials and Georgia Town," *Pittsburgh Courier*, November 14, 1931; "Juliette Derricotte, Dean of Women at Fisk University, Former Student, YW Secretary, Killed in Accident," *New York Age* 14 (November 1931).
33. Kenneth Jackson, interview by Gretchen Sorin, July 21, 2006.
34. Jones, "Where Should a Negro Get Hurt?," 907–8.
35. Ibid.

36. Spencie Love, *One Blood: The Death and Resurrection of Charles R. Drew* (Chapel Hill: University of North Carolina Press, 1996), 32–58.
37. Ibid., 218–22.
38. Johnson, *Patterns of Negro Segregation*, 124.
39. "Courtesy En Route," *Atlantic Monthly* 161 (1938): 699.
40. Green, *The Negro Motorist Green Book* (1947), 80.
41. Johnson, *Patterns of Negro Segregation*, 125.
42. Emily Post, *Emily Post's Motor Manners: The Bluebooklet of Traffic Etiquette* (Silver Spring, MD: National Highway Users Conference, 1949), 19–20.
43. Johnson, *Patterns of Negro Segregation*, 272.
44. Williams, *This Is My Country Too*, 55.
45. James Timothy "Mudcat" Grant, interview by Gretchen Sorin, July 30, 2006.
46. *Pittsburgh Courier*, "Safety Council Lists Summer Motoring Tips," July 23, 1955; *New York Amsterdam News*, "Safe Driving Tips for Night and Twilight," October 26, 1963; *New York Amsterdam News*, "Vacation Driving Tips," June 13, 1964.
47. "Defender Vows to Fight Until Lynch Evil Dies: Four Negroes Murdered by Georgia Mob; Horror Sweeps Nation; Victims of Southern Insanity," *Chicago Defender*, August 3, 1946; "Athens U. S. Grand Jury Hears F.B.I. Testimony: 2 Negroes Among 21 Member Panel Study Evidence; Judge Calls On Jury to Determine What Laws Violated," *Atlanta Daily World*, December 4, 1946; Matt Stevens, "Secrets of 1946 Mass Lynching Could Be Revealed After Court Ruling, *New York Times*, February 12, 2019; DeNeen L. Brown, "Appeals Court Orders Grand Jury Testimony Unsealed in the 1946 Case of the 'Last Mass Lynching in America,'" *Washington Post*, February 12, 2019.

Chapter 6: TRAVEL GUIDES FOR EVERYONE

1. George S. Schuyler, "Views and Reviews," *Pittsburgh Courier*, 1956.
2. George S. Schuyler, "Jim Crow in the North," *American Mercury* 68 (June 1949), 663.
3. For a discussion of rape used as a justification for lynching, see Jacqueline Jones Royster, *Southern Horrors and Other Writings: The Anti-Lynching Campaign of Ida B. Wells, 1892–1900*, Bedford Series in History and Culture (Boston: Bedford Books, 1997); Jan Nederveen Pieterse provides a discussion of the stereotype of the black male as sexual predator in *White on Black: Images of Africa and Blacks in Western Popular Culture* (New Haven, CT: Yale University Press, 1992). Dora Apel uses the imagery of lynching and stories

about lynching in her book *Imagery of Lynching: Black Men, White Women, and the Mob* (New Brunswick, NJ: Rutgers University Press, 2004) to discuss how black men were dehumanized and demonized within American culture to keep them powerless and under control; Jan Gordon and Cora J. Gordon, *On Wandering Wheels: Through Roadside Camps from Maine to Georgia in an Old Sedan Car* (New York: Dodd, Mead, 1928), 56–65, 261–65, 273.

4. Claudia Cranston. "Travel Books for Everybody: The Travel-Loving American Public Has Climbed Out of the Depression," *Publishers Weekly* 129 (January 1936), 113.
5. In the 1930s and afterward, the *New York Times* regularly reviewed the large number of travel books, and some of its feature articles discussed domestic travel by car and train, such as Diana Rice's "Random Notes for Travelers: Series of Auto Tours of This Area Arranged for Visitors," *New York Times* (1857–current file), August 21, 1938, http://www.proquest.com/, accessed November 26, 2008. Articles and reviews of other books transported readers to more exotic places, such as Katherine Woods, "In the South Sea Islands Known as 'Dark.'" Also: John W. Vandercook, *Voyaging in Fiji, New Guinea and The Solomons* (New York: Harper & Brothers), *New York Times* (1857–current file), November 7, 1937, http://www.proquest.com/, accessed November 26, 2008.
6. Katherine Woods, "All Aboard That's Going Abroad: Nine New Books of Travel That Will Take You to England and the Continent, Persia, Yugoslavia and the Caribbean," *New York Times* (1857–current file), October 4, 1936, http://www.proquest.com, accessed November 26, 2008.
7. Ibid.
8. Ibid.
9. Schuyler, "Jim Crow in the North," 665.
10. Many brochures depict African Americans only as porters, bellhops, maids, or chauffeurs. For example, a 1940 ad for the Plymouth automobile touting a "luxury ride" shows a well-dressed white family arriving at a hotel with their vacation bags being carried by a black bellhop who is greatly impressed with their car. A brochure for the Gilbert Hotels depicted a red-suited Sambo caricature in a bellhop uniform smiling broadly with swollen pink lips to demonstrate the type of obsequious service the establishment provided. A variety of images of travel, hotel, and restaurant brochures that include African Americans may be found in the John Margolies collection, accessed at http://www.johnmargolies.com/.
11. In addition to inspiring domestic tourists, the United States Travel Bureau sought to attract foreign travelers to visit. The agency began

operating in 1937, suspended operations from 1942 to 1947 because of severe restrictions on travel resulting from World War II, and then resumed operations briefly. *Travel USA*, a slick magazine designed primarily for travel agents and distributed free of charge, was published from 1948 to 1949. The magazine included brief articles encouraging travel to "Colorful Colorado" or extolling the virtues of Colonial Williamsburg. Articles offered recommendations on how to gauge the weather before a trip and described the construction of new or rehabilitated highways.

12. Elizabeth T. Platt, "Portrait of America: Guidebooks and Related Works," *Geographical Review* 29, no. 4 (October 1939), 659.
13. Christine Bold, *The WPA Guide: Mapping America* (Jackson: University Press of Mississippi, 1999), 3–18.
14. Ibid.
15. Federal Writers' Project of the Works Progress Administration for the State of New Jersey, *The WPA Guide to 1930s New Jersey* (New Brunswick, NJ: Rutgers University Press, 1986), 637.
16. Ibid., 192.
17. Ibid., 193.
18. Ellison, one of the most important writers of the twentieth century, wrote *Invisible Man* in 1953. Zora Neale Hurston, an outstanding writer and anthropologist associated with the Harlem Renaissance, wrote *Their Eyes Were Watching God* in 1937. Jamaican writer and poet Claude McKay was the author of *Home to Harlem*.
19. Federal Writers' Project of the Works Progress Administration for the State of Florida, *Florida: A Guide to the Southernmost State*, American Guide Series (New York: Oxford University Press, 1944), 128, 132, 146.
20. Federal Writers' Project, *New York Panorama: A Companion to the WPA Guide to New York City: A Comprehensive View of the Metropolis, Presented in a Series of Articles* (New York: Random House, 1938), 151; *New York City Guide: A Comprehensive Guide to the Five Boroughs of the Metropolis* (New York: Random House, 1939).
21. Lucia Giddens, "The Happy-Go-Lucky Harlem of the South," *Travel* 53 (July 1929): 40–41.
22. *North Carolina, the Tar Heel State* (Raleigh, North Carolina, Department of Conservation and Development, ca. 1950).
23. *Southeastern Travel Guide* (Automobile Association of New York, 1937), 161.
24. *Southeastern Travel Guide*, 164.
25. Victor Green, *The Negro Motorist Green Book* (New York: Victor H. Green and Company, 1937).

26. A wide variety of guidebooks were published between 1930 and the 1960s to meet the growing number of middle-class African American tourists and business executives. Guides specifically for black travelers included *Hackley & Harrison's Hotel and Apartment Guide for Colored Travelers* (1930–31); *The Negro Motorist Green Book* and *The Negro Travelers' Green Book* (1936–1966); *Smith's Tourist Guide of Necessary Information for Businessman, Tourist, Traveler and Vacationist* (1940); *The Negro Travel Guide* (which was unusual because of its large celebrity photographs and a focus on African American nightclubs and performance spaces) (1948); *The Go Guide to Pleasant Motoring* (1952–1959); *The Bronze American* (unknown dates); *Travelguide* (1947–1963); *Nationwide Hotel Association Directory and Guide to Travel* (1959). The dates listed indicate extant copies located during the course of this research project, but additional issues may originally have been published. A travel guide specifically for Pullman porters and other African American train workers was published in Chicago in the 1940s. The first volume of *The Negro Traveler* was issued in December 1944 (1944–1950?). Other guides, such as *Grayson's Travel and Business Guide* (ca. 1937), were advertised in newspapers and magazines, but no extant copies could be found. Travel sections in popular magazines such as *Ebony* and newspapers such as the *Baltimore Afro-American* also provided details on places to stay and recommended hospitable destinations. The *Baltimore Afro-American* issued the *Afro-American Travel Map* in 1942.
27. Victor Green, *The Negro Travelers' Green Book* (New York: Victor Green and Company, 1959), 2.
28. Smith, "Through the Windshield," *Opportunity* (1933), 143.
29. W. E. B. Du Bois, Letter from W. E. B. Du Bois to The Negro Welfare Council of New London, January 30, 1929, University of Massachusetts, Amherst; Sarah D. Harrison, *The Travelers Guide* (Philadelphia: Hackley & Harrison Publishing Company, 1931), 5.
30. Clay Williams, "The Guide for Colored Travelers: A Reflection of the Urban League," *Journal of American Culture* 24 (Fall/Winter 2001), 3–4.
31. Harrison, *The Travelers Guide* (1931), 5.
32. African American travel guides included myriad appeals to the black middle class, from images of black golfers to the logo used by Victor Green on his letterhead of a suburban couple heading off on vacation. This image also appears on the cover of *The Negro Motorist Green Book*, 1948 edition.
33. Harrison, *The Travelers Guide* (1931), 1.
34. Victor Green, *The Negro Motorist Green Book* (1949), 3.

35. Jesse L. Smith, *Smith's Tourist Guide of Necessary Information for Businessman, Tourist, Traveler and Vacationist* (Media, PA: Smith's Touring Club, 1940), 3.
36. *Travelguide* (1947), 3.
37. The masthead lists 1936 as the publication's start date, but 1937 is the correct date of publication. Another African American travel guide, *Grayson's Guide*, also appeared that year.
38. Henry Johnson, interview by Gretchen Sorin, April 1, 2006.
39. "Grayson's Travel Guide Off Press," *Pittsburgh Courier*, December 1937; "Bronze American National Travel Guide," *Chicago Defender*, June 10, 1961.
40. "Hotels Pledge Better Service," *Atlanta Daily World*, September 21, 1954.
41. *Go Guide to Pleasant Motoring* (Washington, DC: Nationwide Hotel Association, 1955).
42. *NHA Directory and Guide to Travel* (Newark, NJ: Nationwide Hotel Association, Inc., 1959), 7, 21–25.
43. "Travelguide," *Color* (April 1948), 15.
44. "Travelguide Inc. founded in 1946 is now 10," *The Crisis* (October 1955), 462.
45. Leslie A. Nash Jr. "Ten Year Milestone for Travelers," *The Crisis* (October 1955), 462.
46. Ibid.
47. "Philippa Duke Schuyler," W. H. Butler, *Travelguide* (New York: Travelguide, Inc., 1947), 52; Kathryn Talalay, "Philippa Duke Schuyler, Pianist/Composer/Writer," *The Black Perspective in Music* 10, no. 1 (Spring 1982), 43–68.
48. *The Negro Motorist Green Book* (1949), 12.
49. Marguerite Shaffer, *See America First: Tourism and National Identity, 1880–1940* (Washington, DC: Smithsonian Institution Press, 2001), 169–220.

Chapter 7: VICTOR AND ALMA GREEN'S *THE NEGRO MOTORIST GREEN BOOK*

1. Earl Hutchinson Sr., *A Colored Man's Journey Through 20th Century Segregated America* (Los Angeles, CA: Middle Passage Press, ca. 2000), 86–87.
2. "Green Book Points Way to Travellers," *New York Amsterdam News* 19 (1954), 46.
3. Victor Green, *The Negro Motorist Green Book* (New York: Victor Green, Inc., 1939), 2.
4. Hutchinson, 86–87.

5. For example, the 1959 edition of *The Negro Traveler's Green Book* listed seven tourist accommodations in the state of Maine: Mrs. Joseph McLean Tourist Home in Augusta; Bangor House in Bangor; Marigold Motel in Dixfield; Pond View Tourist Home in Gardiner; Mrs. R. Cummings Tourist Home in Old Orchard; Thomas House Tourist Home in Portland; and Brooks' Bluff Cottages in Robbinston. *Travelguide* for 1957 included many of these establishments and quite a few YMCAs across the state.
6. Diary of Hazel Sinclair, transcribed by Gretchen Sorin, Rock Rest Collection, University of New Hampshire.
7. "274 Race Hotels Listed in Federal Census Survey," *New Journal and Guide*, July 23, 1938, 3.
8. Victor Green, *The Negro Motorist Green Book* (New York: Victor Green and Co., 1948), 3–4.
9. Victor H. Green, *The Negro Travelers' Green Book*, Airline Edition (New York: Victor Green, and Co., 1953), 13, 48.
10. Victor Hugo Green was born in New York on November 9, 1892, to William and Alice Green. Census records describe William and Alice as black, but Victor, his sister Helen, and older brother William Jr., perhaps because of their fair skin, were listed as mulattoes. After publishing *The Negro Motorist Green Book* for twenty-four years, Victor Green died in New York's Veterans' Hospital in 1960 at the age of sixty-seven. Information on Victor Green was drawn from the Federal Census of Population for 1900, 1920, and 1930; World War I Draft Registration Card, 1917–1918, Bergen County, New Jersey, roll 1711908, Draft Board 2; "Services Held Victor Green," *New York Amsterdam News*, October 22, 1960. See also Linda Steuerwald and Barbara Iozzia, *The City of Hackensack: Three Centuries of Prosperity*, 1693–1993 (Hackensack, NJ: City of Hackensack, 1994).
11. *National Women's Business Council, Policy and Progress: Supporting the Growth of Women's Business Enterprise*, Report Prepared for National Business Council (Washington, DC, May 2004), 6–7.
12. As part of *The Green Book*'s silver anniversary, an article titled "Janus," by Novera Dashiell, in the 1961 edition described the progress and history of the publication and its staff. In Greek mythology, Janus was the Roman god of gateways and doors. Dashiell noted that *The Green Book* was no longer confined to "the American Negro traveler" but had opened new doorways to foreign countries. Victor Green, *The Travelers' Green Book* (New York: Victor Green and Company, 1961), 4–6.
13. "Dr. Wise Tells Why He Won't Go to Lake Mohonk," *American*

Hebrew and Jewish Messenger, May 26, 1911, 94; "Editorial Article 5"—No Title, The American Israelite, June 1, 1911: 4.

14. In addition to discriminating against "Hebrews," many of the establishments in the Adirondack Mountains also discriminated against tuberculosis patients. Ironically, the Adirondack region of New York State was the first and one of the largest regions in the nation for tuberculosis treatment from the late nineteenth century to the 1940s. For a history of TB in the Adirondacks, see Sheila M. Rothman, *Living in the Shadow of Death: Tuberculosis and the Social Experience of Illness in American History* (New York: Basic Books, 1994).
15. The Adirondack Museum Library, Manuscript Collection: Resort Brochures.
16. Letter to the Editor, *New York Times*, December 24, 1952.
17. Joshua Bendon, "A Jewish Baedeker to America," *Jewish Advocate*, July 24, 1931, 2.
18. Organized Kashruth Laboratories, *Kosher Food Guide*, vol. 6, no. 1 (New York: Kosher Food Guide Publishers, Inc., 1940).
19. There are no extant records of the United States Travel Bureau within the collections of the National Park Service, but the *Travel USA Bulletin* (1948) and *Travel USA* (1949) are held in the Kelvin Smith Library at Case Western Reserve University. The bulletins are published online at http://library.case.edu/ksl/govdocs/travel/about.html.
20. Mia Bay, *The White Image in the Black Mind: African American Ideas about White People, 1830–1925* (New York: Oxford University Press, 2000), 152.
21. *The Negro Motorist Green Book: An International Travel Guide* (New York: Victor Green & Co., 1951), 1.
22. *The Travelers' Green Book* (New York: Victor Green & Co., 1961), 4.
23. Henry Louis Gates Jr., *The Signifying Monkey: A Theory of African-American Literary Criticism* (New York: Oxford University Press 1988), 180.
24. Sullivan, "Don't Do This—If You Want to Sell Your Products to Negroes!" 48.
25. Robert E. Weems Jr., *Desegregating the Dollar* (New York: New York University Press, 1998), 32–34. Federal Census, 1940, http://www.census.gov/population/documentation/twps0056/tabA-10.pdf, accessed October 6, 2007.
26. "Not only Happy Motoring But Happy Travelling by any method is obtainable through Green Book Routing Say the ESSO Special Representatives," *The Negro Motorist Green Book* (New York: Victor Green and Company, 1947), 10.
27. Ibid., 4.

28. *Cleveland Call and Post*, April 13, 1946.
29. *The Negro Motorist Green Book* (1947), 10; *Pittsburgh Courier*, June 9, 1962; *New York Amsterdam News*, June 19, 1954.
30. *The Green Book: Guide for Travel and Vacations* (New York: Victor Green and Co., 1962). The guide's recommended list of museums included the American Museum of Natural History, the American Numismatic Society, the Brooklyn Museum, the Cloisters, the Frick Collection, the Metropolitan Museum of Art, the Museum of the American Indian, the Museum of the City of New York, the Museum of Modern Art, the New-York Historical Society, the Guggenheim Museum, the Spanish Museum, and the Whitney Museum.
31. A. Scott Berg, *Wilson* (New York: G. P. Putnam's Sons, 2013), 303.
32. "In the Face of 'Jim Crow': Prosperous Blacks and Vacations, Travel and Outdoor Leisure, 1890–1945," *Journal of Negro History* 84, no. 2 (1999), 144.
33. The American Automobile Association was founded in 1902 in response to the need for roads and services suitable for the newest mode of transportation—the automobile. They produced a travel guide with a green cover called the *Highways Green Book*—a guide that failed to provide for the needs of African American travelers. Victor Green obviously knew of this book when he named his guide, perhaps tongue in cheek, *The Negro Motorist Green Book*.
34. For a history of golf, African Americans, and civil rights, see George B. Kirsch, "Municipal Golf and Civil Rights in the United States, 1910–1965," *Journal of African American History* 92, no. 3 (2007), 371–91; James Watson, "A Course of Their Own: A History of African American Golfers," *Journal of Sport History* 32, no. 1 (2005), 110–11; Gretchen Cassel Eick, "Fair Ways: How Six Black Golfers Won Civil Rights in Beaumont, Texas," *Journal of Southern History* 73, no. 1 (2007), 227–28; Marvin P. Dawkins, "Race Relations and the Sport of Golf: The African American Golf Legacy," *Western Journal of Black Studies* 28, no. 1 (2004), 327–31.
35. *The Negro Motorist Green Book* (New York: Victor Green, Inc., 1937), n.p.
36. *The Negro Motorist Green Book* (New York: Victor Green, Inc., 1947), 13–25.
37. Chapter 3 discusses the white American vision of southern hospitality. The sexless black mammy in head wrap and slave dress appeared in advertisements, on souvenirs, and restaurant menus, designed to symbolize good cooking and servility.
38. "Louisville, Kentucky," *The Negro Travelers' Green Book* (New York: Victor Green and Co., 1949), 24–29, 74; "What to See in Chi-

cago," *The Negro Motorist Green Book* (New York: Victor Green and Co., 1949), 19–25.

39. Ibid.
40. *The Negro Motorist Green Book* (New York: Victor Green and Co., 1937), n.p.
41. *The Travelers' Green Book: Guide for Travel and Vacations* (New York: Victor Green and Co., 1961), 84.
42. *The Negro Travelers' Green Book* (New York: Victor Green and Co., 1960), 25, 26, 92, 113.
43. This information is based on the 1949 *Green Book*, but other editions include similar listings for each state.
44. "Services Held Victor Green," *New York Amsterdam News*, October 22, 1960.
45. "Wanted, Representatives for the Green Book," *The Negro Motorist Green Book* (New York: Victor Green, Inc., 1939), 29; *Newsweek*, May 20, 1963, 96; Angela Stewart, former archivist, the Piney Woods School, interview by Gretchen Sorin, August 23, 2007.
46. For information on the history of the Piney Woods School and the Cotton Blossom Singers, see Leslie Harper Purcell, *Miracle in Mississippi: Laurence C. Jones of Piney Woods* (New York: Carlton Press, 1956); Alferdteen B. Harrison, *Piney Woods School: An Oral History* (Jackson: University Press of Mississippi, 1982); Beth Day, *The Little Professor of Piney Woods* (New York: Julian Messner, 1955).
47. Victor Green, *The Negro Motorist Green Book, An International Travel Guide* (New York: Victor H. Green & Co., 1949), 7.
48. Victor Green, *The Negro Motorist Green Book* (New York: Victor Green, Inc., 1947), 2–3.
49. The number of black YMCAs listed in the *Green Books* declines steadily in the 1960s. In 1967, the National YMCA officially banned segregation in the organization. The University of Minnesota Library, which houses the Kautz Archives on the history of the Black YMCA, includes an online timeline of the Black YMCA that can be accessed at http://special.lib.umn.edu/ymca/guides/afam/afam-milestones.phtml.
50. Nina Mjagkij, *Light in the Darkness: African Americans and the YMCA, 1852–1946* (Lexington: University of Kentucky Press, 2003), 3–7; Arthur George, "The Young Men's Christian Association Among Negroes," *Opportunity* (1923), 16–18.
51. "Air Transportation," *The Negro Travelers' Green Book, Airline Edition* (New York: Victor Green and Co., 1953), 2–7.
52. NAACP Papers, Letter by District Attorney Charles P. Sullivan of Queens County, n.d.; Memorandum to Legal Staff from Jack Greenberg Re: American Airlines, September 26, 1951; American Jewish

Congress, Memorandum from Leo Pfeffer to Community Relations Councils and Group Relations Agencies, October 8, 1951.

53. "The Project Fun," *Green Book Guide for Travel and Vacations* (New York: Victor Green, Inc., 1962), 4–5.
54. Dunbar, "Memo to LBJ."
55. Such generic "African clothing" became popular when a group of young entrepreneurs in Harlem started a company to create dashikis, capes, pants, and dresses in fabrics that ranged from faux African furs to plaids and real kente cloth from Ghana. Ann Geracimos, "About Dashikis and the New Breed Cat," *New York Times*, April 20, 1969, http://www.proquest.com.ezproxy.oneonta.edu:2048/, accessed March 28, 2009.
56. Victor H. Green, *The International Travelers' Green Book* (New York: Victor Green, Inc., 1965–66), 2–3.
57. Victor Green, *The Travelers' Green Book* (New York: Victor H. Green & Co., 1961), 4.
58. Victor Green, *The International Travelers' Green Book* (New York: Victor Green and Co., 1966), 2–4.

Chapter 8: "WHERE WILL YOU STAY TONIGHT?"

1. *New York Amsterdam News*, July 20, 1946, 23; *Atlanta Daily World*, June 11, 1950, 6.
2. Victor Green, *The Negro Travelers' Green Book* (1952), 4.
3. David Remnick, *King of the World: Muhammad Ali and the Rise of an American Hero* (New York: Random House, 1998), 86–87.
4. *Hill's Fayetteville (Cumberland County) City Directory*, 1941, 1946 (Hill Directory Company, Richmond, VA), https://archive.org/details/hillsfayettevill46hill, accessed July 9, 2018.
5. Paige Williams, "Letter from Nashville: The Spice Trade," *New Yorker*, February 4, 2019, 25.
6. *The Negro Motorist Green Book* and other travel guides indicate that most of the places for African Americans to stay were tourist homes and guesthouses.
7. "By the Roadside: Barred from Hotels, Vacationists Sleep on the Roadside," *Pittsburgh Courier*, August 23, 1941: 13.
8. M. Scopilliti and M. O'Connell, "Roomers and Boarders: 1880–2005." Working paper, 2008, US Census Bureau, Washington, DC, http://www.census.gov/population/www/documentation/paa2008/Scopilliti-OConnell-PAA-2008.pdf, accessed June 29, 2018.
9. Ibid.
10. Eric Lacitis of the *Seattle Times*, interview by Gretchen Sorin, 2019.

11. H. A. Manning Company, *Manning's Portsmouth, Greenland, New Castle, Rye, Durham (New Hampshire) Kittery (Maine) Directory*, 1939–1980; Valerie Cunningham, interview by Gretchen Sorin, 2006.
12. Ibid.
13. Summer Guest Book, Sinclair's, Kittery Point, Maine, 1957–1976, Rock Rest Collection, University of New Hampshire.
14. Valerie Cunningham, interview by Gretchen Sorin, 2006; W. Jeffrey Bolster, ed., *Cross-Grained & Wily Waters: A Guide to the Piscataqua Maritime Region* (Portsmouth, NH: Peter E. Randall Publisher, 2002), 185–86.
15. Saunders Redding, *No Day of Triumph* (New York: Harper and Row, 1942), 96.
16. Ibid., 97.
17. "Cleveland's New Majestic Hotel," *Negro Traveler* (July/August 1948), 8.
18. "Gather for Ball Confab," *New York Amsterdam News*, January 20, 1932: 13; "Cleveland Host to Baseball Meet," *The Chicago Defender*, January 23, 1932; Jeannetta Freeman, "Majestic Hotel Joins America's Top Negro Social Centers," *Cleveland Call and Post*, April 27, 1946.
19. "Majestic's Rose Room to Have Gala Opening," *Cleveland Call and Post*, August 26, 1950.
20. "Majestic's Dances Rate High," *Cleveland Call and Post*, June 7, 1952; "Rose Room's Monday Morn Jump Goes Big," *Cleveland Call and Post*, May 10, 1952; Joe Mosbrook, "Jazzed in Cleveland," *A Jazz History*—a special WMV Web News Cleveland series, Part 61, Blue Monday Parties, http://www.cleveland.oh.us/wmv_news/jazz61.htm, accessed August 2, 2018.
21. *Green Book Guide for Travel and Vacations* (1962), 26.
22. The African American experience of segregation on Miami Beach is documented in a series of online oral histories, http://miamibeachvisualmemoirs.com/blacks-on-miami-beach/ (accessed June 14, 2019). See also "From An Editor's Note Book," *New Journal and Guide*, February 15, 1941: 11; "Satchmo 'First' for Fountainebleau: 1st Big-Name Band to Play Miami Club," *Pittsburgh Courier*, December 15, 1956: A20; "Ink Spots Buck Segregation and Win: Fla. Experiment In Tolerance Scores," *New Journal and Guide*, January 1, 1949: 14.
23. Jerry Markowitz, interview by Gretchen Sorin, 2018.
24. Ibid.
25. Enid Pinkney interview by Kathy Hersh, Close-Up Productions, November 19, 2011, http://dpanther.fiu.edu/sobek/content/FI/14/01/04/49/00001/FI14010449_t_revised%202016.pdf, accessed July 10, 2018.

26. "Order Police Card System to Protect Winter Colony," *Milwaukee Journal*, November 5, 1936; Loewen, *Sundown Towns*, 284.
27. Sondra K. Wilson, *Meet Me at the Theresa: The Story of Harlem's Most Famous Hotel* (New York: Atria Books, 2004); "Adam Powell Raps Castro's Stay in Harlem," *Daily Defender*, September 26, 1960.
28. "U.N. Has Headache, But It's Publicity for Harlem Hotel," *Atlanta Daily World*, September 21, 1960; Max Frankel, "Castro Can't Find Lodging Here; One Hotel Cancels Reservation," *New York Times*, September 16, 1960.
29. James Booker, "Castro Talks: Bars White Press; He Calls Himself 'African American,'" *New York Amsterdam News*, September 24, 1960.
30. James L. Hicks, "Our Achilles Heel," *New York Amsterdam News*, September 24, 1960.
31. Ibid.
32. Andrew S. Dolkart and Gretchen S. Sorin, *Touring Historic Harlem: Four Walks in Northern Manhattan* (New York: New York Landmarks Conservancy, 1997), 125.
33. Minutes of the Central Committee of the Alabama Christian Movement for Human Rights and the Southern Christian Leadership Conference, 1963, Birmingham Civil Rights Institute Archives.
34. Carol Jenkins and Elizabeth Gardner Hines, *Black Titan: A. G. Gaston and the Making of a Black American Millionaire* (New York: One World, 2004); Robert Gordon, "Mother's Day in Birmingham, Alabama," *Chicago Daily Defender*, May 13, 1963; "Bombs Upset Racial Peace in Birmingham," *Chicago Defender* (national edition). *U.S. News and World Report* photographers documented the damage caused by the bombing of the Gaston Motel: Library of Congress, Prints and Photographs Division, "The Civil Rights Era in the U.S. News & World Report Photographs Collection," http://www.loc.gov/rr/print/list/084_civil.html, accessed November 15, 2008.
35. "Sitting on Racial Powder Keg," *Baltimore Afro-American*, September 14, 1963.
36. For information on Georgia Gilmore, see The Kitchen Sisters and Jamie York, "The Club From Nowhere: Cooking for Civil Rights," NPR, December 1, 2004, http://www.npr.org/templates/story/story.php?storyId=4509998, accessed September 5, 2008; Interview with Georgia Gilmore, conducted by Blackside, Inc., on February 17, 1986, for *Eyes on the Prize: America's Civil Rights Years (1954–1965)*, Washington University [St. Louis] Libraries, Film and Media Archive, Henry Hampton Collection.
37. Frederick Douglass Opie, *Southern Food and Civil Rights* (Charleston, SC: American Palate, 2017), 60–61; "The Club From Nowhere."

38. Interview with Georgia Gilmore; Premilla Nadasen, *Household Workers Unite: The Untold Story of African American Women Who Built a Movement* (Boston: Beacon Press, 2015), 20–31.
39. "Paschal Bros. Soda Enlarged as Trade Grows," *Atlanta Daily World*, December 19, 1948; "Dining Room at Paschal's Gives Finest Atmosphere," *Atlanta Daily World*, January 26, 1969.
40. Robbie Brown, "Remembering a Soul Food Legend Who Nurtured Civil Rights Leaders," *Atlanta Journal*, December 5, 2008.
41. *The History Makers*, Oral History with James Paschal, http://www.thehistorymakers.org/biography/james-paschal-41, accessed April 19, 2019.
42. The History of Paschal's, http://www.paschalsatlanta.com/timeline, accessed July 12, 2018; "Robert H. Paschal, Owner of Atlanta Restaurant Where Civil Rights Leaders Dined, Dies at Age 88," *Jet*, March 24, 1997, 18; "Freedom Riders Arrive in City," *Atlanta Daily World*, May 14, 1961.
43. Leah Chase, interview by Ric Burns, November 2017. (She died in 2019.)

Chapter 9: "VACATION WITHOUT AGGRAVATION"

1. Victor Green, *The Travelers' Green Book* (New York: Victor H. Green & Co., 1961), 4.
2. Victor Green, *The International Travelers' Green Book, 1965–66 Edition* (New York: Victor Green and Co., 1966), 2–4.
3. Tapley created *Green Book* covers before he bought the business and illustrated the 1959 edition. Victor Green, *The Negro Travelers' Green Book* (New York: Victor Green, Inc., 1959), 3.
4. James Pierson Beckwourth and T. D. Bonner, *The Life and Adventures of James P. Beckwourth, Mountaineer, Scout, and Pioneer, and Chief of the Crow Nation of Indians* (Minneapolis: Ross & Haines, 1965).
5. W. S. Savage, "The Influence of William Alexander Leidesdorff on the History of California," *Journal of Negro History*, vol. 38, no. 3 (July 1953), 322–32.
6. Victor Green, *The Negro Motorist Green Book and International Travel Guide: Railroad Edition* (New York: Victor H. Green & Co., 1951), 1.
7. *New York Amsterdam News*, May 10, 1969, 43.
8. "Miami Lowers Color Bars for 'Jo Baker,'" *Pittsburgh Courier*, January 20, 1951, 22.
9. "Travel Barriers Lifted for Negroes, Mag Says," *New York Amsterdam News*, June 25, 1966, 36.

10. Summer Guest Book, Sinclair's, Kittery Point, Maine, 1957–1976, Rock Rest Collection, University of New Hampshire.
11. Susan Sessions Rugh, *Are We There Yet? The Golden Age of American Family Vacations* (Lawrence: University Press of Kansas, 2008). For information on discrimination at Hilton Hotels see, for example, Marion E. Jackson, "Sports of the World," *Atlanta Daily World*, June 3, 1955: 7; "Hotel Picketing Hit at NAACP Confab," *Los Angeles Sentinel*, July 12, 1962: A1; "Two Suits Challenge New Orleans Hotel Ban," *The Chicago Defender* (national edition) December 15, 1962: 3; and "NAACP Warns 12 Companies Hotels," *New York Amsterdam News*, May 25, 1963: 1.
12. Cleveland Historical, interview with Russell J. Toppin Sr., https://clevelandhistorical.org/items/show/636, accessed July 9, 2018.
13. Ibid., 84.
14. Melvina Jackson, "Vacationland Notes," *Baltimore Afro-American*, June 9, 1956, 7.
15. "Five Major Myths of Black Business," *Ebony*, December 1971, 156.
16. "Negro Traveler—Still Weary in '67," *New Journal and Guide*, January 17, 1967, 6; "1965 Bringing New Hope in the Field of Civil Rights," *New Journal and Guide*, January 2, 1965, A13; "Supreme Court Fails to Knock Out Jim Crow," *Chicago Defender*, June 15, 1946.
17. "Montgomery Plans to Close Facilities," *New York Times*, January 5, 1962.
18. "Negro Traveler—Still Weary in '67," *New Journal and Guide*, January 17, 1967, 6.
19. Anthony Heffernan, "Must Obey Rights Law: Top Ala. Business Groups Call for End of Jim Crow," *New Journal and Guide*, April 17, 1965, C1.
20. Al Kuettner, "1965 Bringing New Hope in the Field of Civil Rights," *New Journal and Guide*, January 2, 1965.

Epilogue

1. This history is well documented. Sources include: T. Platt, J. Fruppier, G. Ray, R. Schauffler, L. Trujillo, and L. Cooper, *Iron Fist and the Velvet Glove—An Analysis of the US Police*, 1982; Ellis Cashmore and Eugene McLaughlin, *Out of Order?: Policing Black People*, 2013; Stetson Kennedy, *Jim Crow Guide to the U.S.A.: The Way It Was* (Lawrence & Wishart, Ltd., London, 1959); A Day in the Life of a Police Officer in Jim Crow New Orleans, 1917, https://www.nola.com/vintage/2017/09/a_day_in_the_life_of_a_police.html, accessed September 22, 2018.

2. Michelle Alexander, *The New Jim Crow: Mass Incarceration in the Age of Colorblindness* (New York: The New Press, 2010).
3. Brian R. Kowalski and Richard J. Lundman, "Vehicle Stops by Police for Driving While Black: Common Problems and Some Tentative Solutions," *Journal of Criminal Justice* 35 (2007), 169–75.
4. Michael Buerger and Amy Farrell, "The Evidence of Racial Profiling: Interpreting Documented and Unofficial Sources," *Police Quarterly* 5 (2002), 274.
5. Charles R. Epp, Steven Maynard-Moody, and Donald Haider-Markel, *Pulled Over: How Police Stops Define Race and Citizenship* (Chicago: University of Chicago Press, 2014); Sarah A. Seo, *Policing the Open Road: How Cars Transformed American Freedom* (Cambridge: Harvard University Press, 2019); Travis L. Dixon, et al., "The Influence of Race in Police–Civilian Interactions: A Content Analysis of Videotaped Interactions Taken During Cincinnati Police Traffic Stops," *Journal of Communication* 58, no. 3 (September 2008), 530–49; Floyd Weatherspoon, "Racial Profiling of African American Males: Stopped, Searched, and Stripped of Constitutional Protection," *John Marshall Law Review* 38 (Winter 2004), 453–54.
6. Buerger and Farrell, 277–78.
7. Ibid., 272.
8. *Robert L. Wilkins, et al. v. Maryland State Police, et al.*
9. Buerger and Farrell, 280; John Lambreth, "Driving While Black: A Statistician Proves That Prejudice Still Rules the Road," *Washington Post*, August 16, 1998; Weatherspoon, 453–54.
10. "Investigation of the Ferguson Police Department," United States Department of Justice, Civil Rights Division, March 4, 2015, https://www.justice.gov/sites/default/files/opa/press-releases/attachments/2015/03/04/ferguson_police_department_report_1.pdf, accessed March 9, 2019; Jamiles Lartey, "'Predatory police': The High Price of Driving While Black in Missouri," *Guardian*, https://www.theguardian.com/us-news/2018/jul/05/missouri-driving-while-black-st-louis?CMP=share_btn_fb&fbclid=IwAR0s5P_Omk-PGnF2lg3xqYELeko6oFrM8wTiOtefloY3BIeXjelFyyXQD-U, accessed March 9, 2019.
11. The Stanford Open Policing Project, https://openpolicing.stanford.edu, accessed April 19, 2019.
12. President's Task Force on 21st Century Policing, *Final Report of the President's Task Force on 21st Century Policing* (Washington, DC: Office of Community Oriented Policing Services, 2015), http://elearning-courses.net/iacp/html/webinarResources/170926/FinalReport21stCenturyPolicing.pdf, accessed September 22, 2018.
13. Laurie Robinson, interview by Gretchen Sorin, April 30, 2019.

Appendix

1. For information on studies related to implicit bias, see, in particular: B. Keith Payne, "Weapon Bias, Split-Second Decisions and Unintended Stereotyping," December 1, 2006, http://journals.sagepub.com/doi/10.1111/j.1467-8721.2006.00454.x, accessed September 8, 2018; R. Richard Banks, Jennifer L. Eberhardt, and Lee Ross, "Discrimination and Implicit Bias in a Racially Unequal Society," *California Law Review* 94, no. 4 (July 2006): 1169–90.

INDEX

Page numbers in italics refer to illustrations or tables.